John Lennon, Yoko Ono and the Year Canada Was Cool

Greg Marquis

James Lorimer & Company Ltd., Publishers
Toronto

This book is dedicated to Gerry Roney, my favourite person with whom to discuss music.

James Lorimer & Company Ltd., Publishers acknowledges funding support from the Ontario Arts Council (OAC), an agency of the Government of Ontario. We acknowledge the support of the Canada Council for the Arts, which last year invested $153 million to bring the arts to Canadians throughout the country. This project has been made possible in part by the Government of Canada and with the support of Ontario Creates.

Cover design: Tyler Cleroux
Cover image: Pictorial Press Ltd / Alamy Stock Photo
Back cover images: Allan Rock (bottom); Gerry Deiter (second from bottom); Ritchie Yorke (second from top); York University Libraries, Clara Thomas Archives & Special Collections, Toronto Telegram fonds: ASC00912 (top)

Photo Credits
Allan Rock: page 67, 71, 72; AP Images: page 115; Copyright Estate of Gerry Deiter: page 37, 39, 53, 62, 65; Ritchie Yorke Archive Project: page 30, 150, 154, 158, 170; Scott Cisco: page 192, 199, 200 (all), 202 (all), 203, 205; York University Libraries, Clara Thomas Archives & Special Collections, Toronto Telegram fonds: ASC002297: page 21, ASC00912: page 135, ASC00915: page 137, ASC00326: page 139, ASC10011: page 141.

Library and Archives Canada Cataloguing in Publication

Title: John Lennon, Yoko Ono and the year Canada was cool / Greg Marquis.
Names: Marquis, Greg, author.
Description: Includes bibliographical references and index.
Identifiers: Canadiana (print) 20200261312 | Canadiana (ebook) 20200261487 | ISBN 9781459415416 (softcover) | ISBN 9781459415423 (EPUB)
Subjects: LCSH: Lennon, John, 1940-1980. | LCSH: Ono, Yōko. | LCSH: Canada—Civilization—1945- | CSH: Canada—Social conditions—1945-1971. | LCSH: Popular music—Canada—1961-1970—History and criticism.
Classification: LCC FC95.4 .M36 2020 | DDC 971.064/4—dc23

Published by:
James Lorimer & Company Ltd., Publishers
117 Peter Street, Suite 304
Toronto, ON, Canada
M5V 0M3
www.lorimer.ca

Printed and bound in Canada.

Contents

Introduction

Becoming Cool: Canada in the 1960s

Expo has elevated us all, through concrete truth and beauty, to grasp a sure and indispensable confidence in ourselves.

—*Globe and Mail*, October 28, 1967

The aesthetic of cool is a difficult concept to put into words. Think of the "cool kids" in high school or film stars, musicians and writers, such as actors Samuel L. Jackson and singer Chrissie Hynde or novelist Jack Kerouac. The Vespa scooter, the Chevrolet Corvette and the Gibson Les Paul guitar are cool consumer items that never go out of style. In the 1980s, the clothing company Roots, using images such as canoes and beavers, marketed a version of Canadian cool to domestic and international consumers. At various times in history, nations, or their culture, have been deemed cool. And so have cities: London in the 1960s, New York and Paris anytime.[1]

In the 1960s, no one was cooler than the Beatles. This book documents the three visits of then-Beatle John Lennon and Yoko Ono to Canada in 1969. They were important moments in the history of the Beatles, Lennon's final decision to leave the group and launch a solo career and his search for an activist life beyond pop music. The reason for his first trip, despite what many Canadians thought at the time, had more to do with "karma" (a term Lennon often used) than with any conscious, planned strategy. Yet through these visits, Canada was linked to a major shift in pop culture: the death throes of the Beatles. At the time, the public was unaware of the dysfunctional state of the group, and Lennon, in public, acted as if it was still a going concern. The following chapters also remind us that in the late 1960s and early 1970s, Lennon, compared to his posthumous image, especially in Canada, was a polarizing figure.[2]

The visits of Ono and Lennon coincided with and contributed to the first time in history that Canada was considered cool: the late 1960s. Young, educated and urban Canadians were excited by this new sensibility, which was apparent by 1967. Older, less educated and small-town and rural citizens feared or rejected it. In 1969, John Lennon, one of the most recognizable and hippest celebrities on the planet, and Yoko Ono, his controversial and eccentric artist wife, chose Canada to promote peace and advance their solo music careers. Icons of cool are greeted as original and charismatic figures who transform society; they are also denounced as "signs of cultural degeneracy."[3] This was particularly the case during the late 1960s, when John and Yoko were widely admired, misunderstood and reviled. Lennon was cool, but he had not yet acquired his image of secular saint.

In 1969, Canada was a relatively young and prosperous nation of twenty-one million people. Lennon, as a member of the Beatles, had briefly visited its three major cities as part of their North American tours in 1964, 1965 and 1966. But the country he now encountered was different: confident, nationalistic and, at least in its own mind, cool. Canadians dared to think this way in 1967, their Centennial year. Yet the optimism did not last long: best-selling writer Pierre Berton, with some overstatement, later called 1967 "the last Good Year."[4] Three things made Canada cool in the late 1960s: youth-oriented pop culture, the centennial of Confederation and Expo 67 and its new prime minister, Pierre Trudeau. In Quebec, the sense of a new era with unlimited potential had been unleashed by the "Quiet Revolution," an era of political modernization that started in

1960. For many young people and those on the Left, a fourth sign of "hipness" was anti-war and student activism. To be hip, like to be cool, was to be socially progressive and to reject the conformity of mass society. Youth culture was increasingly associated with "defiant anti-authoritarianism and self-expression," and although not every young Canadian dressed as a hippie, smoked marijuana, took part in a sit-in or joined the New Left, these social and political trends symbolized the growing gap between youth on the one hand and their parents and the "Establishment" on the other.[5] The Establishment was a critical term for politicians, business leaders, religious leaders, police, teachers and other authority types who reinforced political and social conservatism.

On New Year's Eve 1966, the small community of Bowsman, Manitoba, celebrated Canada's upcoming centennial — and its own new sewage system — with a mass outhouse burning. The bonfire was one of the quirkier events or projects through which hundreds of thousands of Canadians celebrated the first 100 years of Confederation. Canada in 1967 was not only relatively peaceful, it was also, in the words of Pierre Berton, "in love with itself."[6] Unlike the United States, it was not at war, and its political scene was relatively tranquil.[7] Much of the outside world did seem a dangerous place in 1967. Young people gathered in San Francisco to celebrate the "Summer of Love," but in more than 100 American cities, Black people, in a wave of riots sparked by racial grievances such as police treatment of minorities, clashed with police. The violence took dozens of lives — many at the hands of police and the National Guard — and caused massive property damage. A war between Israel and Egypt and its allies Syria, Iraq and Jordan resulted in a major expansion of Israel's territory and the expulsion of a third of a million Palestinians. The United States ramped up its military activities in Vietnam, at a cost of more than eleven thousand American lives. The South Vietnamese army that year lost even more men. Greece was taken over by a junta of neo-fascist military officers. The People's Republic of China continued to experience

the bloody internal turmoil of the Cultural Revolution, launched
a year earlier by Mao Zedong (Chairman Mao) as an attempt to
purify the nation and reinforce the true version of Communism. In
Central America, the Middle East, Africa and Southeast Asia, civil
wars and insurgencies either simmered or continued.[8]

Before, during and after the Centennial, Canada's media and
political leaders stressed economic prosperity, national unity,
tolerance for pluralism and the nation's prestige abroad. The
centrepiece of the Centennial was Expo 67, the world fair hosted
by Montreal, arguably Canada's most interesting city. In terms
of Canadian unity, the international exhibition, initially planned
for Moscow, gave the Liberal government of Lester B. Pearson a
chance to make a major commitment to Quebec and underscore
that Confederation, to use the language of the time, was based on
co-operation between "two founding peoples," the French and the
English. The celebrations were also an opportunity for the federal
and provincial governments to invest in cultural and recreational
facilities and promote citizen awareness of environmental issues.[9]
During 1967, provinces, communities, organizations and individuals embarked on a frenzy of Centennial projects, most of them
brick-and-mortar facilities such as arenas and libraries. Tens of
thousands flocked to view the travelling Centennial Train exhibit
as well as truck-drawn Centennial Caravans that featured Canada's history and geography.[10] Throughout the year, Canadian
visual art, music and dance were celebrated, often in a multicultural framework. One high-profile event was the Voyageur Canoe
Pageant, in which provincial and territorial teams paddled more
than five thousand kilometres from Alberta to Montreal. Across
the land, Centennial events were designed to attract citizens of all
ages, including youth. On Dominion Day (renamed Canada Day
in the 1980s), Toronto celebrated with a parade, pony and hay
rides and free entertainment at Nathan Phillips Square, where in
the evening young people congregated to wade in the pool, climb
the modern art, play guitars and, in the words of one Canadian

Broadcasting Corporation (CBC) reporter, "grind to the sound of go-go music."[11]

Most Centennial projects were small scale and utilitarian, but Expo was designed to generate excitement, international good-will, and national pride and to display to the outside world that Canada was modern and glamorous, not drab and dour. The people of Montreal and Canadians in general were proud that the fair involved more than sixty nations and attracted sixty million visitors. Heads of state arrived, as did celebrities such as Jacqueline Kennedy, the widow of U.S. president John F. Kennedy; actors Peter Ustinov and Grace Kelly; and Robert F. Kennedy, who would be assassinated when running for the Democratic party's presidential nomination the following year. There were national, private sector and provincial pavilions to tour, as well as many off-site activities, such as concerts at Montreal's Place des Arts and other venues around the city. The 1960s was a vibrant period for the Quebec metropolis, with the opening of Place Ville Marie, an office-retail complex, and the Metro (subway). Big projects were supported by Mayor Jean Drapeau and his Civic party, who, despite being branded the Establishment by the late 1960s, had won office as reformers sympathetic to French-Canadian nationalism. Expanded subway lines that opened in 1967 resulted in an annual Metro ridership of three hundred million during Expo year.

The World's Fair was constructed on Île Sainte-Hélène on the St. Lawrence River. The brainchild of populist Jean Drapeau, the exhibition was viewed within the province very much as a Montreal and Quebec initiative, despite its transnational perspectives and massive federal funding. Montreal was already a dynamic, cosmopolitan and growing city, alive with music, art and young people. The theme of the exposition, "Man and His World," and the futuristic pavilions tended to emphasize modernity, technology and optimism. The focus was on the present and the future, not the past. It included the popular and iconic American pavilion, a large geodesic dome designed by Buckminster Fuller; the Minirail (a monorail); and architect Moshe Safdie's futuristic housing complex, Habitat. To varying degrees, the national pavilions, in terms of design and exhibits, foreshadowed the importance of computers, digital technology and mass communication. Intense media coverage allowed Canadians who were not able to attend to share in the pride and excitement. A common metaphor in associated editorials, television and newspaper coverage and speeches was that Canada was "coming of age."[12] One historian has written that Expo made Canada "suddenly and unexpectedly cool."[13]

In 1967, Canada's summer of love played out in Montreal. Expo 67 celebrated both high and popular culture much like the Centennial Commission, which promoted a steady stream of choirs, dance troupes and musical groups, such as Don Messer and His Islanders, in cross-Canada tours. All genres of music, from choral to jazz, were represented. Youth flocked to internationally known pop acts, including Jefferson Airplane and the Supremes, whereas parents and grandparents enjoyed performers such as Maurice Chevalier and Sir Laurence Olivier. At Katimavik (part of the Canadian pavilion) and other sites, there was a steady rotation of Canadian performers, many of them from the folk music world, such as the Travellers, Oscar Brand, Gilles Vigneault and Gordon Lightfoot. Pop music's heavy hitters, the Beatles and the Rolling Stones, did not appear.[14] As Explosion 67 — Terre des jeunes/Youth and Their World, the 2017–20 conceptual exhibit at Montreal's Centre d'histoire, revealed, Expo, with its large entertainment complex, la Ronde, was particularly intriguing and liberating for children and teenagers who flocked to the site.[15]

According to optimistic reporters and politicians, even relations between French and English Canadians appeared to be improving in 1967. Since Confederation, nationalist writers and politicians in Quebec had favoured a strong provincial rights approach to protect the French language and culture; an independent Quebec had been for dreamers. Despite nationalist rumblings, by the early 1960s, separatism seemed to be a minority opinion, confined to a left-wing, intellectual fringe. Canada's Liberal government, elected in 1963, attempted to make French Canadians feel more welcome in Canada by promises, expressions of goodwill and minor reforms. The Royal Commission on Bilingualism and Biculturalism reported that a majority of English Canadians, even in the West, supported bilingual federal services from coast to coast and the teaching of French in schools.[16] A popular memory of the period is that Canadians in 1967 were proud, contented and optimistic and that the nation was prosperous, humane and peaceful. Compared to the United States under presidents Lyndon B. Johnson (1963–68) and Richard M. Nixon (inaugurated in 1969), "it was the better place to be."[17]

Yet beneath the surface, the Centennial year contained many signs of trouble to come. Montreal hosted the World's Fair with competence and panache, but the Quebec's Union nationale government (a conservative nationalist party) refused to take part in Centennial celebrations. Quebec journalists André Laurendeau and Solange Chaput-Rolland were shocked and disheartened to discover the level of parochialism, strong provincial identity and antipathy toward Quebec and French Canadians in English Canada.[18] Within Quebec and especially Montreal, old resentments over the privileged position of the anglophone minority and the unwillingness of immigrants to speak French simmered. The views of French and English Canadians toward each other bordered on racial stereotyping. These tensions were highlighted when French President Charles de Gaulle, speaking in public in Montreal in July, uttered the memorable statement, "Vive le Québec libre." He had seen similar phrases on placards carried by members of the Rassemblement pour l'indépendance nationale (RIN, Rally for National Independence), Quebec's militant separatist organization, in the crowd in front of him. The Pearson government — and English Canada — was not amused, and for years federal government officials obsessed over any recognition by France of Quebec's provincial government.

In 1967, René Lévesque, a star within the provincial Liberals, left the party as part of his quest for an independent Quebec.[19] The founding convention of the Parti Québécois (PQ), which vowed to use the democratic process to secure Quebec's independence, took place in 1968. Most delegates were described as "cool, young articulate Quebecers who as a group represented the middle class. Many were teachers and students."[20] Under Lévesque, the PQ distanced itself from the ideology and tactics of the Marxist Front de libération du Québec (FLQ) and associated groups that were planting bombs, robbing banks and gathering weapons in a low-level terror campaign against symbols of the federal government and the English-Canadian minority. These raids and bombs had killed four people by 1967. The PQ, which embraced evolution, not revolution, would continue to attract support from francophone artists, writers, poets, academics and musicians, the same types drawn to the New Left and the New Democratic Party (NDP) in English Canada. (The New Left consisted of younger socialist and social democratic activists who rejected the institutionalized approach of the Old Left, the Communist party.) Years later, leading member Bernard Landry would describe the PQ as a "generational party," built on the support of "baby boomers," young Québécois born in the population surge following the Second World War whose aspirations would shape the society of the 1960s, 70s and beyond.[21]

Despite the generally positive feelings in English Canada, the hoopla over 1967 could not mask the basic tensions that had challenged Canada since its inception: the gulf between English and French Canada, widespread anti-French feeling outside Quebec (which, in turn, fed separatism in that province) and concerns about American control of the economy and Canada's foreign policy, as well as the vulnerable place of Canadian culture. Other looming issues were regional disparity and the rights of Indigenous peoples. The latter was highlighted at Expo 67 by the Indians of Canada Pavilion, whose stark challenge to the overwhelmingly positive view of Canada was generally ignored by the hundreds of thousands of visitors seeking fun and excitement. This pavilion, with its message of the rejection of assimilation into white culture, was an early and forthright expression of an Indigenous view of Canadian history, where "nation building" meant colonization. National pride and Canada's cool self-image, in other words, had major blind spots: racial prejudice, discrimination and an ignorance of its own history of dealing with indigenous people.

Many Canadians in the late 1960s were excited by the nation's possibilities, but the heart of cool was youth culture. Youth in this rebellious decade expressed themselves through music and fashion. Pop music had been an important marker of teen identity since the 1950s; by the next decade, inspired by the lyrics of Bob Dylan, songwriters and performers began to tackle political and social issues. Music both reflected the impact of the 1960s "counterculture" and broadened its appeal among young people (the counterculture was the movement, embodied by "hippies," that challenged basic tenets of the dominant culture, such as the work ethic, social conformity, organized religion, sexual control and war as a form of foreign policy). Hippies, typically young people, rebelled by wearing long hair and unconventional clothing, experimenting with drugs and embracing free-spirited attitude toward sexuality. In the words of one author, in the 1960s, the Beatles, along with Bob Dylan and the Rolling Stones, were "part of the Holy Trinity of white pop acts with huge cultural clout. Musicians looked to them for clues as to where the music was likely to go next, and young people were guided by their fashion choices, opinions and beliefs."[22] To use a contemporary term, pop star celebrities were "influencers" whose words and deeds beyond the stage and recording studio were also closely followed in media consumed by adults. After the early Beatlemania period, the group's music, although rarely explicitly political, explored counterculture themes such as drugs and consciousness and drew media and academic attention. Their 1966 album *Revolver*, with its psychedelic sound, signalled the Beatles' experimentation with LSD. By 1967, the group was also identified with the message that love could save the world, the same utopianism that attracted large numbers of young people to San Francisco that summer. That June, via satellite technology, the Beatles performed their song "All You Need Is Love" to a global television audience of four hundred to seven hundred million.[23]

The most outspoken member of the world's first pop superstar group, John Lennon, was one of the most famous people, let alone entertainers, in the world. He became more controversial when he left his wife Cynthia for Japanese-born artist Yoko Ono in 1968 and embarked on a series of musical and artistic projects that confounded most observers. One was Bagism, a type of performance art where John and/or Yoko crawled into a bag as a statement on prejudice. They named their art/music/film production company Bag One and operated out of an office at Apple Corps, the Beatles' business entity. In 1968, the couple released their experimental LP *Two Virgins*, a combination of sound effects and Ono's vocalizations recorded on the night they consummated their relationship. Its front and back covers depicted John and Yoko in the nude, an unprecedented artistic statement/marketing ploy that generated publicity and controversy. The images broke new ground for album covers and tested the bounds of censorship.

The couple continued to capture headlines, often in a controversial fashion. Later in 1968, police raided their London flat and discovered cannabis resin, which Lennon insisted was not his. He entered a guilty plea to possession of illegal drugs and paid a fine to save Yoko (an American citizen) from being deported. At the time, the arrest was depicted within hip circles as harassment of an upstart pop star by corrupt police. But Lennon admitted that the drugs had arrived at the flat in his personal effects from the mansion where he had lived with his wife. This was only a week after Ono had miscarried in a London hospital; the child, who had been conceived when John was still married to his first wife, Cynthia, mother of his son Julian, was proof that he had committed adultery. Through this period, the Beatles continued to be best-selling, critically acclaimed pop artists, following up the ground-breaking *Sgt.*

Pepper's Lonely Hearts Club Band album of 1967 with the equally influential *The Beatles* (also known as the White Album) in 1968. Musically, John Lennon was at the top of his game and a hero to millions of young people around the globe.

Yoko was accepted by some Beatles fans but rejected by many, and her constant presence at John's side (for example, in the recording studio) caused tensions within the Beatles. Often blamed for the breakup of the group, she remained a controversial figure. One of the couple's headline-grabbing events in 1969, a post-wedding bed-in for peace in an Amsterdam hotel, was part of a chain of events that brought the celebrities to Canada not as performers but activists. Lennon was already notorious for telling a reporter in 1966 that the Beatles were "more popular than Jesus," provoking an evangelical Christian-backed boycott of Beatles music in the United States. By 1969, he was an advocate of recreational drug use who had major reservations about drug culture and an opponent of American involvement in Vietnam who spoke out against violent protest and political radicalism. In 1968, the lyrics of his song "Revolution," which questioned radical protest during that dramatic year, set off an intense discussion in activist circles that appears to have sparked Lennon's embrace of peace the following year. Although he could not bring himself to support political violence, he felt he needed to make a meaningful statement against war. This was supposedly prompted by a letter from Peter Watkins, who had directed the controversial docudrama *The War Game* (1966), which depicted the results of a Soviet nuclear attack on Britain.[24]

Following their wedding in Gibraltar and a honeymoon visit to Paris, Ono and Lennon reached Amsterdam, where on March 25 they began a multi-day bed-in for peace. Using their celebrity status, the pajama-clad couple invited reporters and photographers to help spread their message of world peace. The term "bed-in" was borrowed from the term "sit-in," a common form of protest in the 1960s rooted in the American civil rights movement. The goal was to attract the media, and it worked. Reporters were not sure if this was a publicity stunt or a genuine statement in support of humanity (in Ono's world, the two were the same). At the time, Canada was not on their minds, but in less than two months they would embark on a longer and even more publicized bed-in in Montreal, the subject of Chapter 1.

By 1969, Lennon and Ono were preaching revolution in the cultural sense. Lennon had become alienated from the type of confrontational radicalism that created factionalism and ended in street clashes with the police. According to one insider, Ono, through her art and intellectualism, was a major influence on his move into peace work.[25] The utopian society Lennon envisioned was based on a revolution of ideas and lifestyle. And the delivery mechanism for infecting the public with this message was the media, specifically television. Perhaps unconsciously, he shared an optimistic view of television with Canadian media expert Marshall McLuhan at a time when most intellectuals regarded the medium as a cultural wasteland and a bulwark of the status quo.[26] Lennon's idealistic crusade crystallized a fundamental question facing youth culture: Could a peaceful, more egalitarian society be realized through the more confrontational New Left tactics of indoctrination, organizing, protest and civil disobedience or via the seemingly apolitical idealism and hedonism of the counterculture?

Canada in 1969 was a nation alive with possibilities. Two years after the successful Centennial celebrations, its media, political, arts and literary worlds reflected optimism, energy and confidence. Canada appeared to be a country where minorities enjoyed a degree of toleration unknown in other Western democracies and where the welfare state, in contrast to the United States, was considered not a threat to the family and nation but a positive good. Internationally, it was viewed as a strong supporter of the United Nations (UN), peacekeeping and aid to the world's "have-not" nations. After more than two decades of being a reliable supporter of American policy toward the Soviet Union (USSR), the Canadian government was questioning the West's Cold War consensus, such as the rationale behind the North Atlantic Treaty Organization (NATO).[27] One poll suggested that most Canadians (whose parents and grandparents had fought hard in the First and Second World Wars) were predicting that their nation would not be engaging in military operations in the future.[28]

A country with a high standard of living and low crime rates, Canada in the late 1960s welcomed American "draft dodgers" (young men escaping the draft for the war in Vietnam) and military deserters, questioned the American bombing of North Vietnam, maintained diplomatic ties with Cuba, was open to Communist China, no longer carried out capital punishment and was in the process of implementing a national system of socialized medicine. Its federal government was rejecting linguistic assimilation and attempting to make French Canadians feel welcome throughout the country by introducing a policy of bilingualism in the civil service. As a result of changes to immigration policy, the country was becoming more diverse, and within two years the federal government would issue an important statement on multiculturalism. This was more aspirational than a law or a set of policies, but it endorsed a vision of Canada as a multi-ethnic, multi-racial society. Canadian cities had not been torn apart by race riots, although, at the same time, journalists, academics and activists were questioning Canada's reputation for tolerance and civility by uncovering its "polite racism." Canada's youth, although generally less militant than their American counterparts, were both idealistic and alienated from traditional institutions and authority structures. They were also the driving force behind a growing wave of nationalist sentiment in reaction to American economic and cultural domination in the era of the Vietnam War.

Chapter 1

The Montreal Bed-In

I just remember that the people of Canada were
so great. I mean, they were sending us such warm
vibrations ... It was a very nice warm memory and
of course you know they were so good to us that we
probably wouldn't have been inspired to do all that,
Give Peace A Chance, etc., you know.

— Yoko Ono, 2000

On May 25, 1969, with little advance planning or forethought, the most famous member of the most influential pop group in the world and his conceptual artist wife were heading to an unsuspecting Canada. Uncharacteristically, John Lennon had neglected to inform the media of their flight to the Toronto International Airport from the Bahamas. Their plans were changing by the hour. Travelling with Ono's five-year-old daughter Kyoko, they had reached the West Indies after being denied entry into the United States because of Lennon's drug possession conviction. Almost immediately, they decided to head north on "good old Air Canada" (Lennon's words). Toronto's *Globe and Mail* gave the visit of the celebrities and their entourage front-page coverage but below stories on the Apollo 10 mission, layoffs at a Montreal shipyard, a U.S. Army deserter's arrival in Canada and language policy at the University of Ottawa.[1] Lennon expressed surprise at not being admitted to Canada automatically: "We all thought it was sort of like home. Like popping into Ireland, only a bit farther."[2]

John and Yoko were arguably the most recognizable celebrity couple in the world, largely because of his pop superstar status, their counterculture lifestyle and their constant reaching out to the media. Pushed by leftists to do something to better the world, the couple had decided after their recent marriage to advocate for peace. Now their mission was coming to Canada, chosen out of convenience as opposed to any conscious strategy. They hoped to speak to the world's press, but their targeted audience was the United States. John explained that they wanted to encourage American youth "not to be so violent in their non violence" and to give President Richard Nixon acorns that he could plant for peace.[3] Their arrival in Toronto led to a major pop culture moment for late 1960s Canada: the Montreal bed-in for peace, where Lennon and Ono conducted countless interviews, met with visiting celebrities and wrote and recorded a hit song and major anthem for the peace movement, "Give Peace a Chance," arguably the most important legacy of their Canadian visits.

Two of his visits to Canada in 1969 owed more to serendipity than to anything else, but the nation offered certain advantages. Canada granted the couple entry, if only for a short period, despite Lennon's criminal record. After a two-hour meeting with immigration officials, they proceeded to Toronto's King Edward Hotel. The next day, with lawyer Alan Mintz in tow, they met with officials and were told to report back on June 2 for a hearing to determine their eligibility. Canada was also close to the United States, with access to print, television and radio reporters, as well as to activists in the northeastern states. At a press conference, Lennon explained that in addition to having a climate that was more temperate than the Bahamas, Canada was a base from where they could continue their quest for permission to enter the United States.[4] Another reason for coming to Canada, John insisted, was the British media: "I'd have to take me prick out to get the attention of the English press."[5]

John Lennon at the King Edward Hotel in Toronto, May 1969

The reality was that rather than ignoring him, the press in his own country was hostile and even racist toward his wife. Canadian reporters could be cynical and abrupt, but press conferences were somewhat civilized, and many journalists and photographers were genuinely impressed by John and Yoko. Mark Starowicz, then a *Toronto Daily Star* reporter, called coverage of Lennon's Canadian visit "an unprecedented journalistic event."[6]

Canada had one other attraction: its celebrity prime minister, a wealthy, well-educated French Canadian who seemed to epitomize the cosmopolitan single male to whom *Playboy* magazine supposedly appealed in the early 1960s. Although born in 1919, Pierre Elliott Trudeau was physically fit and cosmopolitan and exuded an aura of youthfulness. He was well travelled by Canadian standards, a professor of law, a civil liberties advocate and an author, editing a volume of essays on Quebec's famous Asbestos Strike of 1949, serving as editor of the journal *Cité Libre* and publishing his book *Federalism and the French Canadians* in 1967. In the early 1960s, he became concerned about the growth of separatist feeling in Quebec, which furthered his dislike of ethnic-based nationalism. In 1963, Trudeau was lured to Ottawa and in 1966 became Prime Minister Pearson's parliamentary secretary, followed by minister of justice. Trudeau was a bilingual, cultured bachelor who dated a series of much younger women, drove a cool Mercedes convertible and excelled at skiing, scuba diving, martial arts and canoeing. His habit of wearing flowers on his lapel, and accepting flowers from fans, tied in with the "flower power" image of contemporary hippies who adopted flowers as a symbol of peace and love. He also practised yoga at a time when the Beatles were interesting Western youth in the practice by visiting the Maharishi Mahesh Yogi in India.[7] (The Maharishi was a spiritual leader who popularized transcendental meditation and gained a substantial following in Europe and North America because of his appeal to the counterculture.) Like the early Beatles, Trudeau was also known to ham it up "spontaneously" when reporters were present, dancing and performing acts of physical strength.

As minister of justice, Trudeau rejected the "two nations" solution to national unity that had been adopted by Quebec's provincial Liberals and the Union nationale, as well as the national Progressive Conservatives (PCs) and NDP. Instead, he proposed bilingualism in federal institutions, patriation of Canada's Constitution and a charter protecting individual rights. One of his first concerns was the reform of Canada's *Criminal Code*. This included the decriminalization of homosexual acts in private between consenting adults and the legalization of therapeutic abortion. The Trudeau government's *Divorce Act* created a uniform law across Canada and liberalized the grounds for divorce. In early 1968, as the English-Canadian media began to promote Trudeau as the ideal choice for Liberal leader, many young Canadians were attracted to his "unorthodox and stylish challenge"[8] to the bland politicians who traditionally ran the country. The Montreal MP also became associated with a requisite skill for any 1960s politician or celebrity: the sound bite. During a House of Commons debate in 1967 on the merits of decriminalizing private homosexual acts, Trudeau uttered a phrase borrowed from a newspaper editorial that signalled another step in the sexual revolution: "The state has no business in the bedrooms of the nation." Viewed as an intelligent federalist who understood Quebec and how to deal with its growing separatist sentiment, he was selected leader at a party convention where young delegates were particularly active.[9]

By 1968, Trudeau's attendance at events could be mistaken for the visit of a pop star, with the celebrity (this time a middle-aged politician seeking the leadership of the Liberal party) wading into excited crowds and kissing women of all ages. The media adapted a term to describe the reaction to the Beatles in 1964: sedate Canada was experiencing a wave of "Trudeaumania," which helped the "swinging" bachelor from Montreal become prime minister.[10] In April 1968, following the assassination of civil rights activist

Reverend Martin Luther King, Jr., in Memphis, and coinciding with the outbreak of destructive rioting in many American cities sparked by King's death, Trudeau won the party's leadership at its Ottawa convention, partly on his youth-friendly image.[11] He was vague on policy details but Trudeaumania had created expectations of social reform, partly because of the candidate's pro-labour, civil liberties background. By this point, Canada was moving to the Left, with all three major parties supporting an expansion of the welfare state. The United States, in contrast, was moving toward Nixon, with his racially charged (and successful) campaign against "crime in the streets."[12]

After he took over as prime minister, Trudeau called an election, asking Canadians "to take a chance on the future" to achieve the "Just Society." Although not clearly defined, this was a vision of Canada where government programs would allow individuals to develop to their full potential, minorities would be protected and the nation would be united.[13] Trudeau took part in Canada's first televised national election debate, with PC leader Robert Stanfield, NDP leader David Lewis and Créditiste (Social Credit) leader Réal Caouette. Although only a few years younger than the other men, Trudeau benefited from a media-constructed image of youthfulness. Even with all the hype surrounding Trudeaumania, the Liberal share of the vote was only 45.5 per cent, capturing 154 ridings, enough for a majority.

His reputation as a ladies' man aside, many voters in rural Quebec and elsewhere were convinced that Trudeau was a homosexual because of his *Criminal Code* amendments. In contrast to his reforms of divorce and abortion, because of deep-rooted homophobia most Canadians did not support the partial decriminalization of homosexual acts between consenting adults, viewing it as an unreasonable imposition of the permissive society.[14]

Although viewed as progressive for its day in that 20 per cent of its members were francophone, Trudeau's cabinet did not contain a single woman. Despite the arrival of the sexual revolution in

Canada, women's liberation had yet to make much headway in politics; political parties tended to relegate women to secondary roles and female candidates were judged by their femininity. For years, debates in the House of Commons on women's issues would reflect sexist attitudes bordering on the Neanderthal. In 1969, leading feminist Laura Sabia criticized Trudeau for ignoring women when making references to the "Just Society."[15]

One biographer has written that "Trudeau, like the Beatles, lived part of his life as performance."[16] The British magazine *Spectator* concluded that "Canada had come of age" and that its new leader signalled an end to "traditionalism and mediocrity."[17] He was also the subject of a 1969 *New Yorker* article. American journalist Edith Iglauer, who wrote the piece, had accompanied Trudeau on an eight-day tour of the Canadian Arctic, which underscored another aspect of his mystique: his connection to the land. Iglauer, who would later host the prime minister at a dinner in her New York apartment, recalled decades later that despite his political charisma, she found him to be "socially shy." She also discovered that he shared the values of her sons' "1960s generation."[18]

But the most important audience for Trudeau's image was domestic. Looking back on the era, political scientists Michael B. Stein and Janet Gross Stein claimed that "we Canadians briefly saw ourselves as sassy, irreverent and iconoclastic in a world that was fairly rigid, predictable, and straight-laced."[19] There was less adulation from media outlets and intellectuals in Quebec, where the influential journal Le Devoir was concerned about his lack of support for constitutional reform that would acknowledge special status for the province. Increasingly, Trudeau would be the target of leftists and progressives within Quebec.[20] This began in a vivid manner at the 1968 Saint-Jean-Baptiste parade in Montreal, where Trudeau was a guest of honour. Young RIN protestors clashed with police, threw bottles and other projectiles at the official reviewing stand and chanted, "Trudeau to the gallows." The Montreal police arrested nearly three hundred people, and nearly one hundred citizens and more than fifty officers were injured.[21] The federal election was the next day, and Trudeau's unflinching stance in the face of violence won much admiration in English Canada, but the young nationalist protestors regarded the new French-Canadian prime minister as a traitor to Quebec. On the other hand, his years in office fuelled various conspiracy theories in English Canada. Many opponents of bilingualism feared that Trudeau would engineer a French-Canadian takeover of the country, conservatives were convinced that he was a socialist in disguise and monarchists feared that he would make Canada a republic.[22]

Despite the fact that the minimum voting age in the 1968 federal election was twenty-one, Trudeau captured the imagination of many youth in English Canada. During a well-received speech to foreign correspondents in London in early 1969, he asked a rhetorical question: Why should leaders in chauffeur-driven limousines be taken more seriously than protestors carrying signs? He cited the Indian independence leader and advocate of passive resistance Mahatma Gandhi and Canada's Louis Riel as examples of "protestors" in the past who had legitimate grievances. Riel, a Red River Métis, had led the provisional government that obtained province status for Manitoba in 1870. Later convicted of treason to Canada and hanged as a result of the 1885 rebellion in the Saskatchewan territory, Riel came to be regarded as Manitoba's "father of Confederation."

In October 1968, the prime minister visited the Saskatchewan Legislative Building in Regina to unveil another statue of Riel.[23] One thousand student demonstrators listened quietly while Trudeau spoke on the need to protect minority rights, but they disrupted a second speech with chants of "Just Society — just for the rich."[24] They were upset over federal student loan policy. This and other responses to the new prime minister suggested that young activists were drawn more to socialism, Quebec separatism or the social democracy of the NDP than the left-centre position of the Liberal party.

As early as 1969, much of the Trudeaumania phenomenon was fading, but the prime minister was still treated like a celebrity by many Canadians, such as when he toured Acadian communities in New Brunswick.[25] The media continued to report on his wardrobe — the ultimate marker of celebrity status.[26] At the Canadian Football League's (CFL) November 1969 Grey Cup game in Montreal, the prime minister took part in the opening kickoff wearing a fur coat and white crocheted mitts, a muffler and a Dutch boy cap and sporting a red carnation. Miss Canada, eighteen-year-old Julie Maloney, admitted that she felt "a little envious" that unlike Miss Grey Cup, she did not get to sit with the prime minister. This anecdote suggests Trudeau's star power within Canada in the late 1960s and his attractiveness to youth.[27] His future wife, Margaret Sinclair, who was significantly younger and as a child of privilege had experimented with the counterculture, "found him youthful, willing to listen, and understanding of a young person's dreams."[28]

Earlier in 1969, Canada's leader drew media attention when attending a meeting of Commonwealth leaders in London, and Lennon and Ono may have taken notice. Trudeau, who had little knowledge of international affairs, had considered not attending because he feared that it would be dominated by the issues of Nigeria and Rhodesia.[29] Nigeria, a former British colony, was experiencing a civil war, and Black-majority Rhodesia (now Zimbabwe), controlled by a privileged white minority, had declared itself independent of Britain in 1965 and was on the road to republic status.

Journalists, it turned out, were more interested in his jet-setting lifestyle and the women he dated than Canada's diplomatic initiatives. Trudeau walked through a crowd of protestors outside the meeting and remarked that it was exciting to be exposed to such a large range of political opinions. But the prime minister with the hip lifestyle also expressed anger at the intrusions of Canadian and British reporters, accusing them of acting like "a pretty lousy lot" — an opinion that was often shared by Lennon, whose larger-than-life persona was also partly a media creation.[30]

The Plan Takes Shape

The Lennon-Ono party that landed in Toronto included Apple press agent Derek Taylor, who had accompanied the Beatles on their American tour of 1964. Taylor, who was married with children, was a tasteful dresser and the epitome of correct British manners. He had many friends and contacts in the American entertainment world. And, like many show business types of the period, he indulged in recreational drugs, from speed to peyote and more.

Cinematographer Nic Knowland and a sound technician were on hand to produce footage for a documentary on the peace campaign, possibly to be broadcast on British television with John and Yoko's music as background. They later released the seventy-one-minute documentary *Bed Peace*, based on their Montreal experience. Other footage in Montreal was captured by American underground filmmaker and critic Jonas Mekas, who had known Yoko in her New York years as part of Fluxus, an avant-garde approach to art that emphasized process over finished works.[31]

Lennon explained to the Toronto media that they were trying to interest young people in doing something about peace because "the hippest ones need to help the squares" (meaning non-hip people). He appeared bitter about not being admitted into the United States but also criticized the approach of the organized anti-war movement dominated by the New Left: "The whole scene has become too serious and too intellectual." Yoko explained that for celebrities, a bed-in was a more effective and less disruptive tactic for promoting peace than taking part in demonstrations.[32] Apart from laying "a bit of peace" on the United States, John hoped they could also visit Moscow and "see the Pope" and other heads of state. Yoko stated that "people take war for granted" because they are "conditioned to it."[33]

An American journalist described Lennon as the most unpredictable of the Beatles, who, because of his adultery, divorce, nude record album cover and Dutch bed-in, had alienated many of his fans.[34] If Lennon was embarrassed by any of these controversies, he did not show it and fielded questions from Canadian journalists with a degree of tact and humour. His composure in front of the press in Toronto and Montreal was remarkable given that Paul McCartney later contended that Lennon's heroin use in 1969 "made him devious, paranoid [and] manipulative."[35]

According to Toronto reporter Ritchie Yorke, the celebrity visitors appeared to be sincere in their message of peace.[36] Yorke, an Australian disc jockey (DJ) and journalist, moved to Canada in 1967 and covered pop music for the *Toronto Telegram* and the *Globe and Mail*. Prior to this, he worked for record companies in England and as an international tour promoter for the Spencer Davis Group. Yorke interviewed many heavy hitters in the pop music scene, and his work was read in Canada, the United States and Britain. He was not afraid to be hard on performers, such as when he penned a critical review of Janis Joplin, "the High Priestess of hippie culture," after two shows at Toronto's O'Keefe Centre. He recalled that in the late 1960s pop music writers "hustled [their] own interviews" by hanging out with musicians and their friends.[37] The expatriate Australian wrote liner notes for LPs by American soul singers Aretha Franklin and Jerry Butler and the Canadian pop act the Five Bells. In 1969, under a pseudonym, he produced the first LP by Canadian rock group Edward Bear, released by Capitol Records. One sign that the Australian was an arbiter of hipness was a 1968 fashion piece in the *Globe and Mail* in which he defended bright colours, velvet, leather and frills, as well as clothes by younger designers, as legitimate fashion choices for men.[38] Reporting on John and Yoko for *Rolling Stone, Billboard* and *New Musical Express* over the next year definitely raised his professional profile. Yorke was a well-connected and influential force in the music scene and an advocate for Canadian pop music. One of his greatest frustrations was the unwillingness of radio stations to play Canadian records. As detailed in his 2015 book *Christ You Know*

Ritchie Yorke, John Lennon and Yoko Ono at the King Edward Hotel, May 1969

It Ain't Easy: John and Yoko's Battle for Peace, he was involved with each of Lennon's visits to Canada in 1969, being particularly active with the peace campaign.[39]

Derek Edwards invited Yorke to the King Edward Hotel, where the celebrities asked his advice on the best spot to stage a Canadian bed-in to influence American opinion. He suggested Montreal. At this time, the Quebec metropolis still contained more people than greater Toronto and was home to a number of corporate head offices. Toronto's image (although changing) was relatively boring, whereas Montreal's, by 1960s standards, was cosmopolitan. For example, Montreal had a Playboy Club, which hosted entertainers such as Engelbert Humperdinck. In 2015, Yorke described Toronto in 1969 as "Toronto the Good" — White Anglo-Saxon Protestant conservative and "straight." In contrast, Montreal was "edgy, not traditional English" and in greater proximity to New York City's media and celebrities. This was an overstatement, but there is no doubt that Montreal was livelier than Toronto. With this meeting, the transplanted Australian became part of Lennon and Yoko's team and a key figure in their peace campaign.[40] The *Toronto Daily Star* had a different take on how Montreal was chosen for the bed-in and the genesis of the plan to meet the prime minister with Lennon telling reporters before he met Yorke that he had "heard a lot of Mr. Trudeau" and that he was already planning to head to Montreal, where he mistakenly thought the prime minister lived (he was partly correct: Trudeau's riding, Mount Royal, was located there).[41]

At the King Edward, "teenagers milled about in the corridors," and police attempted to allow only print, radio and television journalists and cameramen into the celebrities' suite. One cynical columnist, describing fans hanging out in the fifth-floor hallway and the hotel lobby, described Lennon as "a rich man behind a locked door," guarded by the police.[42] On the other hand, John and Yoko had travelled without a bodyguard, and Kyoko was allowed to play in the hallway outside the hotel room, at times entertained by teenaged fans, some of whom wore private school uniforms. One notable visitor was popular American novelist Jacqueline Susann, author of *Valley of the Dolls*. Excoriated by critics, the novel was a true blockbuster that told the story of three women damaged by barbiturates and amphetamines. After being invited to meet "the Lennons" at the hotel, where she was also staying, she joined them for a quick chat and drink. After the meeting, she commented to a reporter, "What a darling couple. So peaceful . . . he's sort of fragile. I felt like a mother." She saw no logic in excluding John from the United States for possessing marijuana, explaining that "an artist's passport should be his talent."[43]

One of the most remarkable stories from the first part of Lennon's Canadian visit is the adventure of Jerry Levitan, a fourteen-year-old Beatles fan who not only managed to meet his hero but also scored an exclusive interview while seasoned journalists waited in the hallway outside.[44] As described in his 2009 book *I Met the Wal-*

rus, when he heard via CHUM-FM that John and Yoko had been sighted at the Toronto airport, he began calling hotels. On May 26, helped by a friendly cleaning lady, he managed to bluff his way into Lennon's suite and pitched an idea: Could he return to record an interview for youth about peace? John, Yoko and Derek agreed, and Levitan, with a CHUM reporter and a tape recorder, showed up that evening.[45] Levitan began by asking the couple about their hope to enter the United States. John believed war was "big business" and many vested interests in America supported it on those grounds. Keeping to a theme in many interviews from this period, he spoke of revolutions producing new Establishments and urged "humour and non violence" as the surest route to peace. When the youth brought up Canada's prime minister, Lennon commented, "He seems okay. I don't really know about him." He spoke of Trudeau's "swinging" image in Britain but worried that appearances were more important than a genuine commitment to progressivism. Levitan, who had met Trudeau and was a fan, was optimistic that a meeting with the prime minister would be fruitful.[46]

That evening, taking advantage of their ten-day window of opportunity, the couple prepared to travel to Montreal by air. The departure from the hotel via a fire escape route resembled something out of a Beatles movie as the celebrities, accompanied by Yorke, entered a service elevator and found themselves in the "King Eddy's" enclosed garage. In the limo, John already seemed fatigued by all the attention, commenting that "Ringo was right about not touring," and the bed-in had not even begun.[47] At the Toronto airport, John spoke to Yorke about the negative reaction to the cover of the couple's *Two Virgins* album, the problems of censorship, forthcoming releases by the Beatles and his wish to stage bed-ins in Moscow, Germany, Ireland and Japan.[48] The most satisfying thing to happen to him as a Beatle was not writing songs with Paul McCartney or topping the charts but "meeting Yoko."[49] John admitted that he had misjudged the hostile response to their album cover and explained that he had first thought of the idea when he was in India (which was before his affair with Yoko had begun): "But it was worth it for the howl that went up. It really blew their minds."[50]

Yorke's conversation with Lennon also touched upon the role of nationalism as an obstacle to peace. John spoke of a Toronto cab driver who expressed anti-French views that bordered on racism. "People here are stupid like that," Lennon suggested. "What could be better than a combination of English and French culture in Canada?" Unknowingly, Lennon had hit upon two of Trudeau's core beliefs: a distrust of ethnic nationalism and a hope that the French and the English could work together. Ironically, the celebrities were heading to a city that contained a large anglophone minority that was geographically isolated from the French majority and where English was often the language of business, a situation that fuelled francophone nationalist resentment. For several days, they would be operating in that anglophone world, which was divorced from the reality of most of Quebec.[51]

Canada and the Peace Movement

In the opinion of John Lennon, whose statements were well covered in the international media, Canada in 1969 was a humane and welcoming society, superior to both Britain and the United States.[52] In 2000, Yoko recalled that Canadians in the late 1960s were "kind of liberal people" and that any media event she and John organized in that nation would be well covered south of the border.[53] Yet activists within the country were far from satisfied by the reaction of the Establishment to demands to democratize society and protect it from American economic, cultural and military imperialism. To them, American involvement in Vietnam was illegal and immoral.

Although they hoped to meet Canada's prime minister, John and Yoko's brand of celebrity activism was based on appealing directly to people, particularly the young, and avoiding political parties and established organizations. Lennon's song "Revolution" had expressed his disapproval of "destruction" and "minds that hate," and in interviews throughout 1969 he repeated his dislike of organizations and intellectualism. Although his views appeared to clash with the tactics of the New Left, they often were in agreement with its goals. By 1968, "people were rebelling against disparate issues." What united them in various countries around the world was "a profound distaste for authoritarianism in any form."[54] According to a national stereotype, Canadians were notoriously polite, law-abiding and deferential to authority. Serious political violence was almost unknown, but by 1965 things began to change. The anti-war and other left-wing protest movements were heavily influenced by American organizations, literature and media coverage. Activist (and future academic) James Laxer became convinced that "the student movement in Canada had become totally Americanized," with a distorted focus on civil rights and Vietnam.[55] The University of Toronto planned an orientation festival that addressed social issues such as the city's political structure, "the Americanization of society" and the role of the university. Ironically, one of the special guests, who had to cancel his visit, was American Abbie Hoffman, leader of the Youth International Party (its members were known as "Yippies"), a radical and theatrical branch of the anti-war movement that owed much to the counterculture of the era.[56]

Despite a rising tide of English-Canadian nationalism, Trudeau did not initially support measures to lessen American economic control and adopted, for political reasons, "a passive position on the Vietnam war," seeing no problem with Canada supplying the United States with military equipment.[57] Canada was a founding member of NATO, part of the North American Aerospace Defense Command (NORAD) and a valued American ally. Canadians were not pro-Soviet, but many supported general disarmament by both sides in the Cold War, and in the early 1960s, a sizable minority had feared an imminent nuclear war.[58] In 1963, the newly elected Pearson government agreed to accept nuclear warheads for air defence and for Royal Canadian Air Force and Army units assigned to NATO in Europe. One-third of voters had supported Diefenbaker's PCs, who appeared to be standing up to the United States, and 13 per cent had opted for the NDP, which opposed nuclear weapons and supported an expansion of Canadian peacekeeping under the United Nations. Most of that party's hostility to NATO had to do with nuclear weapons. By 1965, the Vietnam War — specifically America's role — was a major issue for the New Democrats and many Liberals.

As a founding and respected member of the UN credited with inventing peacekeeping in the 1950s, Canada also had a fairly new internationalist perspective. Its peace movement was a combination of the Old Left, the New Left and liberal Christians. The Combined Universities Campaign for Nuclear Disarmament was formed in the late 1950s. Other peace organizations, such the Student Union for Peace Action (SUPA), were organized in subsequent years. Aside from activist organizations, there were many Establishment figures who supported disarmament and opposed nuclear weapons in the early 1960s, including within Diefenbaker's party. By 1965, SUPA activists were in touch with American New Left leaders and responding to the widening U.S. war effort in Vietnam.[59] Starting in 1966, the federal government was under pressure from peace activists, academics and church organizations to adopt a more critical stance toward escalating American military operations in Vietnam. The Liberal party, like the Canadian public, was divided on Cold War issues. The conservative view continued to support containment of Communism, blamed China and Russia for the conflict in Vietnam and regarded the National Liberation Front (Viet Cong) as illegitimate and vicious.[60]

Approximately forty thousand Canadians served in Vietnam as part of the U.S. forces, and four hundred of them were fatal casualties.[61] Yet public reactions in Canada to the American war effort were often hostile. Demonstrations in small towns and major cities protested specific aspects of the American campaign in Southeast Asia, such as the mass bombing of North Vietnam. In April 1968, the Spring Mobilization Committee to End the War in Vietnam, representing a variety of anti-war groups, organized a large demonstration in Toronto against America's involvement in Vietnam. The movement included church, labour, left-wing and student groups. Following a march to the U.S. Consulate, the crowd, which reached in excess of three thousand, convened on Queen's Park for a "teach-in," the term for informal, often open-ended public meetings to discuss political and social issues. There was a clash with a smaller number of pro-war, anti-Communist protestors; police on horseback tried to separate the two groups, and nine demonstrators were arrested. One academic who spoke at the teach-in denounced Canada's role in Vietnam as "lies, spies and hypocrisy."[62]

In November 1968, a four-day conference on Vietnam in Montreal attracted delegates and speakers from a number of causes both at home and abroad. The Hemispheric Conference to End the Vietnam War was marked by internal dissension, with Hispanic and Black delegates accusing others of racism and conservatism. Middle-aged Canadian activists were harangued by youthful Americans, and one group accused the Communist parties of Canada and the United States of engineering the entire meeting to push a reactionary agenda. A number of young dissidents, mainly American, called for the meeting to support guerrilla movements such as the Viet Cong.[63] One somewhat hostile journalist reported that the conference attracted hundreds of seasoned and articulate young New Left activists from the United States who threw their support behind radical causes such as that of the Black Panthers, a socialist political party originating in California that constituted part of the Black Power movement. Although the media focused on its promise to protect African American neighbourhoods with armed patrols from police violence and harassment, the Panthers had a broader program of community welfare. At the Montreal conference, radicals sported "Afro hair dos, black berets,

Judy Marconi, Tommy Smothers, John Lennon, Yoko Ono, Rosemary Leary
and Timothy Leary at the Montreal bed-in, Queen Elizabeth Hotel

leather jackets, drooping New Left moustaches" and "machine gun pendants." The radical turn allegedly attracted young Quebec separatists, who initially had avoided the conference. They were rewarded with a resolution that grouped French Canadians with the Vietnamese and African Americans as victims of "racist and colonial oppression."[64]

The Montreal Bed-In Begins

With one notable exception, Lennon and Ono's peace mission had no contact with Canada's peace movement and concentrated on the Canadian and international media. At 9:55 p.m. on May 25, the celebrities departed on an Air Canada flight to the Montreal airport, where they were met by reporters and hundreds of fans. They headed to the Queen Elizabeth Hotel, located on Dorchester Boulevard (now René Lévesque Boulevard). The modernist building, completed in 1958 by the Canadian National Railway (CNR), was adjacent to the Central Station. Although critics often pointed to the hypocrisy of pop stars of the counterculture variety travelling first class and in limousines, their fans expected no less. According to a hotel representative three decades later, "the Beatle arrived without any money (Apple Records settled the bill later) and he was barely through the door to 1742 when he ordered the living room cleared of its furnishings. The furniture was removed and stacked in the outside hallway."[65] In addition to hotel food and wine, the couple consumed "their favourite macrobiotic food," mainly brown rice, some of it donated by "a yoga camp in the Laurentians."[66] Lennon's health food kick, the result of Ono's influence, was another sign — and a signal to fans — that he had embraced an important lifestyle practice of the counterculture. Yoko had not been in Montreal since 1961 when she attended a local music festival as a conceptual artist. Travelling from New York, she had presented her avant-garde performance piece of "A Grapefruit in the World of Music," a mixture of sights, sounds (including a flushing toilet) and spoken words, a dialogue between a mother and daughter.[67]

The celebrities announced that they were free to talk to reporters from 10 a.m. to 10 p.m. each day, and Derek Taylor asked for "a little help from [their] friends in the press."[68] Although Canadian journalists were welcomed, Lennon really wanted attention from American television networks, major newspapers and magazines and wire services. Over the next week, the suite became a continuous film set, a space for interviews, the end point for special pilgrimages (including a man who walked from Toronto to Montreal for peace), the location of a daily pop music radio broadcast and a recording studio. Lennon left the bed-in only once, on May 29, to visit the U.S. Consulate to apply for a visa. On May 31, the *Montreal Star* printed a cartoon by "Aislin" (Terry Mosher) depicting pajama-clad John and Yoko on a bed. Lennon was holding a paddle and Ono was saying, "The medium is the message," the often-quoted line from Marshall McLuhan, whom the couple would meet on their third trip to the country.

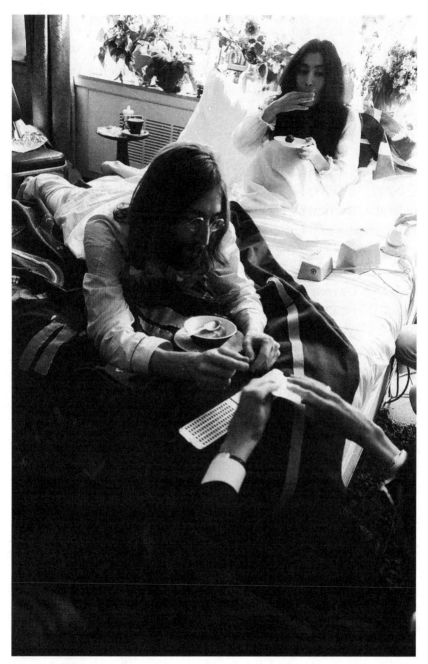

John and Yoko with a blind visitor at the Montreal bed-in

Montreal as the site for a bed-in for global peace was an inter-esting choice given its political and social tensions. According to historian Sean Mills, the city in the 1960s was the site of "one of the most profound, far-reaching and lasting political revolts in North America."[69] The main cause attracting activists, "the decolonization of Quebec," energized intellectuals, poets, artists, trade unionists, feminists, journalists, professionals, students and musicians. Activists also were concerned about the world beyond Quebec. In 1968, Montreal's director of police had called on the federal government to prohibit "red rabble rousers" from the United States and Latin America from attending an anti-Vietnam War conference in the city.[70] Public order was a major issue in 1969, with events such as the occupation by students at Sir George Williams University (now Concordia University) and the bomb-ing of the Montreal Stock Exchange, which injured twenty-seven people.[71] Much of the unrest was caused by francophone resent-ment at anglophone economic privilege and frustrations at the Union nationale provincial government. There were insufficient places in francophone universities for students. In Montreal, French and English feminists banded together as the Front de libération des femmes.[72] In addition, according to journalist Nick Auf der Mur, in the late 1960s the city's working class was fed up with Jean Drapeau and the Civic party, who ran a municipal gov-ernment that appeared to favour elites.[73]

Although cultural politics in Montreal tended to focus on French-English tensions, Black citizens were more self-conscious of their history and organizing to combat prejudice and discrimi-nation. The city was visited by American activists such as Stokely Carmichael and British Black Power advocate Michael de Freitas (Michael X). Carmichael was a former civil rights Freedom Rider (a volunteer who visited the American south to advance desegre-gation and voting rights) who, starting in 1966, preached the logic of Black Power. Two years later, he took part in a Black writers' conference at McGill University. One of the organizers was Rosie

Douglas, who would be targeted as a ringleader of the occupation at Sir George Williams University.[74]

The Sir George Williams University affair began in late 1968 when several Black students, most of whom were from the West Indies, accused a professor of racism. Later in the winter, the situation escalated to the point where several hundred students, Black and white, occupied the computer lab on the ninth floor of a university building. On February 11, 1969, the Montreal police raided the building, and a fire broke out. Nearly one hundred students were arrested, and the suspects were divided into two groups based on race.[75] Racist attitudes were clearly present among spectators outside the building. The legal response to the incident was quite dramatic by Canadian standards: most of the accused were denied bail, riot police blocked friends and relatives from entering the courthouse and a number of lawyers complained that they were denied seeing their clients in jail. The controversy took on an international aspect, with court proceedings monitored by representatives of five Caribbean nations and Martin Luther King's civil rights organization, the Southern Christian Leadership Conference. Most of those arrested were not convicted, but a number did jail time, and some were deported. One of the accused became a Canadian senator, another (Rosie Douglas) the prime minister of Dominica and a third a Quebec judge. The prosecutions at the time fed anti-Canadian sentiment in the Caribbean.[76]

As revealed in the documentary *The Ninth Floor*, the occupation, arrests and prosecutions turned a student protest into a racial confrontation that quickly tested the myth of Canada as an open society.[77] The incident set off a round of editorials and letters to the editor across the nation that condemned lawlessness on campus and called on the university authorities, police and courts to crack down on student extremists. Editorial cartoons portrayed protestors as hairy, poorly dressed anarchists who thumbed their noses at straight society. Editors and columnists railed at "extremist minorities" in places such as Montreal or

Moncton, New Brunswick, who supposedly resorted to "force and blackmail" to stifle debate and force unreasonable concessions from university administrators.[78] Most observers were oblivious to how the Sir George Williams incident — and their own commentary — reflected institutionalized anti-Black racism. The events in Montreal contributed to the awakening Black Power movement in Canada, where Black people were less than one per cent of the population.

The Canadian and international media reported few local or national political or social controversies being discussed at Lennon and Yoko's event. The bed-in is often portrayed as a spontaneous and somewhat chaotic 1960s "happening" (a term for performance art, or in some cases, a hip social event associated with the counterculture). Although many people, especially young Beatles fans, attended or attempted to attend on their own initiative, the event was organized to a degree, and access was controlled. The ever-present Derek Taylor was "handling details and crises and quietly making it work."[79] Assisting him was Capitol Records artists and repertoire man Richard Glanville-Brown. Ritchie Yorke, who sat close to John during his visit to the suite, described a "colourful scene" of flowers, people and sketches and doodles by Lennon.[80] In addition to celebrities and reporters, the rooms attracted a large number of lesser-known visitors and hangers-on. Hundreds showed up, including some blind youths who gave John a Braille watch. Film footage reveals individuals and small groups visiting the celebrity couple, such as three young women with flowers in their hair bearing baskets of more flowers. Alison Gordon of the CBC remembered the bed-in consisting of "self-important people . . . with urgent requests," innumerable room service deliveries and "star-struck fans."[81] Many visits were undocumented, such as when young Montrealer Mike Mendelson, with some friends, managed to reach the suite.[82]

Many of the celebrities who appeared were responding to invitations either from Lennon or the CBC.[83] Some, such as Murray the

K (Murray Kaufman), the former New York DJ who had helped create Beatlemania in the United States in 1964, invited themselves. CBC Radio recorded a long interview with John and Yoko conducted by Fred Peabody, broadcast on June 25 under the title "Give Peace a Chance."[84] At the time, the public broadcaster was attempting to fulfill the mandate of the 1968 *Broadcasting Act*, specifically the goal that "the Canadian broadcasting system should be effectively owned and controlled by Canadians so as to safeguard, enrich and strengthen the cultural, political, social and economic fabric of Canada."[85] The CBC was given the task of preserving and promoting national unity and telling the Canadian story, yet it needed advertising revenues and viewers and was competing with CTV, Canada's private television network. Most of the top shows on both networks were imports. Other than *Hockey Night in Canada* and the odd variety show, Canadians preferred American offerings such as *Rowan and Martin's Laugh-In*, *Gunsmoke*, *Marcus Welby* and *The Mod Squad*. The broadcast regulator, the Canadian Radio-television and Television Commission (CRTC), mandated that only 55 per cent of total programming had to be Canadian. This appeal to viewers and advertisers of mass culture from the United States was nothing new. The networks were also attempting to lure a younger audience.[86]

Young producers working on CBC-TV's *The Way It Is*, in response to Lennon and Ono being denied entrance to the United States, suggested bringing American celebrities to the bed-in to be interviewed by host Patrick Watson, who was generally considered a cool personality. The public affairs show, which began in 1967, had a large budget and a staff that included future media mogul Moses Znaimer and future CBC *As It Happens* and *The Journal* host Barbara Frum. Its head producer was Ross McLean, associated with past current affairs programs such as *Tabloid* and *Close-Up*. Watson had been a creator and co-host of CBC-TV's *This Hour Has Seven Days*, a ground-breaking but controversial current affairs program cancelled in 1966 supposedly for violating journalistic ethics. *This*

Hour, in addition to satirizing politics, practised guerrilla journalism by confronting politicians at their homes and interviewed American celebrities such as actor/director Orson Welles and publisher Bob Guccione, founder of *Penthouse* magazine. Other CBC shows, such as *Front Page Challenge,* the network's long-running news quiz show, regularly recruited American and international authors, politicians, musicians, professional athletes and civil rights activists such as Martin Luther King and Malcolm X.[87] Watson later explained that at the time the idea of inviting celebrities from south of the border to Montreal seemed "goofy and a lot of fun," but it would also allow the CBC to see how serious Lennon and Yoko were about their crusade.[88] Ratings were also a consideration as recently the program had been trailing CTV's current affairs show *W5,* and there were predictions that it would be cancelled. *The Way It Is* tried to be hip and current, running Don Shebib's documentary *San Francisco Summer 1967* on the hippie scene (introduced by Toronto academic John Saywell). But critics found the program dull or inconsistent. For at least one Social Credit MP from the West, it symbolized all that was wrong with the CBC, a combination of "propaganda and perversion" that reflected elitism, anti-Americanism and anti-business and anti-religious feeling.[89]

As the bed-in began, the lobby of the Queen Elizabeth filled with "long-haired Beatle followers" hoping to get an audience with one of their heroes. To a room crowded with journalists, the couple explained that they planned their "lie-in" to last a week, whereupon they would return to Toronto to find out about their visitation status in Canada and possibly the United States. For the most part, access was limited to people with room keys or press passes. Photographers, television crews and radio and print journalists were constant visitors, where the "inner sanctum" was decorated with signs bearing captions such "Vivre l'amour," "I Love Yoko" and "La guerre est fini." Although six-year-old Kyoko, "number one flower child," was often in the centre of the action, she also watched television in another room. Yoko explained that her daughter liked what they were doing and understood the point of the event.[90] One observer recalled that Ono was nervous, but that her experience with performance art helped her endure the lack of privacy and constant presence of strangers in the suite.[91]

The Canadian Press reported that on the first day of the event, staged in a "luxurious downtown suite," cursing and sweating reporters and photographers "elbowed each other for interviews and better camera angles."[92] One reporter remembered journalists, most of whom were over thirty, sharing in "an underlying sense of awe" because a real, live Beatle was in Montreal. Despite this, a number of their questions were "cynical, even sarcastic."[93]

Doris Giller, a features writer for the *Montreal Star*, was one of the few female reporters present in the suite. She had grown up in Montreal on "the Main" (St. Lawrence Boulevard), the city's chief Jewish neighbourhood. A former secretary, she started with the *Montreal Star* in 1963 and infiltrated the macho environment of Canadian journalism. The Montreal Press Club did not allow women as members until 1969. Giller, who became a member of a social circle of anglophone and Jewish Montreal writers and reporters that included novelist Mordecai Richler, eventually moved to Toronto. After her death, her husband established the Giller Prize, Canada's richest and most prestigious literary competition, in her name.[94]

Assistant Anthony Fawcett estimated that the couple gave at least sixty interviews in Montreal. Another estimate was three hundred. Many were with AM and FM radio stations conducted via telephone speaker phones. On more than one occasion, John spoke with students embroiled in the People's Park protest at Berkeley, California, a classic late-1960s New Left confrontation. Deputies with shotguns fired birdshot at demonstrators, killing one person and injuring dozens. More were arrested, and California governor Ronald Reagan called out the National Guard. Lennon urged the students to avoid protesting violently and provoking aggression from "the pigs." Instead, he said, they should use their brains.[95] He also advised protestors who had occupied university-owned property to move to another park or even to Canada.[96] As Jon Wiener pointed out, this advice was not exactly in tune with the tactics of classic non-violent resistance, which was based on passive confrontation, and Lennon had no actual experience with these types of protests. During the bed-in, he conceded that "sit-ins are okay," but he opposed property damage.[97]

In an interview for *Life* magazine, the couple stressed that they had no plans to start a peace foundation or organization to promote their goals but did not rule out co-operating with established organizations. Yoko believed it would be "dangerous" for them to become leaders of a formal movement. Yet, as a pop guru, Lennon had followers. The *London Times* reported that toward the end of the bed-in, two hundred "hippies" entered the hotel and climbed the stairs to the seventeenth floor to see Lennon and Ono; they were told that one of their group could enter.[98] This was a group of young people who had been taking part in a happening on Mount Royal, a "peace-in" event promoted by Montreal radio station CFOX at Fletcher's Field using John in its promotion. Its lone delegate, a teenage girl, left with flowers and a message from John and Yoko: "Return to the mountain."[99] It is not clear how many of the youthful visitors were francophone. There were bilingual Québécois reporters at the bed-in such as Radio-Canada's Gilles Goguen (Radio-Canada is the French-language component of the CBC). He recalled that when Lennon was talking about his musical influences, his song writing and his limitations as a singer, Ono seemed bored.[100]

For photographers, the bed-in was an ideal assignment. Gerry Deiter, a transplanted New Yorker living in Montreal hired by *Life* magazine, was present for the whole week and ended up taking several hundred photographs. The experience had a profound effect on Deiter, who moved to British Columbia and became an activist journalist, sailing on the first Greenpeace voyage to protest American nuclear testing in Alaska.[101] Eighteen-year-old photography student Roy Kerwood used connections with a local radio station to gain access to the celebrities. Lennon liked his photos so much that he purchased several of them. Like Deiter, he became a fixture in Room 1742.[102] In addition to journalists and photographers, the suite hosted a remote radio broadcast by CFOX, the city's lone English rock station. Popular DJ Chuck (Charles P. "Rodney") Chandler scored a major coup when he convinced Derek Taylor that the station could help publicize the bed-in. Chandler and expatriate British DJ Roger Scott set up a remote site in the suite and broadcast pop music daily. This included commercials for soft drinks, beer and other consumer products — a strange twist for a counterculture happening. John got into the act, doing "record intros," voicing commercials and generally having fun.[103]

On May 27, Reuters reported that Lennon had invited Trudeau to Montreal and wanted to give him acorns to promote peace. In the House of Commons, the prime minister did not reply to a query from NDP MP Ed Broadbent as to whether he planned to participate in "the peaceful lie-in." Trudeau told reporters he did not know about Lennon's acorns for peace gesture but would like to meet with the Beatle "if he's around." Suggesting a familiarity with Lennon's best-selling books of wordplay, he added, "He's a pretty good poet."[104] The Montreal happening also affected political debate in Quebec. In the National Assembly, Liberal leader Jean Lesage (whose government had launched the province's Quiet Revolution in 1960) criticized the Union nationale government for a Lennon interview aired on Radio-Québec, the provincial radio network. Lesage, 57, was concerned that John had been interviewed for a series on music that was listened to by schoolchildren. He referred to the celebrities as "those who live in a bed" and who endorsed marijuana use. Fearful for the morals of the province's youth, he noted that the couple had been banned from entering the United States and had been permitted to stay in Canada for only ten days. Premier Jean-Jacques Bertrand had been a Union nationale member of the National Assembly in the dark days of Premier Maurice

Duplessis but as education minister had supported progressive policies. He explained that Lennon, "whether we like him or not, represents an important and undeniable fact in the history and development of music." To dismiss Lennon because of a drug possession conviction, he continued, would be like ignoring a famous author for a past transgression.[105]

On the third day, a crew from New York's WNEW-TV filmed an extensive segment that included scenes of members of the local chapter of the International Society for Krishna Consciousness having a meal and chanting. The "Hare Krishnas" were basically white hippies (with shaved heads) who had been drawn into the movement, which was inspired by Hindu scriptures, because of its easy fit with the counterculture: vegetarianism, communalism, anti-materialism and altered consciousness (attained not by drugs, which were forbidden, but chanting and dancing).[106]

WNEW also covered the visit of Grant Fox, an American soldier who had deserted from Fort Dix, New Jersey. Accompanied by his wife and daughter, he had been assisted by the local American Deserters Committee, which was supported by various American New Left groups as well as a number of Canadian churches. Throughout the Vietnam War, up to ten thousand war resisters came to Montreal, where they often lived in or hung around the neighbourhood of McGill University. As Fox explained: "We were told by the system to go kill." By the time Lennon returned to Canada later in 1969, the world would learn more about American atrocities against civilians, such as the My Lai massacre (the 1968 incident where U.S. infantry killed up to five hundred men, women and children). In one news clip, John helps feed Fox's infant daughter. Lennon reiterated the importance of non-violent solutions, prompting a journalist to ask about the United States aiding Great Britain in 1941. John responded, "What happened then was right for that moment."[107] The segment recorded Yoko's widely reported remark that the Second World War would not have occurred if she had been Hitler's girlfriend and John's advice that the peace movement should employ sex appeal to sell its message, like tabloids used "bikini-clad girls."[108]

Fox's presence reflected another reality for late-1960s Canada: the arrival of thousands of American draft evaders and military deserters avoiding service in Vietnam. The draft dodger issue was a factor in domestic politics and Canadian-American relations and shaped outside international perceptions of both Canada and its leader. One refugee from militarism was Jesse Winchester, a twenty-three-year-old from Louisiana who reached Montreal in 1967. A gifted singer-songwriter, he would launch a professional career in Canada and pen the song "Tell Me Why You Like Mr. Roosevelt," which praised "Lester B." (Pearson) and Pierre Trudeau for welcoming American war resisters. The popular memory that Canada wholeheartedly welcomed American military deserters and draft evaders is largely myth, however. In late 1968, a poll indicated that almost half of Canadians did not agree with "draft dodgers" and that 51 per cent opposed granting them asylum. Opinion softened as the costly war in Vietnam ground on.[109]

Immigration statistics suggest that up to thirty thousand American men who were eligible to be drafted arrived in Canada during the war. Many did not wait for their draft papers, heading north to cities such as Vancouver, Toronto and Montreal, where they found many fellow political refugees and contributed to the emerging counterculture. The 1968 *Manual for Draft-Age Immigrants to Canada* explained that the country "may well be the most functioning democracy in the world" and had "never launched a war and seldom becomes involved in one." According to its author, Mark Satin, because of the nation's toleration of ethnic minorities, "an atmosphere of freedom" prevailed.[110] The arrival of thousands of young men and women, many of them well educated and on the Left of the political spectrum, boosted Canada's activist communities. By 1968, major cities were also attracting American military deserters. They faced greater administrative hurdles and police harassment, but neither draft evasion nor desertion was an extraditable offence, and the Canadian government adopted a largely neutral approach. In late 1968, an American deserters committee was formed in Montreal.

In May of 1969, the Trudeau government seemingly undermined American policy when it announced that border agents would no longer dissuade military deserters from entering the country. The NDP applauded this policy, as did organizations in the United States that assisted war resisters. Several months later, the Department of Immigration clarified its procedures to place deserters in the same category as draft resisters.[111] By the end of the year, tens of thousands of American military deserters and draft dodgers were living north of the border. The influx, which included spouses, girlfriends and others, led to the creation of organizations that assisted the refugees, who often were also helped by their own families. Draft dodgers tended to be middle class and fairly well educated; deserters were comparatively blue collar. Even after the Carter administration offered an amnesty in 1975, many war refugees refused to return home. One was Dick Cotterill, who, while serving in the U.S. Marines, was refused a discharge as a conscientious objector. He deserted to Canada, moved to Nova Scotia, married a Canadian and started a family.[112]

Vietnam seemed to be on the minds of many visitors to the Queen Elizabeth hotel, but the mission of the celebrity activists was broader in scope.

Philip Winslow of the *Montreal Star* secured an interview with John and Yoko after the "tumult" of the initial press conference. Winslow wrote that the "razzle dazzle pandemonium" of the event was causing many journalists to ignore or underplay its actual focus. John explained that they wanted to create a movement of tactical non-violence in the spirit of Gandhi, based on the theory that peace, like war, had to be sold to the public. This viewpoint no doubt reflected the widespread feeling that the American government and military had been using the media to mislead the public on the Vietnam War. Yoko agreed, adding that peace had to be marketed like the most recent models of automobiles from Detroit. There was a need to "indoctrinate" children, "housewives," government leaders and militant students, based on the theory that "we're all responsible for what happens in the world." Yoko believed that many current activist movements were passing fads and that the war in Vietnam was "a symbol of the violent atmosphere of the whole world." Returning to one of his favourite themes, John stressed the importance of converting "urban squares" to the cause. Mothers, he hoped, would identify with a married couple with a daughter. Ironically, given his status within the counterculture, he criticized not only militant protestors who supported the use of violence to effect political change but also supposedly peaceful counterculture types. Hippies and Yippies, he continued, were actually "snobbish and they don't want to talk to squares." This was an interesting statement given that many squares in 1969 would have regarded Lennon, with his long hair and beard, as a wealthy hippie. John questioned whether any "militant revolution" in history had ever succeeded in not producing a new "Establishment." He concluded that "we all have Hitler within us," but "we all have love and peace in us too."[113]

One radio interview connected to an underreported but serious issue in Canada: the plight of its Indigenous peoples. This was in the news in 1969 because in May, despite consultations with Indigenous organizations, the Trudeau government had issued a white paper that called for abolition of *The Indian Act* and the end of reserves and any federal responsibility to "Status Indians" (Indigenous people who were under the jurisdiction of the federal government and who had only become citizens in 1960). This unexpected and controversial policy proposal reflected the individual rights philosophy of Trudeau more than expert opinion and produced immediate pushback from Indigenous organizations.

During the Montreal bed-in, the *Globe and Mail* reported on the activism of Lillian Piché Shirt, an Alberta Cree, in the context of housing discrimination against the urban poor.[114] Although she had support from the broader community in Edmonton,

Shirt's protest was part of the awakening of Indigenous Canada after a century or more of attempted assimilation and neglect by the state and prejudice and discrimination by society in general. With her four young children, she set up her tipi in a downtown park to protest the lack of housing. The situation of the Saddle Lake First Nation woman also highlighted issues facing off-reserve Status Indians, the loss of Indigenous culture because of residential schools (state-sponsored schools run by Christian churches that attempted to assimilate Status Indian children) and discrimination in social welfare. Her story was published in a Montreal newspaper when John and Yoko were in the city. In 2006, Lillian explained that she was approached by Edmonton radio station CJCA to do an interview with a prominent person who was visiting Toronto (this was after the celebrities had returned from Montreal). According to this interview, in 1969 Lillian did not recognize the name John Lennon, but on the telephone he said he wanted to help her. She claimed to have given Lennon a phrase in Cree from her grand-mother, which translated into "Imagine that if, there was no hate, if we loved each other, we loved one another, that there would be no war between us." John allegedly wrote this down. A few years later, she heard Lennon's song "Imagine" and suspected that their 1969 conversation had inspired the lyrics. Lillian Shirt continued her activism and took part in the Native American occupation of the former Alcatraz federal penitentiary in 1969, one of the more dramatic exertions of Red Power in the era.[115] Shirt did not receive a song-writing credit for "Imagine" or royalties.

Celebrities at the Bed-In

The CBC recruited a number of well-known Americans to meet John and Yoko, but the few Canadian personalities on hand could hardly be called celebrities. In terms of the current political situa-tion in Quebec, a media event in Montreal promoting peace was an interesting twist. Activists in that province, although possibly iden-

Quebec sovereigntist Jacques Larue-Langlois at the Montreal bed-in

tifying with the Viet Cong and the North Vietnamese as oppressed peoples, were more interested in the local liberation struggle than in marching on the Pentagon. In a Radio-Canada interview aimed at a francophone audience on May 27, Lennon explained that he wanted to "cool down" revolution and that the combination of "minority, left-wing students," media coverage and police could lead to violence. But young nationalists in Quebec, many of them purporting to be socialists, were frustrated by the pace of political change and increasingly attracted to revolutionary rhetoric.[116]

Jacques Larue-Langlois, a Quebec separatist born in 1934, was no youth, but he was one of the few francophone personalities to officially meet Lennon and Ono at the Queen Elizabeth. Another CBC recruit, Larue-Langlois, who appeared briefly in the documentary *Bed Peace*, looked more like an academic than a revolutionary. A writer and former producer for Radio-Canada, he had become involved with the Comité Vallières-Gagnon, which worked to free two FLQ members charged in connection with two fatal bombings. A founding member of the RIN, Larue-Langlois renounced evolutionary reform after that party joined with the PQ. Like many young, educated separatists of the era, he envisioned Quebec as an independent socialist society. In 1968, he had taken part in the Hemispheric Conference to End the Vietnam War. In the months that followed the bed-in, Larue-Langlois's name would be mentioned by Montreal civic officials demanding an investigation of the Company of Young Canadians (CYC) in Quebec. The CYC was a type of domestic Peace Corps sponsored by the federal government, whose young volunteers, paid stipends, helped disadvantaged communities organize projects. Given that the RCMP Security Service was treating Quebec separatism as a threat to national security similar to Communism, the Montreal writer was probably under surveillance at the time.[117]

Paul McGrath has written that John failed to persuade separatists visiting the bed-in "to abandon the possibility of violence."[118] Ono and Lennon probably knew little of the FLQ or Quebec nationalism, but at this point they were fans of neither political intellectualism nor political militancy. In an exchange captured in *Bed Peace*, Larue-Langlois tries to explain that he is fighting a "monster" and attempting to convince "the people" (presumably Québécois) that they are exploited. He also takes a swipe at capitalism for "making money" from the people. Yoko advises him to fight against his own ignorance and suggests, "You are just advocating hatred." John adds that he risks alienating "the people against other people." The Marxist separatist speaks of the "superstructure" of society, but John is unconvinced, accusing the FLQ supporter of "twelfth-century thinking." Lennon urged radicals to "slow the whole process down," but Larue-Langlois insisted on the necessity of "a fight" or struggle. The FLQ supporter stated that it was necessary to use "all means necessary," including "a certain degree of violence," to fight against "the monster." Larue-Langlois also suggested that John and Yoko were not the first "beautiful people" (celebrities) to offer advice on political problems. As the meeting ended, the tone was more moderate, but when John quipped "Vive la France," the departing revolutionary intellectual retorted, "Québec libre."[119]

Despite its message of universalism, the bed-in, in addition to being an English event staged in a province that was largely French speaking, was an overwhelmingly white experience. At least one Black journalist was present: American art critic and writer Charles Childs, on assignment for *Life* magazine. In the end, his interview with John and Yoko formed the basis of an article in *Penthouse*.[120] American comedian Dick Gregory was the best-known Black person at the Montreal event and apparently the only other non-white visitor of note. Credited for smoothing the path for other Black comedians, such as Bill Cosby and Richard Pryor, his career took off in the early 1960s. By the late 1960s, Gregory had abandoned nightclub gigs for the college lecture circuit, writing and civil rights and anti-war activism. The comedian also supported Native American rights; in 1966, he had taken part in a fundraising concert in Saskatchewan with Indigenous singer and activist Buffy Sainte-Marie. Despite ongoing controversies over racism in Montreal and elsewhere, there is no indication that Gregory's visit produced any discussion of the plight of Black people in Canada, such as the recent convictions of a number of the Sir George Williams University activists by a Montreal court.[121] As writer Lawrence Hill has noted, Canadians, conditioned to think of the United States as a land of racial oppression, were blind to these issues in their own country.[122] John did raise the issue of Black Power in a May 30 interview on WABC-FM with *Village Voice* writer Howard Smith in which he called armed resistance by African Americans "madness . . . what the hell do they think they're gonna do after they've shot everyone?"[123] This was probably a reference to the Black Panthers, who, starting in 1967 were involved in a number of violent confrontations with police. John was echoing a talking point repeatedly put forward by many white politicians and pundits that ignored the Black Panthers' philosophy of self-defence and misconstrued the group as inherently violent, thus perpetuating racist stereotypes.

At the time, the RCMP was concerned that American Black Power activists were radicalizing African Canadians.

In conversation with Yoko and John, Gregory spoke of the need to "bust the Establishment" and to follow the earlier model of the union movement in achieving social change. He stressed the need to value "human rights" over property rights and raised the issue of the death penalty in the United States (in Canada capital punishment was still the law, but no one had been executed since 1962).[124] Gregory asked why, if American democracy was so great, did the United States "have to go all around the world trying to ram it down people's throats with a gun?"[125] His suggestion of a peace conference attracted some attention. In Fredericton, New Brunswick, Walter Learning, director of the Playhouse theatre, sent a telegram to Lennon and Ono, offering the facility for any peace meeting. A conference, more of a media event, would transpire, but its location would be Ottawa.[126]

One of the more influential 1960s figures at the bed-in was LSD advocate Timothy Leary, accompanied by his spouse, Rosemary Woodruff Leary. A clinical psychologist fired from Harvard because of his promotion of the then-legal drug, he was paid the ultimate compliment for someone of the counterculture by Richard Nixon, who described him as "the most dangerous man in America."[127] Leary had emerged as a symbol of the counterculture by 1966, when the Beatles were first discovering it, and was drawn to the anti-war cause somewhat later. He was featured on the CBC television program *Document* that year and was a guest on *Front Page Challenge*.[128] Most famously, he contributed one of the classic mantras of the 1960s, "Turn On, Tune In, Drop Out," supposedly after a discussion with Marshall McLuhan, whom he had met in New York.[129] Leary and the founder of the pop music magazine *Crawdaddy!* Paul Williams had arrived in Montreal on assignment for *Playboy* magazine. In return, Williams was supposed to prepare an article on "the historic meeting between Lennon and Leary."[130] Although no youth, Leary was the much-publicized promoter of a "psychedelic revolution" based on LSD, which governments were criminalizing in the late 1960s. Far from pleasure or hedonism, Leary attributed nobler goals to drug use: greater consciousness, personal fulfillment and societal betterment. These were basic tenets of the counterculture, a lifestyle that was attractive to many young Canadians.[131]

Leary's message on psychoactive awareness predated the newest manifestation of the counterculture: hippies. The Canadian press began to report on this new youth phenomenon, another import from the United States, in 1966. Although critics often derided hippies for their anti-social habits, look and attitudes, many of them were in fact motivated by a strong social conscience. Most were probably simply responding to the newest trend in youth culture, which was an elaboration of the beatnik phenomenon of the 1950s. Singer Jim Morrison of rock band the Doors explained the trend as an expression of middle-class culture; mid-1960s society had created the necessary abundance and leisure time to permit youth to rebel against mass society.[132] One early Canadian manifestation was the March 1967 Human Be-In in Vancouver's Stanley Park. Denied permission, the event proceeded nonetheless, in the spirit of the famous be-in that had recently been staged in San Francisco. The Vancouver happening attracted hundreds and included a performance by the American psychedelic group Country Joe and the Fish and two local bands. Dubbed an Easter celebration "by the peoples of the rainforest," the Human Be-In indicated another reality of the times: counterculture as spectator sport. The press reported that onlookers outnumbered hippies by two to one. In a similar manner, tourists would be drawn to Toronto's Yorkville area (near Yonge and Bloor) to view hippies in their natural habitat.[133] In addition to congregating in certain neighbourhoods, hippies and youth who emulated their free-spirited lifestyle liked to travel, hitchhiking across Canada or backpacking throughout Europe. For the lucky few, the ultimate destinations were overseas counterculture enclaves where drugs were easily available. Young Margaret

Sinclair, a self-described "flower child," sowed some of her wild oats in Morocco before returning to Canada.

Hippies, like young people in earlier eras, tended to congregate in groups and hang out in places such as public parks, coffee houses and bars. In addition, as a study of Yorkville, Toronto's most visible counterculture area, pointed out, there was the larger group of "weekend" hippies, so-called straight or square young women and men who attended school or held down jobs but grew their hair, wore offbeat clothing, listened to psychedelic rock music and spoke a specific argot.[134] True hippies supposedly did not bathe or care about personal hygiene. They often dressed in an androgynous manner, leading to jokes about not being able to tell the boys from the girls. Hippies supposedly were not interested in straight society and its materialism; were attracted to Eastern religions, astrology and communal living; and were free of "hang-ups" about sex. Most worrisome for the authorities (and parents), hippies embraced the use of illegal drugs such as marijuana, hashish and LSD as a liberating experience. A Winnipeg police detective told a 1969 conference on the subject that drug abuse was at "near epidemic levels" in the city thanks to hippies. LSD and marijuana, he claimed, spread from the growing "hippie set" to university students and then to the high schools. In his experience, users of heroin and other hard drugs had started on so-called soft drugs such as LSD and marijuana.[135] The media attempted to interpret the hippie phenomenon. In 1969, the *Winnipeg Free Press* published a twelve-part series, "The Seekers," advertised as "Must Reading for Teens and Parents." One installment explained that hippies wanted to "replace hate with love, materialism with idealism and the instant enlightenment of mind expanding drugs."[136]

In typical fashion, Leary, who a probation officer classified as "an immature exhibitionist," moved into the inner circle at the Montreal bed-in.[137] A transcript of a May 29 conversation indicates that Lennon, Ono and the Learys talked about Leary's Millbrook, New York retreat, the joys of living in a tipi, the student protests at Berkeley, Pierre Trudeau, mass media and the state of America. As John explained: "We wanted to get to Trudeau, but we're really headed to Nixon."[138] Whether Lennon meant that he wanted to meet the American president or help put more anti-war pressure onto the White House is unclear.[139] Rosemary Leary later described the Montreal happening as "a total media event . . . funky and homey too." She discussed issues such as pregnancy, miscarriages and childbirth with Yoko.[140]

Abraham Feinberg, the progressive former rabbi of Toronto's Holy Blossom Temple, was the only documented guest with a connection to Canada's anti-war movement. In April, he had spoken at Toronto's large Easter International Days of Protest, attended by contingents of trade unionists, the NDP, Communists, church organizations and students (many from Rochdale College of the University of Toronto). Fellow speaker, writer and television personality Pierre Berton had denounced the Vietnam War as immoral and inhuman.[141] In 1960, the rabbi had written: "When we fight for true liberty and democracy, we advance the forces chosen by God himself as an instrument of renewed creation."[142] Feinberg had enjoyed a professional singing career on American radio in the 1930s before returning to rabbinical duties in New York. In Toronto, as a serving and retired rabbi, he became involved in civil rights and disarmament work. In 1961, he published a *Toronto Daily Star* opinion editorial that called capital punishment a "threat to the country's moral fibre."[143] Black writer and activist Austin Clarke wrote in his autobiography of taking part in a protest in 1963 with the rabbi against the murder of civil rights worker Medgar Evers in Mississippi. A year later, Feinberg protested against a visit of pro-segregation Alabama governor George Wallace, who spoke at Maple Leaf Gardens in Toronto before twelve thousand Lion's Club members. Feinberg's opinion pieces were published in *Saturday Night*, the *Globe and Mail* and the *Star*. In 1966, writing for *Maclean's*, he defended civil disobedience and encouraged Canada to promote disarmament.[144]

Feinberg had been recruited by the CBC because he was one of Canada's most vocal critics of the Vietnam War. Although Canadian governments from 1965 onward supported American war aims and blamed North Vietnam as the aggressor, Ottawa did not always agree with how the United States operated militarily. In 1965, Prime Minister Pearson had violated his own preferred approach, "quiet diplomacy," in a speech at Temple University, where he urged a temporary halt in the American bombing of North Vietnam to further the aims of diplomacy. This had enraged President Johnson. Two years later, Pearson's external relations minister called for a ceasefire. The Liberal government continued to express concern about the war's escalation and mounting civilian casualties. In 1967, Feinberg and two other clerics visited both South and North Vietnam, which led to his book, *Hanoi Diary*.[145] Many liberal, educated Canadians were troubled by the American role in South Vietnam as early as 1965 as a result of nightly television news reports and images in Beryl Fox's evocative documentary *The Mills of the Gods*, which was shown on CBC-TV. Around this time, New Left publications such as *Canadian Dimension* and *Our Generation* were criticizing American imperialism in Southeast Asia, linking it to the economic and cultural domination of Canada. By 1967, there were almost two dozen campus committees across Canada to end the war in Vietnam. Growing opposition included not only socialists but also the NDP, labour unions and church organizations.[146]

On his trip, Rabbi Feinberg had advised North Vietnamese Prime Minister Pham Van Dong that the U.S. peace movement was weak and that the Americans could not be defeated on the battlefield.[147] Subsequently, he called for Canada to pull out of the International Control Commission, which had been set up to monitor the 1954 truce agreement in Vietnam, because its role was perceived in North Vietnam as biased in favour of the United States. By the time Feinberg returned, many Canadians were viewing the war as immoral — or at least unwinnable. Earlier in 1969, Feinberg had officially welcomed representatives of the Viet Cong at a rally at Massey Hall and spoken at an anti-war rally at Toronto City Hall.[148]

In a *Toronto Daily Star* column written following his time with John and Yoko, Feinberg reported that he was impressed by the Beatle's integrity and dedication, describing him as "a powerful personality and surprisingly religious in the classic sense of the word." Lennon was not just a celebrity but a "mentor" and role model for youth around the world. He questioned the Establishment but in a sensitive manner, and the bed-in was in the spirit of the sit-ins of the civil rights movement. Lennon identified with Jesus, but not in an arrogant way, and opposed war, "the ultimate blasphemy against God." As for John and Yoko living together before they were married, this was a growing practice in Canada and hardly a moral threat. For Feinberg, it was healthier and more realistic to talk about sex in an open way, like Lennon did, rather than to suppress it.[149] A few days after John and Yoko returned to Britain, Feinberg spoke at a Voice of Women meeting at Toronto's St. Lawrence Hall, where he called on the United States to withdraw its forces from South Vietnam.[150]

Rounding out the cast of 1960s pop culture characters at the Queen Elizabeth was American comedian Tommy Smothers. He was part of a brother comedy duo whose hit TV show, *The Smothers Brothers Comedy Hour*, was especially popular with viewers under thirty-five and was increasingly outspoken on social and political issues such as the Vietnam War.[151] Two months prior to the Montreal happening, Smothers, in an interview with a Canadian reporter, complained of network censorship and mused about the American government's lack of honesty about the war in Vietnam, the conservative nature of mainstream politicians and racism in the television industry.[152] In April, at a press conference at Toronto's Park Plaza Hotel, he stated that if the brothers were blacklisted by the entertainment industry in the United States, they would consider producing a show in Canada.[153] In conversations with Yoko and John, Smothers was pessimistic about his nation's

Recording "Give Peace a Chance" in Montreal

political future, stating that even moderates were frustrated by the Establishment's response to protest.[154] He was also frustrated about how the media played up topics such as the sexual revolution but was not very critical of important issues, such as Nixon's planned anti-ballistic missile system or how the government managed public opinion. Yoko remained encouraging: "That is no reason to give up . . . we have to make it."[155]

Recording "Give Peace a Chance"

The main legacy of Lennon and Ono's celebrity diplomacy in 1969 would be the anti-war song "Give Peace a Chance." John appears to have written it by May 30 and played it for the Learys and Paul Williams late that evening. The rehearsal and recording took place between 7 and 11 p.m. on Saturday, May 31, in room 1742, and film footage indicates that around forty individuals were present. The lyrics, written out and pinned to the wall, referred to a number of the participants and played on repeated rhyming phrases ("madism, bagism, shagism, dragism"), reflecting Lennon's love of wordplay. Supposedly singing along was best-selling British pop singer Petula Clark, who had scored a series of major international hits starting in 1964 with "Downtown." She had performed a bilingual show at Montreal's Place des Arts and became upset after the audience appeared to divide into two hostile camps, French and English, rejecting her message of togetherness. This was another sign of the rising tension over language in Quebec. Although she had never met Lennon, Clark visited the Queen Elizabeth Hotel and was admitted into the bed-in, where she asked John for his advice.[156] Tommy Smothers, sitting near John, strummed along on an acoustic guitar. Other credited performers were Tim and Rosemary Leary, Judy Marconi, Paul Williams, Rabbi Feinberg, Joseph Schwartz, Derek Taylor, Dick Gregory, Murray the K and Roger Scott.[157] The visiting members of the Canadian branch of the Radha Krishna Temple did not sing but "kept their eyes closed and wagged their heads in time," swayed to the beat and brandished a drum, small cymbals and a tambourine.[158] Alison Gordon remembered the experience to be fun but never imagined that the song, which seemed a bit rough, would be released commercially and that she would be part of music history.[159] Concert promoter David Tarlton thought at the time that the "chant" was too simple and repetitive to be released but treasured the "spiritual moment" of the actual recording.[160]

Capitol Records' Richard Glanville-Brown had attempted to ship recording equipment from Toronto, but in the end he approached André Perry, a Montreal jazz musician and sound engineer. The setting, with low ceilings and drywall, made sound quality a definite challenge.[161] In a 2014 interview for Le Journal de Montréal, Perry revealed that the recorded tracks were later enhanced by the addition of a rhythm track and new voices on the chorus, including that of Quebec rocker Robert Charlebois. Like a number of prominent singers and artists such as Pauline Julien, in 1968 Charlebois had taken part in a benefit for the Comité Vallières-Gagnon. Yet in 1969, he criticized separatists as "sheep."[162] Early the next morning at his studio in the nearby municipality of Brossard, Perry transferred the four tracks of the raw recording to eight and fixed the rhythm track by using items at hand. He then called on Charlebois and other unnamed Québécois musicians to create a tighter chorus: "I kept 15 or 20% of the atmosphere and I redid the whole thing so that it rings as he [Lennon] would have wanted."[163] The following day, he explained the alternate mix to John and played him both versions. Lennon chose the one with the Québécois performers, so French Canada had contributed in a small way to the history of the Beatles.[164] In 2005, Perry told a reporter that he was not a huge fan of "Give Peace a Chance" at the time but was "flattered that they never remixed it and they're still playing it." He also said that he preferred the "flip side of the 45 [he] recorded with them," the song "Remember Love," a ballad with Yoko singing and John playing finger-style guitar.[165]

Lennon gave McCartney a credit as writer, although he had nothing to do with the song. Released under the name Plastic Ono Band, it became Lennon's first solo single, reaching number one in the United Kingdom, number fourteen in the United States and number eight on Canada's RPM charts. The chorus (if not the verses) was catchy and easy to sing, and it was soon adopted as a protest anthem on both sides of the Atlantic. "Give Peace a Chance" also pushed another barrier: it was an AM radio hit nearly five minutes long, twice the length of early Beatles hits. A number of years later, Lennon explained that he gave Paul credit "out of guilt," as this was his "first independent single." Instead, he should have acknowledged Yoko, "who had actually written it with me."[166]

Aside from "Give Peace a Chance," the meeting in Montreal inspired another piece of pop culture history. The Beatles song "Come Together" supposedly began as an attempt by Lennon to write a campaign anthem for Leary, who was running for governor of California. The day after recording "Give Peace a Chance," Leary supposedly asked for John's help. Lennon picked up his guitar and soon had a rough song, "Come Together, Join the Party." According to Leary, Lennon gave him a tape of the song, and that was the end of his involvement. Two months later, Lennon, having given co-writing credit to McCartney, recorded the finished song with the Beatles. The first track on *Abbey Road*, "Come Together," became a number one single and is considered one of the group's finest songs. Leary planned to take part in the 1970 state election, but his troubles with the law got in the way. He ended up being sent to prison for ten years.[167]

Visitors continued to appear in the suite after the recording session. On June 1, the CBC, "for balance," brought in one outspoken conservative, cartoonist Al Capp, creator of the comic strip *Li'l Abner*.[168] In the tradition of its immediate ancestor *This Hour Has Seven Days*, the producers of *The Way It Is* were providing CBC viewers with a vivid encounter of two opposite poles of 1960s culture. The almost sixty-year-old American engaged in a confrontation with Yoko and John that was captured by the CBC film crew. One biographer subsequently described how the cartoonist had transformed from a progressive into "a student-hating, pro-Vietnam War pal of Richard Nixon and Spiro Agnew."[169] By the late 1960s, Capp, who would soon be embroiled in sexual harassment controversies, regarded left-wing celebrities as naïve, mercenary and insincere.[170]

Capp introduced himself as "that dreadful, Neanderthal fascist," to which John replied, "We're those famous freaks." He went on

Al Capp's interview with John and Yoko

to accuse John of not knowing history and supporting his "friends" in Berkeley, whereas Capp was "cheering on the police." John countered that he was not a fan of any type of violence. The cartoonist (who had a copy of the *Two Virgins* album) then attacked their nude photos as "filth" and rejected the idea that Lennon could speak for him.[171] Capp accused John of staging the bed-in for financial gain: "You got into bed so people like me would come and see you." Lennon replied that an event like the bed-in was not designed for financial gain and that he could make more money by taking an hour to write a song. Capp's parting shot was to question the celebrities' mental soundness, much to the ire of the normally calm Derek Taylor.[172] One witness later wrote that John, a huge pop star usually insulated from direct confrontation, was "flustered" by the aggressive approach of "Al Crapp," which was the norm on a number of American TV talk shows. There was little personal enmity between Leary and Capp, who shared a flight on a small plane back to Boston, courtesy of the CBC.[173] Despite (or because of) his provocative conservatism, Capp had many supporters in Canada.[174]

The Ottawa Peace Seminar

During their first Canadian visit, other than their meeting with Feinberg, Lennon and Ono had no documented interaction with the organized Canadian peace movement. Other established or emerging social movements were also absent; although one press report claimed that "a new wave of feminism" was "breaking over Toronto" and elsewhere, there were no reported visits by women's rights activists.[175] Similarly, there were no delegations from the student movement or the New Left. But on June 2, the *Ottawa Journal* reported on the involvement of the celebrities in an upcoming seminar on world peace. University of Ottawa student union president Allan Rock informed the Canadian Press that he was heading to the bed-in to firm up arrangements.[176] One photograph captured a well-dressed Rock accompanied by a friend, Tom Morry,

Yoko and John with Kyoko and Allan Rock at the Ottawa train station, June 1969

speaking with Yoko and John, making his pitch for a visit. On June 3, it was confirmed that Lennon and Ono would arrive later that day, although their itinerary was not publicized. The plan was for them to take part in a meeting outside the university administration building. The press reported that the university was hosting a three-day conference on peace.[177] In the documentary *John & Yoko's Year of Peace*, Rock admitted that there was no prior commitment from Prime Minister Trudeau to take part in the event and that the conference "didn't exist, except in our minds." In a 2017 interview, he speculated that his clean-cut "corporate look" may have appealed to Apple press agent Derek Taylor.[178]

The University of Ottawa was not immune to the currents of student unrest then buffeting North America. With roots in nineteenth-century Catholicism, it was a bilingual institution that was secularized and modernized starting in 1965. Subsequently, the growing campus was strained by a three-way tug of war over governance among administrators, faculty and students. In 1968, social science students had voted to occupy the headquarters of the faculty to press for their demands. They wanted equal representation on bodies that determined course content and academic policies, reflecting the often-repeated complaint that university courses were not relevant to modern society. The dispute was settled when the faculty council agreed that one-third of the members of these councils would consist of students and another third of "junior professors."[179]

Post-secondary numbers were growing. In the fall of 1968, Ontario universities and community colleges alone expected to enrol a hundred thousand students. Despite a building boom and the expansion of programs, many universities were still turning away qualified students.[180] Even with the expansion of universities and community colleges in the 1960s, only a minority of Canada's youth sought a post-secondary education. More than four in five moved directly from high school into a job market. But these young workers were also swept up in the currents of the age, becoming involved in the trade union movement and challenging both employers and older union leaders.[181] On campus, students began to demand more of a say in how their institutions were run. Their goals usually were far from revolutionary: representation on departmental and faculty bodies, senates and boards of governors; input into curriculum; and a relaxation of disciplinary codes and restrictions on student life. In 1968, for example, political science students at McGill University occupied professors' offices as part of their campaign for seats on departmental committees. This was not only an exercise in democracy; it was also an attempt to "create an intellectually stimulating environment for students."[182] On many campuses, young faculty members, many fresh from graduate school in the United States, supported student activists. Student leaders were attracted to the idealism of the era. In 1968, Gilles Duceppe, vice-president of the Union générale des étudiants du Québec, and Peter Warrian, president of the Canadian Union of Students, appealed to the conference of the Association of Universities and Colleges of Canada (now Universities Canada) for a more "humanist" and critical university. Warrian assailed the university's mantle of liberalism and neutrality as a shield for defending "the capitalist elite." Student leaders of the New Left variety believed that institutions of higher learning should tackle issues such as war, poverty, pollution and racism and adopt a collective moral response.[183] At Simon Fraser University (SFU), the University of Ottawa and elsewhere, activists embraced civil disobedience tactics that included occupying offices or buildings. In some cases, such as at SFU during a protest over its transfer credits policy, the administration called in the police, and arrests were made. In 1969, the university's chancellor accused Canadian students of protesting "phoney issues" and "importing problems from the United States." He admitted that some reforms were necessary but could not understand why student unrest existed, unless it was somehow linked to the "permissive society."[184]

The radical turn among many Canadian youth by the end of the decade provoked anxieties within the halls of power. Earlier in the 1960s, the RCMP Security Service had earned the wrath of the Canadian Association of University Teachers for recruiting informants on university campuses. Trained in seeking out Communists since the 1920s and locked into a Cold War mindset, the RCMP was woefully unprepared for dealing with the New Left, including the student movement. Appearing before a parliamentary committee in 1969, RCMP Deputy Commissioner W.H. Kelly claimed that American Black Power and Red Power radicals (a militant movement among Native Americans in the United States) were making inroads in Canada and reported that the RCMP was "studying" these movements.[185] The vice-president academic of the University of Ottawa's student government in 1969 was Hugh Segal, later a Progressive Conservative senator. Rock, although progressive, was a young Liberal, not a member of the New Left, whereas Segal was further to the right. Later in the year, following the demise of the Canadian Union of Students because of the leadership's espousal of anti-capitalist and anti-Vietnam War sentiments, Segal urged the formation of a new national student lobby, one that would avoid "ideological commitments" and taking stances on international issues.[186] On June 3, he and Rock met John and Yoko and their daughter at the Ottawa train station. Segal recalled that his job at a press conference was to hold Kyoko. He also spoke of the celebrities hanging out for a time at the university chapel. At some point, it was decided that the guests needed to be fed: "They were sort of vegetarian." Segal was despatched to Nate's, an iconic local deli on Rideau Street, and returned with a smoked fish dinner.[187]

Ottawa in 1969 was "an ethnically-divided city, with a French quarter, Lowertown, a French suburb, Vanier, and a French twin, Hull, on the Quebec side of the Ottawa River."[188] But it became more cosmopolitan as the federal government made a concerted effort to recruit more francophones to the public service and immigration policy changed. In the late 1960s, the city, aside from the francophone minority, was not ethnically diverse and contained approximately three hundred thousand residents. Parts of its downtown were in decline, and its reputation was that of a quiet government town. In Ottawa, an exciting event was its annual Tulip Festival. For real excitement, locals and tourists alike hit the bars and nightclubs of Hull.

For John, the real attraction of Ottawa was the prime minister, who, as it turned out, did not attend the university event. Several hundred waiting students were told that the celebrities would not show up until 6:30 p.m. This appears to have been a ruse to keep the seminar on track as the party arrived at the Arts Building at 5:00 p.m. The panel on world peace was set up in the lobby and attracted many reporters and a small number of apparently invited students. Interviewed in 2017, Allan Rock speculated that if Yoko and John had arrived during the regular term, a huge crowd would have been on hand.[189] Although billed as a panel discussion, the event was more like a "ninety-minute press conference" dominated by Lennon.[190] Rock recalled that "it was a chaotic, circus-like scene, and I was a young, green ringmaster. I'm sure I made some opening remarks, but the main event was John Lennon, supported by Yoko."[191] In addition to Ono, Lennon and Rock, the panellists included Bruno Gerussi, a stage actor turned CBC Radio personality. At one point, an impatient Gerussi stated that academic terms

John Lennon and Allan Rock at the University of Ottawa

"really don't mean a hell of a lot" and that "philosophy isn't what you think, it's what you do."[192] Other University of Ottawa participants were student Alexis Blanchette and Professor Colin Wells, chair of the Department of Classics and vice dean of arts.

Representing the New Left was Martin Loney, a British-born student radical from SFU who was president of the Canadian Union of Students, which supported North Vietnam, opposed American corporate power in Canada and was concerned about the predominance of American professors in Canadian universities. He had already been arrested twice in British Columbia and was a teaching assistant in SFU's departments of Political Science, Sociology and Anthropology, which would be taken over by the university administration the following month. Faculty and students associated with the department would go on strike in the fall; SFU countered with an injunction that disrupted New Left activities on campus.[193] As

Allan Rock and Bruno Gerussi with Derek Taylor in the background (left) at the peace conference

part of the radical student movement, Loney was monitored by the RCMP Security Service, especially later on in the wake of the 1970 October Crisis when FLQ members in Montreal kidnapped a British diplomat and a Quebec provincial politician. By 1971, the RCMP was concerned that he had a network of radical "disciples" within the federal public service. The federal solicitor general suspected Loney of plotting "socialist revolution."[194]

During the panel discussion, Lennon did most of the talking.[195] He advised the audience of students and journalists that more sophisticated methods were required to achieve a peaceful world. Rather than demonstrations, he urged people to "plug peace" through advertising and other methods. Violence, he repeated, would play into the hands of the Establishment by allowing it to discredit the movement. He advised young people to "infiltrate the system rather than try to fight it, and don't be a snob about it." Lennon criticized radical "snobs," defended the police as "human" and explained that prime ministers were forced to compromise their principles to govern. Yoko, like John dressed in white, also spoke of the power of advertising, suggesting that if the medium could be used to sell products, it could also sell peace. People should be convinced that violence was "obscene." John pointed to the importance of persuading "the kids" in the same way Coca-Cola did: "We're the so-called hip generation, so smart, but if we can't outsell businessmen, that's it."[196]

The Ottawa visit was overshadowed by a new controversy: the lyrics in the recently released Beatles single "The Ballad of John and Yoko," which documented the couple's wedding and honeymoon in Europe. The word "Christ" and a reference to crucifixion dredged up memories of the 1966 uproar when Lennon had been forced to apologize for remarks on organized religion made to a British reporter. Pressure from conservative Christians forced many radio stations to ban the current single.[197] In Montreal, Lennon had told Yorke that radio censorship was "insane" and "pure hypocrisy," suggesting that conservatives hated "what Christ stood for" and could "only bear to hear his name in church."[198] Toronto's influential CHUM station stopped playing the song on June 3; CKFH in Ottawa broadcast it with certain words edited out. Despite the controversy, the single reached the top ten in the United States and number one in many nations.[199]

Following the event, John spoke briefly to students outside Tabaret Hall, and then he and Ono were taken on a tour of Ottawa by Rock in his Volkswagen (VW). They stopped at the Sussex Drive residence of the prime minister, who was not at home. According to Derek Taylor (as reported by Ritchie Yorke), a lone "Mountie in scarlet" at the gate was given a note and some flowers for Trudeau.[200] Rock's memory was that they proceeded directly to and knock on the front door, spoke to a housekeeper and left a note for Trudeau.[201] The time that Lennon and Ono were in Ottawa was a busy period for the prime minister as Parliament was in session, discussing in a special committee the official languages bill that would introduce bilingualism in the civil service and handling questions on a number of important domestic and foreign policy issues, including a new budget that

attempted to address the problems of inflation and regional disparity. It is not known if the celebrities expressed disappointment at
not meeting Canada's leader. The Lennon that Rock met was polite,
gentle, generous and down to earth — a far cry from a larger-than-
life rock star.[202] In 2000, Rock recalled that when they were driving,
a Beatles song came on the radio, and John, in the back seat, yelled
for the volume to be turned up.[203]

The party departed from Ottawa for Toronto by train and
arrived at Toronto's Union Station at 6:30 a.m. on June 4. At the
Windsor Arms Hotel in the Yorkville neighbourhood, John met
with his new manager, Allen Klein, who briefed him on sales
of "The Ballad of John and Yoko." (Klein, although opposed by
McCartney, had started to represent Lennon, George Harrison
and Ringo Starr earlier in the year.) Later Ono and Lennon made a
quick trip to Niagara Falls to shoot documentary footage. The visit
was cut short because too many fans and curiosity seekers were at
the tourism attraction. As of June 5, Lennon was telling the press
that he still hoped to receive last-minute permission to enter the
United States.[204] *Rolling Stone* readers later learned that, according
to John, "they" (unnamed American authorities) had wanted him
to "cop out" by making a commercial or public service announcement with an anti-drug message to acquire a visa.[205]

That evening, Lennon's party checked out of the hotel as fans gathered outside. The press reported young girls screaming Beatlemania
style and young men snapping photos. At the Toronto airport earlier
that day, the Department of Immigration advised that Lennon could
apply for a new visa. Taylor explained to journalists that they had
decided to withdraw their application for an extended stay in Canada
and return to London "to be with our [their] friends and families."
Lennon told reporters that he was "very happy with the results of our
[their] visit and with the Montreal bed-in." He continued: "You can't
change things overnight, but I believe that we've made a lot of people
think about peace. We've got to keep plugging away." Lennon was
unsure if he would return to Canada to continue his peace mission

but said it was possible. According to Yorke, the effort had involved many interviews and the distribution of a large number of photographs and autographs.[206] CBC's *The Way It Is* episode "A Bedtime Story" was broadcast on June 8 and featured footage of visiting celebrities and Watson's interview with Lennon. In the future, the CBC, by virtue of its involvement, would become a major contributor to the public memory of Lennon and Yoko's visits to Canada in 1969.[207]

Aftermath

In the weeks following John and Yoko's visit to Canada, the Beatles were busy: two singles and the LP *Yellow Submarine* climbed the charts, and preparations were made to return to the studio to work on what became the album *Abbey Road*. Yet in terms of publicity, none of the Beatles seemed as busy as Lennon. At the time, views on both the sincerity and the success of the Montreal bed-in were mixed. Not all reporters who interviewed the couple were convinced that their campaign was genuine or could work. Letters to the editor indicated divided opinions, likely pre-programmed by the "generation gap," the difference in political and social attitudes between baby boomers and their parents' generation.[208] One Ontario clergyman denounced the event as an "exercise in futility," claiming that Lennon's "absurd actions" were opposed by 99 per cent of Canadians.[209] Notwithstanding his flattering and optimistic statements about their nation, many Canadians feared, derided and objected to Lennon because of his associations with the permissive society and the counterculture. To them, the couple's peace crusade was a self-indulgent publicity stunt by celebrities with a superficial understanding of the issues and little knowledge of Canada. Al Capp's comments on celebrities, anti-war protestors, hippies, student activists and feminists were crude and abrasive, but his opinions reflected those of many Canadians, including former PC prime minister John Diefenbaker. Speaking in the United States in July 1969, Diefenbaker opined that draft dodgers were "of no use to Canada." Although he had disagreed with the initial American decision to send troops to South Vietnam, he now opposed a withdrawal, fearing that a victory for the Communists would endanger all of Southeast Asia.[210] A few weeks earlier, Diefenbaker had lambasted the Trudeau government for allowing Yippie leader Jerry Rubin to attend an event at the University of Toronto in February 1969. The American radical had been ruled ineligible to enter Canada because of provocative remarks made at SFU in 1968.[211]

Others, such as Rabbi Feinberg, Gerry Deiter, Jerry Levitan, Ritchie Yorke and Allan Rock, were inspired, — or at least impressed — by the bed-in. The fact that Lennon and Ono were campaigning for peace from Canada and speaking positively about their nation excited many. Large numbers of Canadians subscribed to the view that their society was morally superior to that of the United States; in the words of one historian, by 1968, "the American dream had become a nightmare."[212] Despite the reality that not all citizens shared equally in the "Canadian dream," Lennon's flattering comments reinforced the sense of self-congratulatory nationalism that had been brewing since 1965 and was reinforced by the Centennial and Expo 67. One of the most extreme responses came from the University of Toronto's progressive Rochdale College, where students staged a sympathy bed-in. One student vowed: "We'd be willing to go even further with a nude-in. We would not only strip our bodies, we would strip our souls."[213]

Rolling Stone contended that the Montreal bed-in, location aside, had been aimed at "the center of world vibrations," the United States, where "the movement" (the Left) was split and demoralized after Nixon's inauguration. In the opinion of editor Jann Wenner, Lennon's campaign, despite its outward appearance of "hippie earnestness," was "not bullshit."[214] The Montreal happening assumed a larger significance after Lennon's murder in 1980 and his emergence as a global prophet of peace. Writing in 1984, Jon Wiener described the bed-in as part of Yoko and John's "bold campaign of New Left media politics."[215] But immediate impacts that translated into action in Canada and beyond were limited; in 1969, the student and anti-war movements, even if the latter borrowed the chorus of the song written in Montreal, were marching to the beat of their own drums, and their tactics clashed with the ideals that Lennon professed at this time.

The most tangible outcome of Lennon's first visit to Canada in 1969 was "Give Peace a Chance," which would be recorded and performed live by many artists over the years. Its biggest impact, despite its lack of a clear New Left message, was as an anthem for the peace movement. In the fall of 1969, anti-war demonstrators, dismissed by Vice-President Spiro Agnew as being led by "an effete corps of impudent snobs," sang choruses of the song in Washington, New York and other centres.[216] For John, seeing Pete Seeger, Mitch Miller, and Peter, Paul and Mary via television perform his song at a massive November demonstration in Washington "was one of the biggest moments of [his] life."[217] Two weeks later, *Newsweek* reported that the "peace anthem" was a key part in mobilizing the 250,000 people who showed up to protest against the war.[218] The song was easily adapted to the "Age of Aquarius" (a name, borrowed from astrology, given to the late 1960s and early 1970s by those with an optimistic view of the power of the counterculture to transform society). In early 1971, to celebrate the end of the successful run of the "folk-rock, tribal, anti-war" musical *Hair* (which had produced a hit song "Aquarius/Let the Sun Shine In") at Toronto's Royal Alexandra Theatre, the cast linked arms and sang multiple choruses. Three decades later, Yoko Ono considered the song as the most important legacy of the bed-in, claiming that "it went around the world" and inspired other songwriters to create music with political messages.[219] In 2009, André Perry described "Give Peace a Chance" as a "major document" of the Montreal event and "an all-time international hymn for peace, spanning the decades."[220]

Chapter 2

Rock 'n' Roll Revival in Toronto

It gave me a great feeling.

— John Lennon, 1969

When the Beatles invaded North America in 1964, rock and roll was a decade old. The breakup of the group six years later, which did little to end its influence on popular culture, coincided with a trend of commemorating, celebrating and commercially exploiting rock music's past. Before 1969 was over, John Lennon returned to Canada to perform at one of North America's first concerts organized around the new concept of rock nostalgia. Like his first trip to Canada that year, the September visit was the product of a number of coincidences. According to Johnny Brower, one of its organizers, the Toronto Rock 'n' Roll Revival was the venue where John "made his break from the Beatles."[1]

Despite Ritchie Yorke's opinion that Toronto took second place to Montreal in terms of the cool factor, Ontario's capital was changing by the late 1960s. Population and infrastructure growth, ranging from private projects such as the Yorkdale Mall to the new modernist city hall that opened in 1965, were impressive. Although the population in the city of Toronto remained static, it took off in the suburbs. By 1971, the metropolitan area's population reached almost 2.7 million. In 1966, columnist Richard Needham claimed that Torontonians liked to talk about "subways and sky-scrapers."[2] The urban region's growth was reflected in the 1950s by the creation of Metropolitan Toronto, whose council often was in conflict with that of the City of Toronto. There was a new vibrancy as "Toronto the Good" was transformed from a city of Protestant churches, the Loyal Orange Order and pro-British respectability to a more pluralistic community of competing interests. One notice-able change was the growth of the Italian-Canadian community. As liquor laws were modernized and the standard of living improved, so did the restaurant scene and nightlife. By the 1960s, Toronto was the music and entertainment capital of Canada. On the provincial level, progress was shepherded by PC Premier John Robarts, an outwardly bland but capable politician. Although he resisted imple-menting medicare until 1969, Robarts created a community college system, several new universities, GO Transit (a regional public transit system), the province's first nuclear power station and a large number of new schools and other public facilities, such as Ontario Place. His government also enacted legislation to control pollution, reflecting a new public concern.

Many residents of the Toronto area in the 1960s dreamed big. Yet growth and progress did not bring consensus. As political cleavages surfaced over housing, transit, social welfare, policing, heritage conservation, city planning, urban renewal, pollution and urban development in general, activists increasingly targeted City Hall. Population growth, immigration, migration from other parts of Canada and increased diversity revealed social tensions. Many of these strands would coalesce in the successful battle to stop the Spadina Expressway, a grassroots movement to protect inner-city communities from a series of highway expansions. These quests for a livable city reflected the more humanistic ideals of the 1960s and produced a new breed of young, articulate politicians such as John Sewell, an independent candidate elected alderman in 1969.

They also reflected the generation gap: many of Toronto's politicians and business leaders had served in the Second World War. Sewell, a lawyer, wore sandals and blue jeans to council meetings and supported causes such as tenants' rights and municipal grants for community organizers. He also wanted City Hall to be more transparent and representative of Toronto's neighbourhoods. The immediate response of status quo politicians was not to accommodate citizens' groups, some of whom were funded by the federal government, but to oppose and denounce them for stirring up problems, slowing down growth, impeding civic administration and tarnishing the city's image.[3]

The Baby Boom and Pop Culture

It was not the new politics or community activism that brought Lennon back to Canada in September 1969, but the music business. He returned not as an apostle of peace, but as a member of a band — not the Beatles — to play a gig at the University of Toronto's Varsity Stadium. This performance turned out to be an important moment in both Canadian and global pop culture. Baby boomers — children, teens and young adults at the time — supplied the demand for popular music, and musicians, record companies, record stores, radio stations, talent agents, promoters and venue owners supplied the product.[4] Although the genre by the late 1960s was romanticized by critics and fans as sincere, authentic and even a new form of art — something to which the Beatles contributed — rock music was a business, and the decision to buy a record or attend a concert was an act of consumption.[5]

The baby boom, which began just after the Second World War and lasted until 1965, was a population surge resulting from a higher rate of marriage, a younger age at first marriage, a higher birth rate and couples starting to have children early in their marriage. It was also fuelled by postwar prosperity and the era's general optimism. The result was that half of the population of Canada by the middle of the 1960s was under 25, and many were teens. The boomers, as well as Canadians of Lennon's generation (born in the early 1940s), both contributed to and were affected by the social and cultural changes associated with the 1960s: the sexual revolution, experimentation with recreational drugs, a questioning of tradition and authority and, in many cases, support for social causes, such as civil rights, peace and women's rights. Younger Canadians tended to adopt more liberal opinions on almost any political or social issue, such as birth control, capital punishment or foreign investment, than their parents.

The baby boom generation also reflected Canada's ambivalent relationship with the United States. During the 1960s, Canadians could not escape the reality that America, in addition to its global military and economic power, "became the mainstream of Western civilization" in terms of popular culture.[6] English-Canadian cultural nationalism, evident in the arts, literature, drama and film, was expansive in the 1960s, largely in response to the threat of Americanization. The generation born after the Second World War helped propel the Canadian economic and cultural nationalism of the late 1960s and early 1970s. Yet it was heavily influenced by American media and popular culture and activist movements against racial segregation, poverty, the Vietnam War, sexism and pollution. Starting in 1964 and extending into 1967, British pop acts such as the Beatles, the Rolling Stones, the Animals and Dusty Springfield — the "British Invasion" — dominated North American record charts. In general, however, American pop music saturated Canada's airwaves and created a larger, imagined North American "youth nation." Historian Doug Owram stressed that rock and roll highlighted "generational differences" at the expense of national identity.[7]

During the 1950s, the combination of the early baby boom, affluence and new technology created a profitable market: the teenage consumer. Teens bought comic books, magazines, clothing, sporting equipment, fast food and, above all, records.[8] The "top 40" format of AM radio stations was aimed at adolescents.[9] As white American performers adopted Black rhythm and blues (R & B), rock and roll became popular and profitable, and American musicians began touring Canada. When Bill Haley and the Comets performed in Vancouver in 1956, the music critic for the *Vancouver Sun* dismissed the concert as "the ultimate in musical depravity" and concluded that rock offered "nothing of social value." He worried that impressionable teens could be driven into a frenzy by the hypnotic rhythms and cacophonous sounds.[10] In 1957, Elvis Presley appeared in Vancouver, Toronto and Montreal, his only live shows not in the United States. A snooty *Toronto Daily Star* reviewer wrote the following about Presley's show at Maple Leaf Gardens: "He has all the appeal of one-part dynamite and one part chain lightning to the adolescent girls, but to one like myself who is neither a girl nor an adolescent, I could only feel that he was strikingly devoid of talent."[11] Journalist June Callwood, writing in *Chatelaine*, attempted to explain "the strange and sometimes frightening career" of Presley in a less alarmist manner, reassuring readers that teen fans were neither immoral nor delinquent but exercising generational solidarity and displaying normal adolescent behaviour.[12]

Fear and anxiety had surrounded adult attitudes toward the young for much of the twentieth century, but by the middle of the 1960s, there were increasing concerns that the generation gap was a permanent and insurmountable divide. Like jazz before it, rock and roll music was blamed for encouraging premarital sex, illegal drug use and general irresponsibility. The explicit song lyrics and suggestive dances of rock supposedly promoted immorality and anti-social attitudes among teenagers.[13] More liberal-minded adults viewed generational differences either as a passing phase or an inevitable process of social change to which they had to adapt. Social conservatives feared that politicians, clergy, teachers, university presidents and other authority figures were giving in to unreasonable youthful demands because of sentimentality or fear of appearing old-fashioned — a major sin in the 1960s.

In the 1950s, Canada was part of the circuit for touring American performers of various genres. Conway Twitty, then a rockabilly artist, played the Flamingo lounge in Hamilton in 1958. He was booked by Harold Kudlets, later described as "the man who brought rock n' roll to Canada."[14] In addition to solo acts, Canada was also part of the circuit for early rock and roll package tours. In September 1959, Dick Clark's Caravan of Stars reached Montreal and Toronto; the performers included Canadian crooner Paul Anka as well as the Coasters, the Drifters, Annette Funicello and other American hit makers. Significantly, these shows were racially integrated.[15] Canadian acts in the late 1950s tried to land major record deals and break into the Canadian and American hit parades. Most failed. There were exceptions, such as teen idol Bobby Curtola of Thunder Bay. An early domestic rock recording, "Clap Your Hands" by Montreal's the Beau-Marks, topped the Canadian and Australian charts in 1960. This group, formed in 1958, wrote its own material and recorded in French and English.

In the late 1950s, word spread in the American South that Ontario had a shortage of R & B acts. This attracted Arkansas singer Ronnie Hawkins and his band the Hawks. Hawkins would become a fixture of the Toronto music scene, and alumni of his band would include members of the Band and Crowbar. Although Canada had produced pop crooners such as Anka, the first real rock and roll recording, in the opinion of Jason Schneider, was cut by Hawkins on the Quality label and included songs penned by African-American performers Chuck Berry and Bo Diddley.[16] In 1963, Levon Helm, also from Arkansas, and the rest of the Hawks, all Canadians, split from Hawkins. For the next few years, Helm, Robbie Robertson, Richard Manuel, Rick Danko and Garth Hudson toured the United States and Canada playing R & B, ignoring the British Invasion.[17] They were not alone. According to David Clayton-Thomas, Black blues and R & B artists from the United

States "were booked into the top clubs in Toronto and played to mixed audiences." Wilson Pickett performed in Toronto in 1966, backed up by a then unknown Jimi Hendrix.[18]

Canada, one of the biggest popular music markets in the world, attracted both British Invasion acts and their American challengers. Dick Clark's tours responded to the popularity of British performers by hiring groups such as the Zombies, who stopped at Vancouver, Calgary, Edmonton, Regina, Winnipeg and Ottawa in 1965. At the Caravan's final show in Montreal, it was joined by doo-woppers Little Anthony and the Imperials and England's Herman's Hermits.[19] In April of that year the Rolling Stones, rivals to the Beatles, performed in Toronto. The opening act was David Clayton-Thomas and the Shays.[20] The Stones returned to Maple Leaf Gardens later that year and displayed the edgy behaviour that was making them known as the bad boys of rock. In 1966, a rowdy Stones concert in Vancouver caused licensing and police officials to consider the future of rock shows in the city.[21] By the late 1960s, Toronto was a busy place for both local and touring pop music artists. In 1967 and 1968, James Brown and his polished R & B act performed in Toronto four times. In the space of a few weeks in early 1968, California's Creedence Clearwater Revival appeared at The Electric Circus, the Who played at the Rock Pile and the Mothers of Invention performed at Massey Hall. The Canadian National Exhibition (CNE) was a venue for family-friendly American pop and country performers such as Johnny Cash, Bobby Vinton and the 5th Dimension.[22]

The British Invasion and the American music scene inspired an explosion of local rock bands, most of which never got beyond high school auditoriums and Legion halls. Quebec cover bands played French-language versions of British pop hits in a style called "yé-yé." Groups such as the Lincolns of Truro, Nova Scotia, who favoured R & B over the Beatles, became local legends and provided many happy memories for those who attended their dances and concerts.[23] Most Canadian rock musicians worked part time, and although some obtained local star status, opportunities for recording contracts and radio airplay were limited. As rock writer Ritchie Yorke later explained, Canadian musicians were challenged by "the quandary of closeness" to the American pop culture behemoth. Radio stations played American and British hits, and club owners and promoters tended to favour touring American acts over local ones.[24] For decades, English-Canadian publishers, authors, artists and other cultural producers had worried that the massive American pop culture industry inhibited the domestic cultural sector and even Canadian identity. Things were somewhat different in Quebec, where popular music was "closely associated with (Quebec) nationalism and the sovereignty movement," despite the lure of recordings and performers from the United States, Britain and France.[25]

From British Columbia to Newfoundland, every Canadian city had its local youth-oriented music scene; Vancouver, for example, had many rock bands and a fledgling recording industry. But because of its size, Toronto was the headquarters of popular music in postwar English Canada. According to singer Neil Young, the Toronto sound circa 1966 was represented by R & B-based rock and groups such as the Sparrow, featuring singer John Kay, and the Hawks, Ronnie Hawkins's former sidemen. Young had left the music scene in Winnipeg for Toronto, where he hung around the Yorkville coffee house scene, dabbled in folk music and was recruited into an R & B group. By this time, Young, like many other Toronto musicians, was experimenting with marijuana, amphetamines and hashish, a sign of the growing connection between pop music and psychoactive substances.[26] The king of Yonge Street, Ronnie Hawkins, had a regular gig at Le Coq d'Or.[27] Hawkins usually hired the top musicians in the city, including singer David Clayton-Thomas, who grew up in Willowdale, Ontario. Clayton-Thomas later joined the Fabulous Shays, who enjoyed a local hit with a cover of a John Lee Hooker song.[28] In 1966, Mandala (formerly the Rogues), fronted by singer George Olliver, was a Toronto band on the rise. The group, which included guitarist Dominic Troiano, opened for the Rolling Stones, The Animals and The Byrds.[29] Toronto's psychedelic rock sound was represented by the Paupers, who signed with a New York label and were represented by Bob Dylan's manager, Albert Grossman. In 1967, the group performed at San Francisco's Fillmore Ballroom and the Monterey Pop Festival. Before the Paupers broke up, they carried out a second U.S. tour and were part of a CNE concert that included Jimi Hendrix.[30]

Another reason why Toronto was significant for Canadian pop music was that it was home to the nation's most influential rock radio station, 1050 CHUM. Song-writing and performance talent, promotion, appearances at the right clubs and luck were all part of pop success, but nothing trumped airplay on AM radio. CHUM, with its star DJs and top 40 format, published a weekly chart of hits; in many cases, record stores simply ordered the singles and LPs from the charts. In 1968, the station's Bob "Mac" McAdorey was perhaps the most influential radio music director in Canada. DJs also interacted with visiting pop stars such as the Rolling Stones and Beatles when CHUM sponsored concerts.[31] With AM radio dictating the fortunes of pop music, Canadian songwriters, performers, recording studios and record labels were severely disadvantaged. In 1968, for example, only between 4 and 7 per cent of AM programming involved music written, performed or recorded and produced by Canadians.[32]

The Genesis of the Toronto Pop Festival

By the late 1960s, outdoor festivals were the newest manifestation of rock performance. During the decade, more than three hundred rock festivals in the United States attracted up to fifteen million patrons. The promoters of the Toronto Pop Festival of 1969 were inspired by the Monterey Pop Festival of 1967; the associated documentary *Monterey Pop*, directed by D.A. Pennebaker, was released a year later in 1968.[33] The outdoor festival was emulated in regional and local markets and built on the success of jazz and folk festivals. Promoters, either genuinely or for marketing purposes, adopted utopian language in justifying large live-performance events. An American promoter involved with Woodstock and other American festivals, for example, told a reporter that the purpose of a three-day event planned for rural Quebec in 1970 was not to make money but to "turn people on" — in other words, to provide them with a communal counterculture experience.[34]

Rock festivals, because of the high profile of the performers, their counterculture cachet and controversies with municipal, state and provincial authorities, received considerable media attention.[35] In Canada, one well-known immediate ancestor to the rock festival was the Mariposa Folk Festival, held in Orillia, Ontario, until 1964, when it was hastily transferred to Maple Leaf Gardens. By 1963, the event was associated with logistical problems, underage and binge drinking and rowdyism, which prompted the local municipality to refuse permission the next year. One music writer described it as "a beer-soaked brawl."[36] Following two years at Innis Lake, the festival, which included well-known American folk acts, relocated to Toronto Island. The non-profit event featured educational workshops and a panel discussion, and most performers were paid a modest flat fee.[37] In time, Mariposa, which helped launch the careers of a number of American performers, such as John Prine, developed an earnest image and a well-behaved, almost middle-class audience, with few policing or drug problems.[38]

On July 5, 1969, two days after the death of founding member Brian Jones, the Rolling Stones staged a massive free concert in London's Hyde Park. It was filmed by a television network and broadcast in Britain two months later. On August 31, John Lennon was part of a group of celebrities who attended the Isle of Wight Festival of Music in Britain. The star attraction was Bob Dylan, who had not performed at a public event in twenty-seven months. These high-profile pop culture moments, combined with the Woodstock festival, influenced John and Yoko's return trip to Canada in September 1969. But local promoters played a key role.

By the late 1960s, a new generation of "hip entrepreneurs" was moving into Canada's fledgling entertainment industry. One example was Revolution, a Toronto recording studio run by musician/arrangers Doug Riley and Mort Ross and engineer Terry Brown.[39] Another was twenty-year-old Johnny Brower, one of Toronto's most ambitious rock promoters. Along with Peter Gracey, Rick Taylor and two "silent partners," he was a founder of the Yonge Street club the Rock Pile. Brower had been a member of the Toronto rock band the Diplomats in the early 1960s. Inspired by the success of the Fillmore Auditorium in San Francisco, he saw the need for a new venue for touring acts. In April 1968, when still living at home with his mother, he organized the first Toronto concert by the Doors. Next, he was involved in a Jimi Hendrix show in Detroit. Brower and his partners secured financing and use of the Masonic Temple, a large building that had been hosting soul music acts. The Rock Pile was an all-ages venue; there was no liquor licence, but pot smoking was not unknown. Brower explained that they aimed to attract "big name, underground acts" that appealed to older high school and university students. The opening act in September 1968 was the American group Blood, Sweat & Tears, featuring David Clayton-Thomas.[40] The club booked some impressive American and British acts during its brief existence. Deep Purple, Muddy Waters, Iron Butterfly, John Mayall and the Bluesbreakers, the Ohio Express, Procol Harum, the Small Faces and the Who. The underground quotient was provided by acts such as Frank Zappa and Jethro Tull.[41] Twice in 1969 the venue hosted Led Zeppelin, destined to be one of the most influential rock groups of the 1970s. The Rock Pile, although short-lived, was part of North America's "psychedelic ballroom circuit."[42]

In 1969, Brower and partner Kenny Walker were behind the promotion of the Beatles' television film *The Magical Mystery*

Tour, shown at Toronto's O'Keefe Centre, Montreal's St. Lawrence Centre and Ottawa's Capitol Theatre.[43] In a 2015 interview, Brower claimed that because of flagging ticket sales in Ottawa, he helped start a rumour via an AM radio station that George Harrison would be attending the screening. The ruse was successful.[44] The partners also promoted shows for Scottish pop artist Donovan at Varsity Stadium and American singer Ritchie Havens at Massey Hall. According to Brower: "I branched off and partnered with Kenny Walker and started doing shows at Massey Hall and the O'Keefe Centre, [as well as in] Buffalo, Niagara Falls, Montreal and Ottawa."[45] Walker, who had a business degree from Ryerson Polytechnical Institute, had grown up in comfortable surroundings in Toronto's Forest Hill neighbourhood. These experiences inspired the partners to try something bigger. By 1969, agents were encouraging promoters to create festivals where more bands, on tour to promote new records, could be booked. According to Brower, "Everything revolved around commerce."[46]

Profits were not ensured in the pop music promotion game. Bernie Fiedler, owner of the Riverboat, the Yorkville coffee house for folk music lovers, brought in the American group The Lovin' Spoonful, which was starting to make it big. After paying the performers (who included guitarist Zal Yanovsky from Toronto), the fee for Massey Hall and a 10 per cent hospital tax, the impresario netted $125 — and this was after he had arranged for free advertising in the *Toronto Telegram*'s youth supplement and a CHUM interview with the band that boosted ticket sales at the door. Timing was also important: booking the American pop group The Mamas and The Papas for Maple Leaf Gardens on Dominion Day in 1967, for example, had been a mistake; fans did not turn up on this summer holiday.[47]

Walker and Brower's next venture, the Toronto Pop Festival, was one of the first of its kind in Canada. At some point in 1969, the young promoters were joined by two young members of Canada's "royal family," the Eatons. Thor and George Eaton were two of four sons of John David Eaton, who ran the family's department store empire until 1969. He was also an owner of the *Toronto Telegram* (it was actually a trust for his children and those of publisher John Bassett). The family maintained a compound in Antigua and an island in Georgian Bay, and John David owned and flew a Hughes helicopter. In the late 1960s, going into business with the fourth generation of one of Canada's most successful families not only made financial sense, it also brought prestige. The retail giant, which employed fifty thousand people across Canada, began in 1869 when Irish immigrant Timothy C. Eaton and his wife opened a dry goods store in Toronto. The business expanded under his son John Craig Eaton, who married Flora McCrea, a nurse from small-town Ontario. When her husband was knighted for his contributions to Canada's war effort, she became Lady Eaton and was a noted supporter of various causes. Years after her husband's death, Flora moved to Eaton Hall, a Norman chateau-style mansion on Lake Simcoe in King township north of Toronto. After her death, it became a campus of Seneca College of Applied Arts and Technology.

As documented in books such as *The Canadian Establishment* by Peter C. Newman, the life of an Eaton included private schooling, travel, working for the family business, joining private clubs, hosting and taking part in society functions, collecting art, sitting on prestigious boards, building large homes with pretentious names and being recognized by various public honours. In short, the Eatons were at the top of a pyramid of several hundred individuals who constituted "Canada's unelected government — invisible, inbred, secretive, puritanical and tough-minded business-men dedicated to preserving the status quo — *their* status quo."[48] This elite was overwhelmingly white, Anglo-Saxon and Protestant. For Toronto bluebloods, it was more important to be born rich than to become rich, and belonging to the right clubs was key. The correct address (Rosedale, High Park, Forest Hill) and tasteful country estates were *de rigueur*. The role for women in this preliberated era was to be supportive spouses, gracious hostesses and guests at society events and benevolent philanthropists. By 1966, however, the "invisible men" who exercised power in Toronto and beyond were facing a new breed of energetic entrepreneurs[49] and a "celebrity elite" that was influencing public opinion.[50]

T. Eaton Company profits were enhanced by keeping unions out of its fifty-two stores across Canada, which were staffed mainly by women. The Canadian Congress of Labour attempted a union drive in the late 1940s and early 1950s but failed. In 1961, Lady Eaton, the matron of Toronto society who had engaged in decades of philanthropy, gave a speech in which she argued that unions in modern society were no longer necessary. The former director and vice-president of Canada's largest retailer explained that unions were no longer fulfilling the functions for which they had been created and questioned why any well-paid worker would want to go on strike.[51] A feature in *Maclean's* on John David Eaton explained that he "does not like taxes, waffling, civil servants, politicians or socialism."[52] As future events would indicate, the 1960s flirtation of the baby boom generation of Eatons with hipness would not necessarily translate into a conversion to genuine progressivism. In other words, a "mod" lifestyle (wearing hip clothing and youthful hair styles, maintaining an interest in pop music) was not inimical to the status quo.

Although the family was clearly part of the Establishment in the 1960s, its department stores attempted to ride the hip trend in retailing by offering mod clothes to adolescents and young adults. Business writers assumed that most of the buying power of teens was aimed at clothing, but it is not clear that fashion was based on traditional, store-bought garments alone. Clothes and music did seem to go together, with young people attempting to mimic the current look of their favourite performers. An account of the Centennial Cool-Out at Maple Leaf Gardens in 1967 stressed not only the music (one band was the Guess Who) but also the styles imitated: Cher, the Beach Boys, the Mamas and the Papas, the

Lovin' Spoonful and Carnaby Street, the shopping street in London, England, that became associated with the mod fashions of the time. That year, British model Twiggy visited Toronto to promote her clothing line at Eaton's. The store's fall 1969 look for women was described as "anti-establishment."[53]

Yet in reality, the company was failing to match the competition, especially in lucrative suburban markets. In 1966, Eaton's, working with the Fairview Corporation, announced plans for a major office-retail development to modernize the area around its flagship store on Queen Street and move the city's financial district to the north. Working with an investment company connected to the Bronfman family, Eaton interests were also planning the redevelopment of two blocks of central Vancouver. In 1967, facing opposition over the plan's call for the demolition of the old City Hall and the valuation of that property, the Eatons abandoned the $260-million Toronto project.[54]

In the 1960s three of the Eaton brothers (the four were known as "the boys") became involved in the music business. The first to try his hand was John Craig Eaton II, born in 1937. In 1965, he bought equipment for the R & B group the Mynah Birds and arranged a line of credit at Eaton's for members of the band, who included Neil Young. Despite a record deal with Motown, the group broke up because of a management problem, and in 1966, Young and bass player Bruce Palmer sold their gear, bought a hearse and drove to Los Angeles, where they formed the successful group Buffalo Springfield with Stephen Stills. "Johnny" Eaton reportedly later tried to collect on his debt when Young returned to Toronto.[55] In 1969, when their father retired, John Craig and brother Fredrik were appointed chairman and president of Eaton's of Canada, the holding company for T. Eaton and Co.

Brother Thor, born in 1942, attended Upper Canada College (a private school for boys dating back to 1829) and graduated from the University of New Brunswick with an arts degree in 1962.[56] His lifelong passions were horse racing, salmon fishing and duck hunting. He later owned 25 per cent of Eaton's assets, which included shares in the Canadian Television (CTV) network. In 1969, he was working as a stockbroker with Dominion Securities.[57] Younger brother George Ross, born in 1945, began racing sports cars when still a teen. At age 19, driving with a partner, he won the Sundown Grand Prix at Mosport, Ontario. That year, he told a reporter: "The further away from reality I get, the better. I'd rather live to 21 than have a dead life and die at 81."[58] Also a stockbroker, Eaton took part in Formula One competitions in Canada and the United States in the mid- to late 1960s. Eaton had the money and leisure time to pursue this hobby but also the talent.[59]

Liberation Days in Toronto

Press accounts claimed that Brower-Walker Enterprises Ltd. laid out $150,000 to $200,000 for their pop festival.[60] The money presumably came from Thor and George Eaton, whom Walker knew from Forest Hill. The festival was scheduled for June 21–22 at the University of Toronto's Varsity Stadium on Bloor Street. Built in 1911, the facility hosted the Toronto Argonauts of the CFL until the late 1950s. *Billboard* noted that Ottawa promoter John Benwell was another partner.[61] As Jack Batten explained to *Toronto Daily Star* readers, Brower, despite his youth, was "cagey" in dealing with agents who demanded cash advances for their clients and routinely tape-recorded his business calls as security against shady dealings. During this early era, the festival circuit was well known for no-shows, last-minute lineup changes and rip-offs.[62] In 2018 Brower explained that they were fortunate "to get some of the best acts in the world." One was Steppenwolf, which was making its debut return to Toronto. The keyboard player, Goldy McJohn, who gave the band its distinctive sound, had been in a group with Brower.[63] Pop festival tickets at the door cost $7 per day (at the time, the typical minimum wage in Canada was around $1.25/hour) and $12 for the entire weekend. Publicity was in the hands of Richard Flohil of Concept Associates. In keeping with other large concerts where promoters attempted to exploit connections — real or imagined — between pop music and the counterculture, one poster featured the slogan "Liberation Days." Pre-event publicity mentioned a wide range of pop and rock acts, not all of which ended up on the final lineup. A number of them were Canadian groups who had been working in the United States. One of the more interesting additions was the Band, former members of Ronnie Hawkins's band who had honed their skills in the bars of Yonge Street. Although their set would be impaired by technical problems, Ritchie Yorke viewed the Band as "the most important pop group to emerge since the Beatles."[64]

Yorke described the festival as "one of the most significant events in the city's pop history."[65] The scale of the event and its technical aspects were unprecedented for Toronto. The sound system was provided by Bill Hanley, who had been in charge of amplification at the Monterey Pop Festival, and was supposedly "the largest amplification system ever used in Canada."[66] It was also an exciting opportunity for rock journalists to encounter prominent musicians of the era. Yorke, for example, met Johnny Winter, the albino blues guitarist from Texas, at the Toronto airport at 3 a.m. and accompanied him into the city.[67] Perhaps the coolest act booked for the event was the Velvet Underground of New York. Its 1967 album *The Velvet Underground & Nico* had received virtually no airplay — usually a requirement at the time for bookings for clubs and festivals.

Toronto was already, in the words of *Billboard*, one of the world's "music capitals," but the lineup was impressive by the standards of the day.[68] It included Blood, Sweat & Tears, fronted by David Clayton-Thomas, who sang "with the force of an express train."[69] Clayton-Thomas, who had spent time in the Guelph Reformatory and the Burwash Industrial Farm (the latter was a type of provincial jail that stressed rehabilitation through work), was a streetwise musician "gifted with one of the best voices in rock."[70] The veteran of the local scene recalled his "triumphant homecoming" at the Pop Festival, which made his mother proud but failed to impress his difficult father.[71] Another group with local connections was Steppenwolf, now famous because its hit "Born to Be Wild" had been featured in the hit movie *Easy Rider*. Originally an Oshawa-based fake British Invasion group (Jack London and the Sparrows), it became more of a blues rock band, adding singer-guitarist John Kay. In 1968, under its new name, the group began to enjoy hit singles and play large American venues.

Another prominent act was the progressive British rock ensemble Procol Harum, which in 1967 had scored a huge hit with "A Whiter Shade of Pale." The lineup also included Al Kooper and his band of New York studio sidemen; the Chicago-based psychedelic group Rotary Connection (which included singer Minnie Ripperton); SRC from Detroit; Man, psychedelic rockers from Wales; Teegarden & Van Winkle, a Southern duo based out of Detroit; and Slim Harpo (James Isaac Moore), an influential Louisiana blues singer, guitarist and harmonica player who would die the following year. For novelty purposes, the organizers booked Tiny Tim, the falsetto-singing, ukulele-playing media personality who happened to be a huge Toronto Maple Leafs fan (his favourite player was defenceman Tim Horton).[72] Alice Cooper, a replacement for another group on Saturday, was originally from the American southwest. With a stage act influenced by vaudeville and cheap horror movies, it became one of the top-grossing acts of the 1970s.[73] For Brower, highlights of the festival other than Steppenwolf and the Band included Johnny Winter, backed up on keyboards by his brother Edgar, and Dr. John, the New Orleans-based blues-rock singer. Brower recalls that when rain threatened his set, Dr. John performed some "voodoo": the clouds disappeared, and the show was on. The finale was provided by Sly and the Family Stone, then at the height of their powers, who put on an "amazing show."[74]

The lineup also included Canadian bands, who, according to Yorke, "were not outclassed by the heavy competition."[75] In fact, the organizers proudly explained that one-third of the groups involved were Canadian. Ottawa's Modern Rock Quartet was booked, as was Toronto favourite Kensington Market. Nucleus was formerly the Lords of London, a British Invasion clone that scored a few Canadian hits in 1967 and 1968. Motherlode, based out of London, Ontario, was a short-lived pop-soul act responsible for "When I Die," a number one hit in Canada and a minor hit in the United States. It morphed into Dr. Music, a jazz-rock ensemble founded by Doug Riley. The other local act was Stone Soul Children. The festival had been promoted in the Montreal area, and in recognition of the "French fact," the organizers booked Robert Charlebois, who, as noted in the previous chapter, had helped supply vocal harmonies on the remix of "Give Peace a Chance." Wearing a red Montreal Canadiens jersey, Charlebois delivered an intense performance that wowed Toronto critics but appeared to be lost on most of the crowd, which was focusing on big American names. At the time, the charismatic singer had a hit record in Quebec and Europe. His lack of a fan base in English Canada was a vivid example of how Canada's two solitudes were not always bridged by youth culture.[76]

According to Yorke, the festival attracted around fifty thousand people, with perhaps fifteen thousand coming from outside the city. Coincidentally, Varsity Stadium was located within a newly emerging hip zone between College Street and Spadina Avenue. Yorke described "disorganized, long-haired hip youngsters" flooding into the city in search of the venue.[77] Many concert-goers slept in cars, on the grass at Queen's Park or on university property or at nearby Rochdale College, the eighteen-storey building that housed the University of Toronto's progressive, student-run college. The experiment in alternative living and radical pedagogy was portrayed by the police, the media and many politicians as a hippie dystopia ruled by drugs and violence. To supporters such as resource person (and poet) Dennis Lee, Rochdale, with its humanistic values and consensus-based decision making, was the way of the future. In 1969, the college attempted to remove speed (injected amphetamines) and heroin users from the building and updated residents on the purity of other street drugs as a harm reduction tactic. It also established a drug clinic. Rochdale continued to be in the news, usually for negative reasons, such as vandalism, illegal drug sales and consumption or squatters.[78]

Newspaper reporters, editors and cartoonists loved (and partly manufactured) the hippie phenomenon, and both angry and supportive letters about hippies appeared in Canada's newspapers. The media often framed the discussion in pathological terms. Reactions from the adult world were a combination of tolerance, amusement and fear. In 1967, Toronto City Council had discussed LSD use among local hippies and compared the problem to San Francisco's Haight-Ashbury district. Toronto's mayor proved his square credentials in 1968 when he vowed that his city would not become a refuge for hippies and voiced support for the Toronto police department, which had dispersed street demonstrations in Yorkville and arrested twenty-five people for drug possession and disturbing the peace.[79] Vancouver's mayor, Tom "Terrific" Campbell, was another outspoken enemy of hippies; in one CBC clip from 1968, he lambasted "loitering louts," "scum," "first-class troublemakers" and draft dodgers who flocked to his city. He also criticized "do-gooders" who mindlessly helped these "parasites" and spoke in apocalyptic terms of hippies "destroying Canada."[80] To authority institutions such as the RCMP, hippies were a threat to public order and morality, particularly because of their drug use.[81]

Drug enforcement and the attitude of police toward young people caused much bitterness in Toronto and other Canadian cities by 1969. A general trend of questioning authority made the police, who in Canada historically faced little opposition or public criticism, an obvious target of suspicion and resentment. Stories of police harassment of the young were common fare in Toronto's underground newspapers, *Tribal Village* and *Harbinger*. Drug enforcement in the past had been a minor concern, and users were regarded as deviants deserving little public sympathy. In October

1969, the Le Dain Commission (a federal inquiry formally known as the Commission of Inquiry into the Non-Medical Use of Drugs) held an informal hearing at the Penny Farthing, the iconic York-ville coffee house, where hippies, students and social workers gave commissioners an earful. The police were accused of persecut-ing suspected drug users, and users were afraid to go to hospitals when in need of help because they feared the information would be passed on to the police.[82] There were abuses from time to time, but the reality was that although the chief of the Metropolitan Toronto Police viewed marijuana as a gateway drug whose dangers were minimized or sentimentalized, many front-line officers were prepared to turn a blind eye to its use, especially at rock concerts. Although not in favour of legalization, an issue that the Le Dain Commission was studying, the president of the Canadian Associa-tion of Chiefs of Police admitted that it was impossible to eradicate marijuana by enforcement.[83] More on the hawkish side was W.H. Kelly, a former deputy commissioner of the RCMP who, already troubled by Canada's reception of draft dodgers and military deserters, feared that drug liberalization would make the nation "a haven for drug-smoking hippies."[84]

Controversies over drug use in Toronto's Yorkville neighbour-hood and the spread of the habit from "freaks" to the young teens and transients who began to congregate there resulted in not only research on the new hallucinogenic substances but also new approaches to public health. By 1968, psychiatrists were working with youth workers, and the Trailer and the Queen Street men-tal health clinic were attempting to assist "acid heads," while the Toronto Western Hospital dealt with "meth-freaks" — metham-phetamine users. The Trailer, consisting of paid staff and volunteers, was a counselling and referral service that sought out youth in need at Yorkville, Rochdale College and pop festivals and among meth-amphetamine users. Police officials and other conservative voices blamed increased drug use on the substances themselves, criminal elements and the troublesome atmosphere of the 1960s. To them, a more permissive society was not a healthy society but a threat to morality, public order and the work ethic. Reporting on drug issues often was framed in terms of the generation gap. For example, one journalist explained that youth were escaping into "their own chemically created world" rather than facing "the frustration and stress of a society created by their parents."[85]

Attending a pop festival was another way for young people to escape the square world of their parents. Peak crowds at the Toronto Pop Festival ranged from twenty-five to thirty thousand. Details about profits or revenues were not disclosed, but one estimate is that the promoters began to break even late Saturday morning. Not all feedback was positive; *Village Voice* columnist Richard Goldstein criticized the crowd for not being sufficiently patriotic toward Canadian bands, found the sound quality poor and was frustrated by the long set-up time between acts. San Francisco promoter Bill Graham (owner of the Fillmore Ballroom) wondered how a high-quality rock spectacle could be mounted in a football stadium.[86] For those who feared drugs, nudity and general disorder, organizer Brower had reassured the public that "the kids" would be "responsible enough to handle this sort of freedom."[87] Later, he credited the Toronto police with helping to guarantee an orderly event and claimed that many visiting Americans had commented favourably on the approach of law enforcement in Canada. He declared the event an "artistic success" as well as a financial one, estimating that fifty to sixty thousand tickets had been sold. Steve Katz, guitarist for Blood, Sweat & Tears, considered the Toronto festival to be in the same league with the famous one in Monterey. Kenny Walker, predicting that it would become an annual event, informed Ritchie Yorke that the partners were planning a "rock 'n' roll spectacular" for the fall that would include Chuck Berry, Alice Cooper, Creedence Clearwater Revival and others.[88]

Brower complained that Toronto's mayor, William Dennison, had refused to welcome the festival to the city, possibly because of alarmist media coverage of rock shows south of the border.[89] Dennison, elected mayor in 1967, was an old-school social democrat who had served as a Co-operative Commonwealth Federation member of the provincial parliament. Despite a background that was more progressive than that of the average Toronto politician and being considered "a good socialist" by a Metro Toronto Labour Council official, he spoke out against draft dodgers and hippies. Yet Dennison was not without compassion for the young, speaking in favour of a youth shelter proposed for the Bathurst-Queen area in 1968.[90] With strong support from Toronto's east end, he defeated hip candidate (and Liberal) Stephen Clarkson in the 1969 election for mayor. Dennison grew more conservative and by 1971 was accusing various ratepayers' organizations (such as the Riverdale Community Organization) of being infiltrated by "political and academic misfits" who were plotting to "destroy our way of life and system of government."[91]

On many levels, the Toronto Pop Festival was a success. According to Brower, "this was the big festival before Woodstock."[92] Most media reports stressed its peaceful nature. Police were aware of marijuana use but decided to refrain from making arrests rather than antagonize the crowd. The Toronto weekend was in stark contrast to Saint-Jean-Baptiste celebrations on June 24 in Montreal when an unauthorized parade organized by the Front de libération populaire (a socialist separatist movement) protested the "bourgeois tendencies" of the traditional parade. Young protestors shouted slogans such as "Québec for the Québécois" and denounced Nixon as an "assassin" and Trudeau as a traitor. When they spotted PQ leader René Lévesque, they gave three cheers. Things came to a head when nationalists attacked a float and tore apart the statue of the parade's patron saint. Fleeing the police, some demonstrators broke store windows and looted goods. Twenty were arrested.[93]

Walker and Brower's event took place several weeks before the most famous pop festival of the era, the Woodstock Music and Art Fair in upstate New York. Even before it had ended, Woodstock had acquired legendary status and was branded a signature event of the sixties decade. A *New York Times* piece suggested that U.S. culture had produced "a new kind of mass phenomena." There was widespread drug use, but overall the crowd was well behaved and "at peace with themselves almost to the point of ecstasy." Participants spoke of the memorable music, the spontaneity, the positive vibrations ("vibes") and the sense of community, with people helping pick up garbage and volunteering to assist those experiencing bad LSD trips.[94] The lineup of thirty-two acts included many of the major performers of the day such, as the Who, Janis Joplin, Creedence Clearwater Revival, the Grateful Dead, Sly and the Family Stone, Joe Cocker, Santana and Jimi Hendrix. The promoters had contacted Lennon asking if the Beatles would perform; four decades later, producer Michael Lang recalled that organizers had worked on a way to permit Lennon to enter the United States in 1969. Lang found a letter from Apple offering a performance by John Lennon and the Plastic Ono Band. This is an important historical footnote behind Lennon's decision to take part in the Toronto event in September 1969. With his wife as his collaborator, his new musical interest was the Plastic Ono Band, which had no formal membership.[95]

A number of Canadians performed at Woodstock, including Ontario guitarist John Till, who was part of the band backing up Janis Joplin for her much-publicized performance. David Clayton-Thomas sang with Blood, Sweat & Tears, riding the success of its recent hit "Spinning Wheel," which he had written in Yorkville. The group was one of several acts not paid (or fully paid) for its gig, prompting its manager to refuse to sign off on film and soundtrack rights. The result was that many forgot that the best-selling group had performed at Woodstock.[96] The biggest Canadian contingent consisted of the Band former sidemen guitarist Bob Dylan. All members of the Band, except drummer Levon Helm, who was from Arkansas, were Ontarians, despite the group's musical homage to Americana. Both a critical and a commercial success, the group had released only one LP, *Music from the Big Pink,* but it was taking popular music in a new direction. After arriving by helicopter to the venue, the group performed what Guitarist Robbie Robertson later recalled was "a slow, haunting set of mountain music" to the massive crowd.[97]

Neil Young performed as part of Crosby, Stills, Nash & Young, who did not realize what they were facing until after they arrived on the site. In his memoir, Young wrote," It was big, it was scary. No one could be heard."[98]

Canadians were also in the audience at Woodstock, but not all of those who tried to attend made it across the border. On August 15, immigration officials at Buffalo turned back more than one hundred Canadians attempting to reach the concert. The Buffalo police explained that the travellers had been blocked because they were attempting to smuggle drugs into the United States. Two chartered buses had left Toronto's Rock Pile club, a tour organized by promoter Ossie Parsons. Police at Buffalo also arrested fifty-three Americans travelling through Canada from Wisconsin and Michigan on drug charges and seized thirteen vehicles.[99] Interviewed four decades later, Clay Borris, a veteran of Toronto's Yorkville scene, recalled Woodstock as crowded, messy and dirty, a rainy and mud-soaked endurance contest. After witnessing Hendrix's finale, "The Star-Spangled Banner," he and a female companion, sleep deprived and hungry, hitched a ride to New York City.[100]

Other large festivals followed Woodstock. On September 1, 50,000 heard performers such as Janis Joplin and B.B. King at the Texas International Pop Festival at Lewisville. According to film critic Roger Ebert, it was not the concert, or Abbie Hoffman's book of the same name, but a film that created the idea of the "Woodstock nation."[101] *Woodstock*, released in the spring of 1970, ran for three hours, won an Academy Award for best documentary feature and was popular with audiences, grossing $50 million in the United States alone. Typical of the era, the media was obsessed with the "meaning" of Woodstock, the most hyped musical event in history. Some observers feared that mass gatherings that focused on drugs, music and tribal communalism signalled a shift away from organized New Left politics and protest. The *Toronto Daily Star* worried that "the Movement" was breaking up, that young people were losing their interest in the Vietnam War and pursuing "a passionate interest in personal lifestyle."[102] Activists realized that music could attract young people to their events. In August, the Toronto Vietnam Mobilization Committee organized a pop music festival at Nathan Phillips Square to commemorate the atomic bombs dropped on Japan in 1945. This and a similar event in Ottawa were monitored by the RCMP.

Reviving Rock 'n' Roll

Brower and his colleagues began to plan another festival for Varsity Stadium in the fall. In a 2018 interview, he explained that the inspiration had been Chuck Berry, who had had the audience "in the palm of his hand" at the pop festival. Unlike many younger performers, the veteran knew how to communicate with an audience.[103] Their event would be called the Rock 'n' Roll Revival, and it would blend the new rock with the sounds of rock and roll pioneers. The date was chosen in large part because several legends from the past, including Berry, were available. Other acts with recent hit records would be added. Brower always wanted to put local bands on the bill as he knew many of them personally. The Rock 'n' Roll Revival was possibly one of the first events to use the nostalgia label and probably inspired successful revival shows south of the border.[104] The Toronto organizers scheduled the concert for September 13, less than a month after Woodstock. Despite the "oldies" theme, they booked one of rock's most controversial acts, the Doors, whose singer Jim Morrison was facing obscenity charges in Florida.

The day-long event was part of a wave of concerts in the late 1960s and early 1970s that paid tribute to the foundational music of 1950s and early 1960s. In pop music, two years was a long time;

a decade was an eternity.[105] As Jim Morrison explained on CBC Radio in 1970, "generations now happen every year."[106] Yet the term "revival" was in the air in 1969. In many cases, the "old" performers (with the major exception of Elvis Presley) had continued to tour, but without the publicity or radio airplay of the earlier years. Although many were only in their thirties and forties, this made them ancient by pop music standards. Other signs of rock nostalgia were radio stations featuring "golden oldies" and documentary histories of the genre and record labels releasing greatest hits albums. Fans in the know (and all guitar players) were aware that rock, like jazz, had a lineage.[107] A further manifestation of revival was the return of package tours, where singers and groups who had peaked in the late 1950s and early 1960s performed their most popular songs. Audiences did not expect any new material. These were the rock and pop acts of the Golden Age, whose fan base consisted of not only early baby boomers but also people born in the late 1930s and early 1940s (like John Lennon). A number of these acts, who had been overshadowed by the British Invasion and newer American performers such as the Beach Boys and the Doors, were still labouring in the trenches because they needed the money.

The audience for the Toronto event consisted mainly of youth who were too young to have directly experienced doo-wop, R & B and other earlier pop music trends. But through the Beatles and the Rolling Stones, who had covered the songs of these artists, they appreciated the influence of the pioneers on the modern sound.[108] One of the first signs of the commercial potential of rock nostalgia was the reception Bill Haley received in London in 1968 when he performed "Rock Around the Clock" and other classics from ancient times: the mid-1950s. In the summer of 1969, American booking agent Richard Nader began planning a series of revival concerts in New York's Madison Square Gardens. The first show featured Bill Haley, Chuck Berry, the Shirelles, Jimmy Clanton, the Coasters, the Platters and the tribute ensemble Sha Na Na. The shows, which attracted teens and those in their twenties and thirties, who often dressed in 1950s fashions, were commercial successes.[109]

A conjuncture of personalities and circumstances came together to bring the Plastic Ono Band to Canada — and to save the organizers of the revival from financial disaster. A week before the event, they had sold only two thousand tickets — several thousand were required to break even — and were frustrated by the lack of support from CHUM and other radio stations. Brower has speculated that the fact that the Doors were the headliners may have prevented some parents from giving ticket money to their teens. Key financial backer Thor Eaton, possibly taking financial advice from within the Eaton organization, was hesitant to provide the next pot of money needed for production and artists' fees. Brower explained that Ritchie Yorke advised contacting American DJs Kim Fowley and Rodney Bingenheimer for advice. Fowley was an influential DJ, publicist, manager and producer who had been the lead singer in the Hollywood Argyles. In 1969, he produced an attempted comeback album by rock legend Gene Vincent. He ended up being the master of ceremonies (MC) for the Rock 'n' Roll Revival, as he explained in a 2013 interview:

> I got the Toronto job because I was the voice of the Love-Ins in L.A. 1966, '67, '68 and '69. I did some pop festival shows with The Doors, The Seeds, Jimi Hendrix and The Jefferson Airplane. I did all those shows and knew what to do with a large audience like 100,000 people. Ritchie Yorke, Billboard editor in Canada and a contributor to Rolling Stone and NME at the time, knew about me and persuaded the promoters to hire me. $4,000.00 and a plane ticket. I also got a hotel room a week before the gig. My job was not only to announce the date but also be a consultant and tell them how things were going.[110]

Ritchie Yorke (who also wrote the liner notes for a new LP by Fowley) interviewed him in Los Angeles, where he spoke of a "back to basics" movement in rock; it was better to appeal to fourteen-year-olds, especially girls, he said, rather than adopt artistic pretensions with "cerebral trip records" and promote imitation Sergeant Pepper bands.[111] In a Toronto interview to promote the event, Fowley explained the appeal of rock and roll nostalgia to the younger generation. This would be "a revival by default, since it doesn't represent the times. It reminds us of home." At a promotional rally at Varsity Stadium, he attempted to whip up the crowd while a DJ from CKFH-AM threw free record albums into the audience.[112] By this point, there was no mention of John Lennon taking part.

Local music critic Jack Batten viewed Fowley as over the hill for a hip rock festival, but behind the scenes he was indispensable.[113] Fowley recognized the importance of the show and suggested that Brower call Apple Records, on a hunch that John and Yoko were there daily conducting "peace business." His idea: make a pitch for the couple to fly to Toronto to act as masters of ceremony at a festival that included Gene Vincent, Chuck Berry and other classic performers beloved by the Beatles. He advised Brower not to mention the Doors in case this scared off Lennon. Brower made sure that Thor Eaton was in the room when he made the call to London. He got through to the Apple office, and someone, either a receptionist or Anthony Fawcett, wrote down the particulars of his invitation. To his shock, John Lennon suddenly came on the line. At the same time the Toronto organizers were attempting to make contact, their friend Ritchie Yorke was visiting the Apple building on Savile Row. At Derek Taylor's suggestion, he was planning to interview George Harrison about the new Beatles album. Yorke happened to be present when Brower made contact by phone and was invited into the Bag Productions office to provide "some advice."[114] At first, Lennon was convinced he had been talking to "Canadian immigration" about an invitation to a festival. Yorke knew this was probably the event planned by Walker and Brower and promised Yoko and John that he would find out more about it. He also personally vouched for the organizers. It took several calls to get the reluctant Lennon on board.[115]

Following Fowley's advice, Brower asked John and Yoko to attend the Rock 'n' Roll Revival as special guests, but Lennon replied that they would be "sitting in the audience like a king and queen bee number." Yorke (as he reported) then posed the question, "Why don't you play then?" to which John responded, "Yeah, why not." Brower, interviewed in 2018, recalled blurting out something such as "We can squeeze you in," and the wheels were set in motion. Brower and Walker still needed to convince business partner Thor Eaton to invest more funds and faced a last-minute promotional blitz. They also had to secure visas and necessary documentation for the new additions to the program. According to Yorke five decades later, the impending Toronto gig was "the show that would end the Beatles."[116]

Walker and Brower had scored a major coup as promoters. The Toronto performance of the Plastic Ono Band would be the first time Lennon played before a sizable live audience since 1966, and he would be the only Beatle on stage.[117] But five days out from the festival, many refused to believe their good news. They phoned Apple Records the next day to speak to John and find out the names of his band and any support staff, hoping they could record Lennon's voice for promotional purposes. Instead, they reached Anthony Fawcett, who provided the necessary information. Armed with a recording of his voice, they visited CHUM radio, where they were given a frosty reception. Their contact there became angry, thinking that the recording was a ruse designed to save the troubled festival. Still determined, Brower contacted his friend Russ Gibb, a Michigan DJ and promoter. Gibb played the tape on his FM radio program — which was popular with young music fans in Michigan — and it worked. Thousands of tickets for the Rock 'n' Roll Revival had to be sent to Detroit: "Russ Gibb had saved the day," according to Brower.[118]

On the other side of the Atlantic, Lennon needed to assemble a band overnight. He asked Derek Taylor to contact George Harrison, who possibly could help. John admitted to being nervous at the prospect of playing in front of a large audience for the first time in four years.[119] One account is that John was so interested in playing live with the Plastic Ono Band that he demanded no fee. Manager Allen Klein, however, had Brower assign the film and recording rights of the performance to Lennon. Klein also hired a filmmaker to document the event.[120] According to Yorke, the Plastic Ono Band was paid the standard fee, as well as the cost of air travel. Phillip Norman, who spent several weeks hanging around Derek Taylor in the Apple press office, recalls that George and Ringo were skeptical of John's plan to fly all the way to Toronto to play a single gig.[121]

News spread quickly of the last-minute addition of a Beatle and friends to the Toronto lineup, which was announced only fourteen hours before the opening of the festival. According to Brower, this publicity helped save the event and explained the large number of Michigan licence plates on vehicles parked near Varsity Stadium.[122] When Lennon spoke to the press before he boarded his flight to Toronto, the story was picked up by media on both sides of the Atlantic, and CHUM radio finally came on board. The show was sold out, which guaranteed a profit.

John called the group the Plastic Ono Band, the same shadowy group attributed to "Give Peace a Chance." Although thrown together at the last minute, it included seasoned musicians. Eric Clapton played lead guitar and helped with backing vocals. A friend of George Harrison, Clapton had played on "While My Guitar Gently Weeps" on the White Album. A graduate of the Yardbirds and John Mayall's Bluesbreakers, he later joined Cream, a short-lived but influential trio known for its powerful sound. Clapton had left the Yardbirds because he worried that it wanted to emulate the Beatles and leave behind the purity of blues music. With its American tour and record of 1967, Cream emerged as an influential exponent of the new psychedelic sound.[123] This was not Clapton's first visit to Canada, the homeland of his father and the residence of his mother and step-siblings. In July, he had played Varsity Stadium as part of the new supergroup Blind Faith, which consisted of fellow Cream alumnus Ginger Baker on drums, British prodigy Stevie Winwood on keyboards and Ric Grech on bass. The concert, which drew only three thousand and lost money, had been organized by Johnny Brower.[124]

The second recruit, Klaus Voormann, was a German graphic artist and musician who had played bass for the British group Manfred Mann from 1966 to 1969 and was a session player/sideman for Lennon and a number of other well-known performers, such as Lou Reed, James Taylor and Carly Simon. Voormann, a former art student, had met the Beatles in a Hamburg bar in 1960 in the company of Astrid Kirchherr, who as a photographer would influence the Liverpool group's early look. Voormann had won a Grammy for the cover art on the Beatles album *Revolver*. Alan White, recruited by John, was hired as drummer. White would play on a number of Lennon's solo records and in 1972 joined the English progressive rock band Yes.[125]

According to roadie Mal Evans, there had been a "mad scramble" to put the band together. Clapton could not be reached by phone, so a telegram was sent to his residence. This delayed the departure of the entire entourage. At one point, Lennon appeared to change his mind and suggested that they send flowers to the event; a persistent Anthony Fawcett convinced him to go. In addition to the musicians, the travellers included Fawcett, Terry Doran and Jill and Dan Richter, whose job was to film and photograph the experience.[126] On the Air Canada flight out of Heathrow, the improvised group, equipped with handwritten song lyrics, discussed a set list and reviewed keys and chords.

Once the Rock 'n' Roll Revival started, Brower recalled that so many people crowded outside one section of Varsity Stadium that the police were concerned about safety. Much to the ire of

Kenny Walker, Brower and the police decided to allow fifteen hundred people to enter for free. Others jumped the wall. Young journalist Melinda McCracken, a self-described "refugee from the middle class," penned a generally positive review that captured the excitement generated by the performances. She claimed that the revival "outdid the Pop Festival in several ways, if not attendance." The presence of "all the old rock and rollers was dramatic and historical." There were no delays between acts, and the music was of a higher quality than the previous festival. Although film and still images of the event reveal few true hippies, there were stereotypical pop festival attributes, such as naked people, bikini-clad young women being body painted and a poetry reading. For McCracken, some of the performances were "awe inspiring," although she found Kim Fowley, who was neither witty nor charismatic, an odd choice for MC.[127]

The music started at noon, and the first performer to animate the crowd was Bo Diddley (Elias McDaniel), whose songs and distinctive rhythm guitar style influenced many rock musicians. Dressed in a "dark red metallic suit" and accompanied by his "pretty girl singer Cookie," he sang numbers such as "Hey Bo Diddley." Next was Chicago Transit Authority (later known just as Chicago), a soft rock group with a horn section that ended up selling more than forty million records in the United States. Tony Joe White was a Louisiana "swamp rocker" whose single "Polk Salad Annie" had sold well in Canada that summer. He was backed by the influential rhythm and blues group Booker T. and the MGs, something that was not even mentioned in the Toronto press. Nostalgia fans were treated to Jerry Lee Lewis and the Memphis Beats, which, in McCracken's opinion, sounded like a country and western group. Their set included "Mystery Train," "I Got a Woman" and "Great Balls of Fire." Lewis was only five years older than Lennon but looked and talked as if he came from a different era and gave off a vibe of hip bemusement.[128]

At forty-three, Chuck Berry was probably the oldest rocker

on the program, but he delivered his usual energetic set, which included "Johnny B. Goode" and other hits, as well as his current novelty song, "My Ding-A-Ling." Berry was not quite a nostalgia act. Although he had not had a major hit since 1964, his songs were covered by artists, he was still touring and he was featured in a major *Rolling Stone* interview in 1967.[129] Berry had first played Maple Leaf Gardens in 1956 and as recently as 1967, the same year his greatest hits album was released. Because of travel scheduling, Lennon did not meet Berry — another one of his heroes — at the Toronto gig.[130] The crowd at Toronto was receptive to Berry's animated, athletic performance and his "aura of slick vulgarity." Melinda McCracken, from the viewpoint of the counterculture, acknowledged Berry as "one of the rock 'n' roll greats."[131] He had no formal set list; his backup band consisted of local musicians Ron Marinelli, Hugh Leggat and Danny Taylor.[132] Trinity College English professor Dennis Duffy, who was in the crowd, explained that the older rock and roll lacked the seriousness and pretension of modern rock but appealed to young people because of its driving beat.[133]

Gene Vincent, who was overcome emotionally when Lennon sang, was another blast from the past. In 1956, Vincent had a massive hit with "Be Bop A Lula" and became a highly sought-after artist, appearing on *The Ed Sullivan Show* and in the early rock and roll movie *The Girl Can't Help It*. He also was featured in *Hot Rod Gang*, a B movie about teen hot rodders that included Vincent songs in its soundtrack. In the late 1950s, he found a new audience in Britain.[134] He met the Beatles when performing in Germany, and at one point they began to copy his signature look of black leather outfits. The Beatles played on the same bill with Vincent several times and recorded his signature song.[135] Vincent's bad boy image and *Hot Rod Gang* made him popular with car and motorcycle enthusiasts. Looking fatigued, he was accompanied on stage by members of a local motorcycle club, the Vagabonds, as well as their girlfriends, who wore jackets proclaiming that they were the "property" of the club. Their leader, Edjo (Ed Leslie), was a well-known Toronto character who ran a motorcycle shop and a charter boat business. In the era before the Altamont festival in California, where members of the Hell's Angels murdered a Black audience member as the Rolling Stones performed, biker gangs were viewed as a legitimate counterculture tribe. As depicted in a 1966 National Film Board documentary on Satan's Choice, rivals to the Vagabonds, club members, like beatniks before them, rejected many of the values of mainstream society. There is no record of the songs Vincent performed, other than his best-known hit. Vincent, described as "portly and flagging," was not a healthy man, and the Toronto gig was not enough to turn around his career. Two years later, he died at age thirty-six.[136]

Another showstopper was Little Richard (Wayne Richard Penniman), sporting his trademark "enormous pompadour." Based on his flamboyant appearance and tremendous energy, McCracken could see how he had been "too much for the time" in the 1950s.[137] Penniman was a hugely influential African-American singer and songwriter who helped preside over the creation of rock and roll. His energy and showmanship, derived from the Black gospel tradition, were legendary. In the first half of the 1950s, he laboured in the R & B world but had a crossover hit in 1955 with "Tutti Frutti." This was followed by other successes, such as "Long Tall Sally," which became a Beatles staple. Little Richard's live shows were credited with helping to break down the colour barrier, at least among pop music fans.[138] On stage in Toronto, he wore "silver lamé pants, silver boots and a top covered in little mirrors."[139] One critic reported the "electricity" of the set, delivered by a "rock 'n' roll drag queen," complete with "fright wig, impeccable eye shadow and gay mannerisms."[140]

Another American at Varsity Stadium was fiddler and singer Doug Kershaw from Louisiana, a popularizer of Cajun music, a branch of American roots music. In the early 1960s, he had written "Louisiana Man," which was released as a country single. A multi-instrumentalist, on this occasion he played electric violin backed up by "the raw sound of a Nashville country band" that included David Rea, an American who had moved to Toronto in the 1960s and collaborated with Canadian folk duo Ian and Sylvia Tyson and Gordon Lightfoot.[141] Also on the bill was Screaming Lord (David) Sutch, a theatrical and eccentric English singer who performed early rock standards backed by local blues act Whiskey Howl. This three-man group had already opened for Led Zeppelin and was complimented by one reviewer for its musicianship.[142] In *Rolling Stone*, McCracken described the festival as "a seemingly haphazard potpourri of old timers, relative newcomers and weirdos,"[143] and Sutch fit into the last category. Cat Mother and the All Night Newsboys was a New York group that performed the Coasters' classic "Along Came Jones," as well as their recent hit, "Good Old Rock and Roll," a single that paid tribute to three of the "giants" at the Revival — Berry, Lewis and Richard — as well as Buddy Holly and Elvis Presley.[144]

The "wildest act," in McCracken's eyes, appeared just before the Plastic Ono Band. Most critics agreed. Alice Cooper, wearing "ghoulish costumes," performed a tribute to Myra Breckenridge (the character in a recent Gore Vidal novel who underwent sex-change surgery), smashed a pumpkin on stage, blew feathers into the audience, fired off a flare gun, released an obscene balloon and threw two pigeons and a live chicken from the stage. Alice Cooper "were not great musicians, but (constituted) great theatre."[145] Dennis Duffy described Alice Cooper as "a hard, kinky group" whose lead singer wore makeup. In contrast to the professionalism and relative innocence of Chuck Berry, it "played with cruelty and violence."[146] Alice Cooper had already found many fans in Canada, the country that had also produced the producer who helped make the group one of the biggest-grossing acts of the early 1970s, Bob Ezrin.[147]

The Plastic Ono Band in Toronto

The Plastic Ono Band, met by Brower at the Toronto airport, was delayed being admitted into Canada because Yoko had not been vaccinated. By the time they reached Varsity Stadium, the music was well underway. Film footage showed members of the Vagabonds (apparently hired as security by Brower) providing a motorcycle escort for a limousine, implying that the passengers were John and Yoko on the highway. In reality, the vehicle carried the Doors, who supposedly were frightened by the experience. By the late 1960s, the Vagabonds, like other Ontario motorcycle clubs, were under increased police scrutiny. Their 1967 Christmas party had ended in a major brawl with the Metro Toronto police, with twenty-seven people charged with various offences and a number of bikers and cops treated for injuries. In late 1968, police raided their Toronto clubhouse and seized two handguns. A few days later, Mississauga police arrested several members travelling with shotguns, a rifle, a baseball bat and motorcycle chains. As time went on, the Vagabonds and similar groups lost most of their romanticized image as counterculture rebels and were viewed as anti-social misfits. This happened as early as May 1969 when the RCMP cleared the Aldergrove Beach Rock Festival in British Columbia of unruly bikers, some of whom were supposedly armed. Initially an accepted part of Toronto's Yorkville scene, eventually the Vagabonds were viewed as predatory opportunists profiting from the sale of speed and preying on male and female hippies and part-time hippies dubbed "weekenders." By the early 1970s, evidence of assault, robbery, rape, drug trafficking and murder made them a top organized crime threat in the eyes of police.[148]

When Lennon and party, also provided with a Vagabonds escort, arrived at Varsity Stadium, fans closed in on their limousine Beatlemania style and rocked it back and forth. Beatles roadie Mal Evans set up their amplifiers on stage. John seemed excited to be preparing to play in front of a live audience but "was not feeling very well."

Yoko and John perform at the Toronto Rock 'n' Roll Revival, September 1969

Backstage, there was an impromptu practice, with Lennon, Clapton and Voormann all plugged in to the same amplifier.[149] The dressing room/warm-up space was actually a locker room, which did not impress Ono, but it was something to which all rock musicians were accustomed.[150]

In 1971, John confessed that his condition at the stadium was not simply a case of nerves but the result of drug use:

We were full of junk too. I just threw up for hours till I went on. I nearly threw up in Cold Turkey — I had a review in *Rolling Stone* about the film of it — which I haven't seen yet, and they're saying, "I was this and that." And I was throwing up nearly in the number. I could hardly sing any of them, I was full of shit.[151]

The "shit" could have been heroin, but Yorke has written that Lennon was supplied with cocaine.[152] Lennon never mentioned drug use in Canada in subsequent interviews, but it is unlikely that he would have risked trying to bring heroin or other drugs into the country. Lennon later recalled that he been nauseous before the performance.[153] In his memoir of 2012, Dan Richter (also a heroin user at the time) wrote that "John wanted some blow before he went on," and that help appeared in the form of Gene Vincent, who claimed that Little Richard had a supply. Vincent left and soon appeared with a small vial of white power that looked "suspiciously like speed." Richter attributed John's subsequent vomiting to "nerves, heroin withdrawal or the lousy dope."[154]

Allen Klein, who was present in Toronto, had arranged for the set to be filmed for promotional purposes.[155] D.A. Pennebaker, director of the 1967 Dylan documentary *Don't Look Back* (in which Lennon made an appearance), was in charge of the project. Mal Evans recalled that when the Plastic Ono Band took the stage at midnight, Kim Fowley did a really great thing. He had all the lights in the stadium turned right down and then asked everyone to strike a match. It was a really unbelievable sight when thousands of little flickering lights suddenly shone all over the huge arena.[156]

Lennon, dressed in a tropical suit with a black shirt, announced: "We're just goin' to do numbers we know, as we've never played together before." They opened with rock and roll classics but delivered an eclectic assortment of songs. One was John's new composition "Cold Turkey," a straight-up rock tune that was "a brutal exercise in truth-telling without any of the nightmare surrealism of his psychedelic period."[157] The subject was the scourge of heroin addiction. According to McCracken's piece in *Rolling Stone*, the effect of the song was to produce "a quiet, stunned audience."[158] Other songs included "Money," "Dizzy Miss Lizzie," Suede Shoes" and other standards from the late 1950s and early 1960s, as well as Lennon's "Yer Blues." In 1969, there was a certain novelty about John Lennon playing rock and roll classics and not his own material, but the Beatles had cut their teeth on Elvis, Buddy Holly, Little Richard and Chuck Berry.[159] Lennon was touched by the fact that his idol Gene Vincent had been standing at the side of the stage when they performed and that Vincent had recalled their days in Hamburg.[160] In the *Toronto Daily Star*, McCracken told little about the set, other than noting that by the time the celebrities took to the stage, the crowd was exhausted but "full of happy smiles."[161] As Lennon remembered: "Everybody in the audience was with us . . . leaping up and down and doing the peace sign."[162] Clapton later would describe the gig in Toronto as "a glorified jam session."[163]

In terms of pop music history, the presence of John Lennon, who was still a member of the greatest pop group of all time, was more important than the venue, the makeup of the group, the songs played or the quality of the performance. Fans who were excited to see one of rock's superstars could be forgiving if the set was rough around the edges. Most could even look past the stage antics of Yoko, which, in the spirit of the late 1960s, were perhaps more eccentric than bizarre. At different times performing aspects of Bagism, she emerged out of a large white bag to wail or whoop. The crowd eagerly joined in on the first live performance of "Give Peace a Chance"; Lennon probably did not know that local radio stations CHUM and CKFH had stopped playing the song because of "poor quality." On the other hand, Canadian stations were giving heavy airplay to "The Ballad of John and Yoko." After this, John announced, "Yoko's gonna do her thing all over you." The strange sounds began in earnest, with Yoko repeating, "Don't worry, John, don't worry. Let's hope for peace." This was "John John (Let's Hope for Peace)," another avant-garde offering from their forthcoming record *The Wedding Album*. Meanwhile, Lennon and the other musicians made feedback sounds with their instruments or smoked cigarettes.[164]

Yoko's role in Toronto was the subject of some controversy. Wiener described her performance as "powerful and disturbing."[165] Ono had studied classical music and understood musical notation; according to supporters such as Richter, her contribution simply reflected "traditional Japanese singing techniques."[166] One journalist suggested that the crowd was too hip to be phased by her far-out performance, but Jack Batten was more direct. He complimented John for being "an enchanting, good-hearted, talented, witty, appealing man" but said that his wife was "awkward, demanding, difficult and weird." Moreover, her antics on stage "almost drove the crowd insane with boredom."[167] Stagehand Brian Simmons remembered that the audience "booed the Lennons, especially Yoko. John helped her off the stage with his arm around her. He was saying, 'don't worry baby, I'll make it up to you.'"[168] Britain's *Daily Mail* claimed that Ono had been booed off the stage, but John had only positive things to say about her performance, describing her second song as "completely freaky."[169]

Immediately after the set, seventeen-year-old Godfrey Jordan, a freelance photographer on assignment for the *Toronto Daily Star*, accompanied the celebrities into a small room beneath the stadium. Jordan took four photographs in the space, which was lit by a single bulb. They depict a subdued Lennon lost in thought. Writing in 2005, he recalled that John's demeanour changed little after he left the stage: "He exuded the same shy, controlled nervousness, whether playing with his under-rehearsed pick-up band before an ecstatic audience of forgiving fans, or, now, sitting on the bench in this bunker-like dressing room awaiting whatever was to happen next."[170] In a short meeting with the press, Yoko brushed off any negative feedback, explained that they were "exploring new sounds" and that something new could not be "accepted overnight."[171]

The Plastic Ono Band was not the Rock 'n' Roll Revival's head-liner; this honour went to the Doors. The group's debut album in 1967 had been certified as multiple platinum in Canada, and the next three albums, including the July 1969 release, *Soft Parade*, would be certified as platinum. The group had played the CNE in Toronto the previous year.[172] Hiring the California-based band in 1969 was a risky move for any promoter. Brower acknowl-edged that their lead singer had been accused of obscenity during a Miami performance earlier in the year but explained that the local promoters were not going to "demonstrate immaturity" by demanding an anti-obscenity clause. Brower has argued that book-ing the band was actually an adept move as they were bound to appeal to younger fans for whom the 1950s was too remote, and their notoriety was guaranteed to attract the curious.[173] The Doors represented a new trend in psychedelic pop that stressed hyp-notic, primal rhythms and lyrics that emphasized despair, agony and sexuality. Charismatic singer Jim Morrison was regarded as a symbol of his generation. Like John Lennon, he was also viewed as something of an intellectual.[174] McCracken described the band's performance, which followed the Plastic Ono Band, as "almost anticlimactic" but acknowledged Morrison's "pure and clear" voice and his "controlled emotional tension." In keeping with a trend in psychedelic and early hard rock, many of the songs were extended jams lasting a dozen minutes or more.[175] On stage in Toronto, Morrison spoke of the liberating nature of rock and roll and paid tribute to "the illustrious music geniuses" on the bill. The set — and the Rock 'n' Roll Revival — concluded at 1:45 a.m. with the contro-versial song "The End."[176]

Aftermath

To avoid being mobbed by fans at a hotel, Lennon, Yoko and entourage stayed with Thor Eaton. After the concert, the Plastic Ono Band was driven to the Eaton estate in Caledon, north of the Toronto airport. This was the last residence of Lady Eaton, the well-known grandmother of the business partners of Brower and Walker. Flora McCrea Eaton had died in July, and her funeral was a gathering of the corporate and political elite. The Caledon residence had hosted prominent people in the past and would in the future, but world-famous musicians associated with the counterculture were on a different level. According to Brower, the visiting celebrities and festival staff were treated to a catered meal, which must have taken place in the early-morning hours. The guests caught a few hours' sleep. After breakfast the next morning, they rested before departing in limousines for the airport. A photo shows the band members relaxing by the pool, making peace signs and sporting Toronto Rock 'n' Roll Revival T-shirts.[177]

For many, experiencing the Rock 'n' Roll Revival was a consolation prize for missing Woodstock. In 2018, Brower remembered it as "a truly iconic experience."[178] The Toronto gig, according to a McCartney biographer, was significant for the Beatles: "Once John found the courage to step onstage with his own band . . . he could finally see his way into a post-Beatles future."[179] In the words of biographer Jon Wiener, Lennon enjoyed the Toronto experience so much that "he decided to hold his own, a more political and non-profit version of Woodstock."[180] As will be explained in a later chapter, Lennon's peace festival never materialized, but his public musings planted the seed with the media and rock fans that such an event could be held in Canada.

McCracken wrote that events such as the Toronto Pop Festival and Rock 'n' Roll Revival "could become a way of life."[181] This was written in the afterglow of Woodstock, which for many signalled a new trend in youth culture. In his retrospective, Batten again praised the quality of most of the performances at Varsity Stadium but worried about the "passivity" of festival audiences, who were being "manipulated and regimented." Many, no doubt, had been high on LSD or marijuana, but most seemed "stoned on rock and roll." Roughly one hundred youth had been treated by the Trailer, the Yorkville outreach service, for adverse drug reactions. The crowd had projected "a warm and loving feeling to the performers" as well as to each other, and even the police had shared in the good vibrations.[182] Earlier in the summer, Dennis Duffy had described the Toronto Pop Festival as a "tribal rite," suggesting that these gatherings were important bonding exercises for baby boomers.[183]

Brower and Walker had spawned the Toronto Pop Festival and the Rock 'n' Roll Revival and helped create a buzz that the Canadian city was about to become a major centre for pop music, But within weeks of Lennon's visit their partnership had sundered. On October 17, Ritchie Yorke reported that Johnny Brower was leaving the partnership, hoping to sell his share, and was done with the music business. Walker confirmed the breakup, citing Brower's "involvement in certain activities." The announcement came after Brower had returned from Turkey, where he had been arranging a shipment of Afghan sheepskin coats (another fashion trend jump-started by the Beatles). He supposedly had also met with Lennon in England.[184]

Back in London, Ritchie Yorke (who had missed the performance) reported that both John and Yoko were positive and energized by the Toronto gig. Yorke's *Rolling Stone* article described it as "historic." Lennon considered their brief visit to Canada "bloody marvelous." As had been his habit since 1968, he was careful to praise his collaborator, comparing Yoko's performance art to her show at Cambridge University and explaining that her work was ahead of its time and too sophisticated for the average pop music fan. In Yorke's piece, addressing press reports of his wife being booed, Lennon said he thought this had been confined to a handful of people.[185] He continued: "I'm really glad we went. And because of it we plan to be doing more things like it." According to John, "something did happen in Toronto, the start of something new." He further explained: "It convinced me to do more appearances, either with or without the rest of the Beatles."[186] In an early 1970 interview, Lennon explained that he enjoyed the Toronto gig because "there was no Beatlemania. There was a bit of an atmosphere because John and Yoko came, but there was no Beatlemania and people just listened."[187]

The Plastic Ono Band's performance was recorded and became the album *Live Peace in Toronto 1969*, released by Apple three months later. John mixed the album himself at Abbey Road Studios. Although Capitol initially was reluctant to release the album in the United States, it did surprisingly well. It included a calendar that featured poems by John and photos. The second side of the LP consisted of Ono's contributions. As a reviewer later explained: "In those days, if you wanted John you had to take the whole package."[188] This was the first live album by any Beatle. "Cold Turkey," which chronicled Lennon's experiences with heroin, was released as a single in October but did not fare as well on the hit parade as he had hoped. John later claimed that the song was banned on some radio stations, but the lyrics made no direct mention of drugs, and it is possible to interpret it as a cautionary tale. In retrospect, he referred to it as a "rock 'n' roll version of *The Man with the Golden Arm*," the novel and movie about the struggles of a heroin addict. It was the first song totally credited to John.[189] The LP reached number fourteen in Britain and number thirty on the Billboard Hot 100, and this was likely because of the novelty effect in that it was Lennon's second solo release.

Working for Allen Klein, Pennebaker recorded much of the Rock 'n' Roll Revival. His seventy-minute movie, *Sweet Toronto*, was released in 1971. In its rough-cut version, it was projected on John and Yoko's bedroom wall at their Tittenhurst Park mansion, and Lennon was excited to see the performances of his heroes; he had arrived too late at Varsity Stadium to see most of them. In the editing stage, Pennebaker explained that he was focusing on Bo Diddley, Jerry Lee Lewis, Little Richard and Chuck Berry. He described these performers as "the originals" whose music had created the foundations of rock but who were now ignored by the music press and television.[190] The final version featured only one song by each of these masters and eight by the Plastic Ono Band, including "Give Peace a Chance" and "Cold Turkey." This segment also featured Yoko's controversial contributions. The entire film can be found on YouTube. Pennebaker also produced a version that omitted the Plastic Ono Band set, called *Keep on Rockin'*.[191]

Despite the good vibes reported by Yorke in *Rolling Stone*, things were tense in Beatle circles after the Toronto trip. At a meeting on September 20, Paul McCartney suggested performing in small venues in Britain or on a TV special; John resisted, stating, "The group is over! I'm leaving."[192] As the Beatles tried to hide their inner turmoil from the public, Paul and his wife Linda moved to Scotland. Allen Klein, who was in negotiations with record company executives, asked Lennon not to go public with his solo plans. Klein said nothing to Capitol Records about John leaving the group but explained that its members would be focusing on solo efforts in the future.[193] By the end of the year, all four members of the Beatles were involved in solo or side projects. On October 1, the LP *Abbey Road*, with its classic cover photo of the group, was released in North America.[194] Although there is no evidence that he was refusing to profit from the Beatle's continued success, John seemed more excited by the promise of the Plastic Ono Band, a feeling the Toronto experience reinforced.[195] Even fans who had no animus against Yoko on a personal level were perplexed by his claims that his new solo songs were the best of his career and the insistence that his spouse was a creative force superior to Paul McCartney. The next time the couple visited Canada, in December, their energies would be devoted not to music but peace.

Chapter 3

War Is Over

Canada is American without being American . . . You are the new country.

— John Lennon, 1969

From 1968 and into the early 1970s, John Lennon appeared to vacillate between vague support for the apolitical counterculture and more activist causes such as freedom of expression, pacifism, anti-apartheid in South Africa, civil rights in Northern Ireland and drug decriminalization. His Canadian visits coincided with his more utopian phase. Lennon continued his flattering pronouncements during his third and last visit to Canada in 1969. He told reporters in Montreal just before Christmas: "It seems we get more smiles from Canada, genuine smiles and help, than we get from anywhere else. So that is why we come back here all the time."[1] Despite his positive statements about their country, not all Canadians, especially squares, admired John and Yoko or took them seriously, largely because of their counterculture image and celebrity status. Yet they had a friend in Rabbi Abraham Feinberg, who wrote:

> The love that the two of them have for each other extends itself to all humanity . . . it really does.

I've already heard from leaders of the movement in the United States and Canada how happy they are that John and Yoko have undertaken to be the spearhead (they don't like to be referred to as leaders but they are leaders because of what they are). And, there's no couple in the world behind whom the young people will organize themselves more enthusiastically than behind John and Yoko. Not only because of their fame and their acclaim and prestige and influence, but because of their personal qualities of character.[2]

The main purpose of the December visit was to promote the couple's "War Is Over!" campaign, a natural extension of their bed-ins. It involved trips to Toronto, Ottawa and Montreal; a working vacation with rocker Ronnie Hawkins; in-camera testimony before the Le Dain Commission; a filmed interview with Marshall McLuhan; and the announcement of a planned peace festival for Canada in 1970. The high point was a brief meeting with Canada's hip leader, Pierre Trudeau.

Trudeau and Canada in 1969

Was Canada in 1969 the peaceful and egalitarian nation John Lennon purported to have experienced? Was its leader not only cool but also open-minded? The answers to both questions are yes and no. Trudeau's private life continued to suggest a cool factor. In late August and early September, he added to his jet-setter image with a sailing vacation based out of the French Riviera. On the yacht was an unidentified woman described as "very pretty."[3] When he returned, he attended a gala fundraiser in Montreal — where the guest list included names such as Molson, Bronfman and Kennedy — in the company of actress Louise Marleau. Press accounts that fall suggest that many people did not realize that the Trudeaumania wave had passed. At the Governor General's Ball in October, the prime minister, displaying a degree of hipness, explained that he would have preferred Jefferson Airplane over the military orchestra that provided the dance music. According to the *Globe and Mail*, "eager young things in microskirts" waited to meet the celebrity politician, one sighing, "I think you're just groovy."[4]

Trudeau faced a number of serious foreign policy issues, some of which impacted domestic politics, in 1969. The prime minister was not overly excited by the British connection, but he was gradually appreciating the importance of the British Commonwealth. In 1968, he had spoken of the need to change the focus of Canada's foreign policy. Under Pearson (1964–68), Canada had played a "helpful fixer" role.[5] In contrast, Trudeau was a realist, yet many Canadians at the time thought of their nation's role in the world in terms of idealism and reasonableness. Many supported Canada's peacekeeping role within the United Nations as it was prestigious and reflected their evolving vision of their nation. They also supported a ban on arms to the apartheid regime in South Africa. Another important international focus was la francophonie, the world's French-speaking nations.

Trudeau, who famously compared the U.S.–Canada relationship to that of an elephant and a flea, could not escape the complicated realities of that relationship. He was too sophisticated to adopt anti-Americanism as a political posture or set of policies, and he was wary of commenting directly on U.S. domestic policies. Foreign policy was another matter. One point of contention was the proposed underground nuclear test at Amchitka in the Aleutian Islands. In September 1969, the Department of External Affairs sent a diplomatic protest to Washington based on the advice of seismologists. Canada rejected the American view that the test carried no risk and announced that it would hold the U.S. government responsible for any damage.[6] Opposition to the tests, which symbolized an escalation of the arms race, provoked

spirited university student protests in all regions outside Atlantic
Canada in early October and helped jumpstart Canada's environmental movement.[7] Another point of conflict with the United
States with both environmental and sovereignty implications was
the fall 1969 voyage of SS *Manhattan*. The Humble Oil's super-
tanker navigated the Northwest Passage to pick up crude oil in
Alaska, prompting the Trudeau government to pass environmental protection legislation.[8]

Vietnam, although not a major priority for Trudeau, was
embedded into Canada's historical distrust of its neighbour and
was a growing domestic issue. Younger Canadians were more
likely to object to the war and to Canadian connections to the
"military-industrial complex." The developing revelations of
the My Lai massacre prompted a group of Canadian academics
to call on the United Nations to investigate war crimes and to
develop a better international legal response. Allegations of the
killing of Vietnamese civilians had appeared sporadically in the
media earlier in 1969, but by December it was front-page news. In
Montreal, three American deserters spoke at a McGill University
event where they described how army training taught recruits
to dehumanize and racialize so-called "gooks." William Whit-
man recalled how his tank crew had slaughtered eight villagers,
all men and women over the age of sixty.[9] In October, relatively
small Moratorium to End the War in Vietnam protests were held
in Montreal, Toronto and other Canadian cities. In November, as
news circulated of large, planned anti-war events in the United
States, things were different, with students, Communists, unions,
church organizations and academics taking part in a second wave
of moratorium events. This was the high point of Canada's anti-
war movement in terms of turnout, but regionally inconsistent.
In part because of Montreal's bylaw against demonstrations,
events in that city were smaller and held indoors. At a teach-in
held in the Paul Sauvé Arena, Deputy NDP Leader David Lewis
denounced the "imperialist" war.[10]

After the September visit to Canada, Lennon and Ono — and the Beatles — had continued to capture headlines. Rumours about the future of the group were circulating, as well as a strange conspiracy theory that Paul McCartney was dead. The couple was involved with various causes in Britain, and Lennon continued to speak of the musical possibilities of the Plastic Ono Band. In late November, he drew both praise and condemnation by returning his Member of the British Empire (MBE) award to Queen Elizabeth. As reasons, he cited the British government's support of Nigeria in the Nigerian–Biafran conflict and of the United States in Vietnam. More tongue-in-cheek was a complaint that his single "Cold Turkey" was "slipping down the charts." At a press conference, he spoke of the My Lai massacre allegations as another example of the immorality of war. Unlike the New Left-associated peace movement which fixated exclusively on the Vietnam War and tended to excuse or overlook atrocities carried out by the Viet Cong, John and Yoko were speaking up against war in general. Lennon's slight of the monarchy may have offended many older Canadians, who still valued the institution. Although a minority of citizens favoured republicanism, most continued to support Canada's status as a parliamentary democracy. A combination of tradition, apathy and inertia meant that the monarchy continued to influence national identity. "O Canada," for example, did not replace "God Save the Queen" as the national anthem until 1980.

Lennon's MBE gesture connected with another issue resonating with many Canadians in 1969: humanitarian aid. In 1968, the Liberal government had created the Canadian International Development Agency (CIDA), a Crown corporation dealing with foreign aid. In 1969, Canada was increasing its aid budget, on both humanitarian grounds and the realization that much global unrest was caused by famine and disease. One related issue where the Trudeau government was criticized for not moving fast enough was Biafra, the breakaway province involved in the Nigerian civil war. Over the course of the conflict, hundreds of thousands died of starvation. The Trudeau government cancelled its predecessor's plans to supply two transport aircraft, and when pressed about Canada's response to the humanitarian crisis, the prime minister arrogantly retorted, "Where's Biafra?" Public support for famine relief mounted and produced Canairelief, a volunteer organization to deliver aid by plane. Trudeau did not want to be seen as supporting a separatist movement; he may also have feared being asked to contribute Canadian forces as UN peacekeepers. Canairelief pilots continued delivering supplies by night, despite threats from the Nigerian authorities. Two Canadian volunteers died in a crash. In the House of Commons, all opposition parties hammered the Liberal government for its cautious and legalistic response. Canairelief also criticized Trudeau's support of Nigeria and his refusal to denounce Britain's sale of weapons and military equipment to its government.[11] The prime minister doubled down on his criticism of the Biafran rebel leader, accusing him of exploiting the humanitarian crisis for propaganda purposes. In the end, the government agreed to donate $1 million to Canairelief, but by this point, the war had ended with a Nigerian victory.[12]

Under Trudeau, Canada continued its official support of disarmament. The Liberal government hoped that the Strategic Arms Limitation Talks (SALT) underway between the United States and the USSR would limit the number of nuclear weapons. The Soviet crushing of the Czechoslovakian reform movement in 1968 aside, there was public support for Canada focusing less on American-dominated Cold War priorities. Trudeau wanted a Canada-first defence policy but recognized the importance of helping the United States defend North American airspace. This could still lead to disagreements, such as in March 1969 when the prime minister criticized Nixon's anti-ballistic missile plan, which many saw as a threat to Canada's safety and world peace. On September 19, the defence minister confirmed that Canada's NATO ground forces in Europe would be cut in half and that the fighter squadrons would be phased out. One poll suggested that 51 per cent of the public

supported the move.[13] The government also promised that its
NATO contingent would give up nuclear weapons by 1972; there
was no similar commitment for NORAD forces in Canada.[14]

The idea that Canada was a civilized alternative to the United
States was hardly new, but by 1969 public opinion was increasingly worried about U.S. influences. Much of this hinged on the
foreign investment debate: Canada's manufacturing, energy and
mining sectors depended heavily on American investment, and
many academics and activists saw this as a type of colonialism.
Although Marxism influenced many of these writers, they often
struck a chord with younger Canadians. In 1969, Mel Watkins
and James and Robert Laxer launched a movement within the
NDP to promote an independent, socialist Canada. Supported
by the NDP Youth, the so-called "Waffle" also endorsed Quebec
self-determination. The Waffle represented a small percentage of
party members but challenged the party establishment and its trade
union allies. Its manifesto employed the language of the New Left,
calling the United States a nation dedicated to imperialism abroad
and racism at home. The main threat to Canada's survival, according to the Waffle, was American economic domination, and the
answer was not simply replacing the American capitalist class with
Canadian capitalists but replacing capitalism with socialism.

Trudeaumania had been based in part on the enthusiasm of
Canadians who were too young to vote. By 1969, all political parties were attempting to deal with the generation gap. National PC
leader Robert Stanfield, the moderate face of the party, claimed
that many radical causes were simply American imports that
impeded a true national identity and that Canada's only hope
was for the young to "accept personal responsibility."[15] At the
annual Couchiching Institute on Public Affairs conference in
July, PC organizer Dalton Camp denied that the country was
undergoing a revolution; in his view, dissent was being pushed
by small numbers of students, "Indians" and separatists, and it
was important not to overreact. Protest, he charged, was largely

imported from the United States and was "paranoid" and "hallu-cinatory."[16] Trudeau was less cynical on youth, but his responses were ambivalent. On occasion, he sounded and acted like a middle-aged Establishment male; at other times, he appeared hip and understanding. At times, he spoke negatively about radical students, protestors and militant trade unionists. When visiting British Columbia and in the company of his future wife (who was then 19), he angrily tore a sign out of the hands of a women's liberation protestor. For all his urbanity and supposed rationality, Trudeau was not above trading barbs with individual protestors, such as "Rick the Freak," a hippie draft dodger he encountered on a visit to Winnipeg in July.[17] Yet in September, he announced that he had faith in Canada's youth and that his government would lower the federal voting age to 18 before the next election, giving many university students the franchise. He also claimed to be open to speaking to demonstrators as long as they refrained from obscenities, personal attacks, threats and "mob behaviour."[18]

Quebec was one province where many hip young people were not just immune to Trudeaumania but also openly hostile to the French-Canadian prime minister. Prior to the 1968 Saint-Jean-Baptiste Day riot in Montreal, it is not clear if any demonstrators had ever thrown rocks and bottles at a Canadian politician, let alone the nation's leader. On June 23, 1969, young protestors in Quebec City built a barricade and lit bonfires as the ruling Union nationale held a leadership convention. The police responded with tear gas. Montreal clearly was the most turbulent city in Canada that year in terms of public order, with dozens of marches and demonstrations, a number of which turned violent. Trudeau had been invited to the celebrations at Sherbrooke, but the event was cancelled when the office of the host organization was bombed. Separatist students at the Université de Sherbrooke had threatened violence if the prime minister visited.[19]

In 1969, many young people in Quebec were motivated by concerns over the future of the French language. The pro-separatist

Ligue pour l'intégration scolaire (LIS) wanted all schools and colleges to be unilingual French. The message of these young sovereigntists was that the only true Québécois was a francophone (at this time, anglophones were around 14 per cent of the population). In early September, fifteen hundred protestors who supported French-only schools gathered in the Montreal suburb of St. Leonard, which was 30 per cent Italian Canadian. The mayor read the *Riot Act*, police wearing riot helmets deployed tear gas and a number of Italian-Canadian businesses were vandalized. More than ninety were arrested, and a greater number required medical treatment. In the end, thirty-nine were charged, many of them educated and middle class. A few days later, sixteen sticks of dynamite, presumably planted by the FLQ or supporters, demolished the home of Montreal mayor Jean Drapeau.[20]

Waging Peace in Canada

John Lennon and Yoko Ono returned to Canada in December 1969 to launch the next round in their peace offensive. In addition to having a fairly positive media environment (based on their two previous trips), Canada was a convenient location from which to connect with their real target audience, the United States. This would be accomplished not through a third bed-in but radio, television and print media interviews, as well as a billboard and poster campaign. Like the Montreal bed-in, it would not involve co-operating or interacting with any Canadian peace organizations. Other than Rabbi Feinberg, the elder statesman of the movement in Canada, Lennon had no connections with the national movement, and there is no evidence that it ever reached out to him. Planning began just before October, with John Kosh, the creative director for Apple Records, tasked with designing the slogan, handbills and billboards. Perhaps unconsciously, the campaign's concept and slogan "War Is Over (If You Want It)" seems to have been borrowed from a poem by Allen Ginsberg and a Phil Ochs song ("The War Is Over") released that year.[21]

Canada was not foreordained to be the site of the full launch of the campaign. In 2018, Johnny Brower explained that he brought John and Yoko back to Toronto to help promote "a festival like Woodstock, except for peace." Brower credited Richard Miller, a friend of American producer Shep Gordon (Alice Cooper's manager in 1969), with the concept, known as "the Music and Peace Conference of the World." In late 1969, as noted above, Brower underwent "an acrimonious split" with his business partner Kenny Walker, which complicated matters. On a visit to England Brower met with John and Yoko and shared his idea about staging a festival at Ontario's Mosport racetrack, "a wonderful facility." After hearing about the peace campaign and that Montreal was designated as the Canadian city for billboards and posters, he convinced Lennon to focus the Canadian campaign on Toronto and promised he would contribute financially. They agreed that once the War Is Over campaign had been launched, they would announce the peace festival.[22] In his 1976 memoir, Anthony Fawcett confirmed that Brower and Yorke had visited the Apple offices in early December to discuss plans for a large festival. There was talk of establishing a peace foundation, a meeting with Canada's prime minister and an ill-defined "peace vote" based on mail-in coupons.[23]

On December 16, the couple, accompanied by Fawcett, arrived in Toronto on a British Overseas Airlines Corporation flight. Before they departed from London, John informed the media that Canada was "one of the key countries in the new race for survival."[24] They had been well treated by its immigration officials, and the country's attitudes toward Vietnam, China and NATO were "very sensible," according to Lennon. For a young nation, Canada was mature. Brower, agreeing with Lennon about Canadian reasonableness, described his country as "groovy" and "hip."[25] Once in Canada, John explained to the *Toronto Daily Star* that they planned to launch a major peace publicity campaign and work on a Canadian peace festival for 1970. The peace effort was being assisted by Brower, who explained that thirty War Is Over billboards would be rented in Toronto, five thousand posters would be put up and young people would be hired to distribute ten thousand circulars. When asked why he had chosen Toronto for the launch of this new effort, Lennon explained, "I like the place."[26]

The celebrities were given the VIP treatment at the Toronto airport, exiting a rear door into a white Phantom Rolls-Royce owned by singer Ronnie Hawkins. Recently, he had landed a major record deal with Atlantic Records that allowed him to improve his lifestyle. Hawkins, who had never met the Beatle, had agreed to host his entourage at his farm near Streetsville, now part of Mississauga. The suggestion had been made by Yorke. The idea was to shelter the celebrities from prying fans and journalists and give them a base from which to work on the next stage of their peace crusade. In a later interview, Hawkins claimed that at the time he did not know much about the Beatles but that John knew his songs well.[27] In his autobiography, Hawkins wrote that Lennon impressed him as a "pragmatic, business-savvy guy."[28] Lennon liked the LP *Ronnie Hawkins* and agreed to record a promo for Atlantic Records. The Hawk's current group of talented young musicians included Hamilton singer and harmonica player Richard Alfred Newell, known as King Biscuit Boy. At the time of playing host to Lennon and Ono, Hawkins, a burly man, had reached the weight of one hundred and eighteen kilograms (260 pounds) and was trying to get in shape for his rejuvenated career.[29]

In a less than critical piece penned for *Rolling Stone*, Yorke stressed the human side of John and Yoko's winter visit to Canada. Ronnie and his wife Wanda lived in a five-bedroom Tudor-style house with French Provençal décor and frescoes on the ceilings. In one passage, John and Yoko were depicted watching a rerun of the Beatles appearing on *The Ed Sullivan Show*. Despite his recent negative comments about Beatlemania, Lennon was excited and crouched down, like a child, near the television screen. The article also mentioned

Lennon's plan for a "massive pop festival for peace" in Canada that he hoped would involve all the Beatles (he referred to them as individuals, not members of a group).[30]

One reporter described the Mississauga Road farm as a secure site, protected by a gate and "bodyguard" Walter "Heavy" Andrews.[31] The entourage included two macrobiotic cooks. Extra telephone lines were installed to handle the volume of communications with radio stations, newspapers and magazines. In later years, Hawkins recalled that at one point

John and Yoko at Ronnie Hawkins's Mississauga home, December 1969

a bathtub in the room where his guests stayed overflowed, damaging the ceiling below. The host supposedly was left to pay a hefty telephone bill, but his temporary association with John and Yoko was good publicity.[32] Photos from the visit show a genuinely happy Lennon driving a snowmobile and an Amphicat, a six-wheeled amphibious vehicle designed and built by Ron Beehoo from Streetsville. Yoko supposedly resented when her spouse and their host spent too much time enjoying the Canadian outdoors.[33] She was reportedly frightened by these contraptions (possibly because earlier in the year she and her daughter had been injured in a road accident with John behind the wheel), but in one photo Yoko was on the back of a Moto-Ski snowmobile with John driving. Brower remembered Hawkins and Lennon "racing over open fields" on the snow machines.[34] Their host later revealed that during their visit, Yoko did most of the talking (a pattern reported by friend and assistant Dan Richter when describing the couple's daily life at Tittenhurst Park). The hyperintelligent Ono was the "boss," and John was quiet.[35] This was the reverse of the pattern at press conferences. Ronnie Hawkins, whose views on women were old-fashioned to the point of misogyny, believed that Lennon was "hen-pecked" by his smart but controlling wife, whom he nicknamed "Loco." In his view, the whole peace festival idea was a "power trip" for Yoko. His wife Wanda found it difficult to interact with her.[36]

One incident at the farm was not so peaceful. A *Toronto Daily Star* photographer claimed that he was roughed up by two men near the Mississauga residence where the celebrity couple was staying. Early in the new year, Brower and fifty-three-year-old Walter Andrews, who worked for Brower, were tried for common assault. Andrews pleaded guilty; Brower fought the charge but was convicted. Both men were fined $50.[37] According to Yorke, after he and Brower had taken Ono, Lennon and Fawcett to the Hawkins home, they became involved in a confrontation near the gate of Hawkins's property with a car containing photographer Frank Lennon and reporter Marci McDonald. Andrews punched Lennon, and Brower grabbed a camera and destroyed the film. As detailed in Yorke's 2015 book, when John and Yoko learned of the incident via television news, they were not too pleased.[38]

Despite the location of its headquarters on the outskirts of Toronto, the Christmas peace campaign had global ambitions. The celebrities' core message was "War Is Over! If You Want It. Happy Christmas, John and Yoko." Not all authors have been enamoured of the couple's activism in this period. One has described it as "a travelling carnival of put-ons and misbehaviour, rhetoric and activism," which extended into 1970.[39] Whatever its merits and impact, the War Is Over campaign involved the same mixture of "performance art, humour and sloganeering" that the activist couple had been practising since they met.[40] Large numbers of posters were distributed, and billboards were hired in Toronto, Montreal, New York, Los Angeles, Rome, Paris, Berlin, Athens, Tokyo and Port-of-Spain, Trinidad. In Toronto, Capitol Records paid for advertisements in the newspapers. Taking his marketing of peace to the next logical level, Lennon was appealing directly to the public through Madison Avenue techniques. According to Kaplan, the billboards were part of "communications guerrilla warfare," with John and Yoko "envisioning the world as a global communications network."[41] The most prominent billboard was in New York's Times Square. The message was repeated in a large ad in the *New York Times* on December 21, 1969.[42]

Within days of the arrival of the celebrities, Yorke had left his job at the *Globe and Mail* to work for Karma Productions, recently formed by Brower and his associates to advance the peace festival and other Lennon concepts. It had an office on Toronto's Avenue Road. The Peace Network, promoted by Yorke, consisted of dozens of radio stations in North America that publicized the Mosport festival and John and Yoko's peace ideas and asked their listeners

Ritchie Yorke with Yoko and John at Ronnie Hawkins's home

to forward information on local peace activities. The radio campaign was launched with an announcement in *Billboard*. The fact that the informal network was announced in Canada, as Wiener notes, caused the FBI to list it under "New Left — Foreign Influence."[43] *Rolling Stone* reported on the buzz in the hip community, which included the rumour that the Beatles, Dylan and the Stones would be at the festival in Canada.[44] One radio station manager in Delaware was approached by the Peace Network to broadcast a five-minute peace message. Listeners were hostile to the idea, but a delegation of youth tried to get the station to change its mind. The manager then wrote the RCMP for information on the Peace Radio Network as he had his "suspicions." The RCMP replied that it communicated only with the FBI on matters of this type. The RCMP provided the FBI with information on Lennon's planned Mosport festival. Years later, the Canadian Security Intelligence Service (CSIS), which took over from the RCMP Security Service in the 1980s, asked the FBI not to fully declassify its files on Lennon, despite that fact that the subject was dead.[45]

On December 17, at a press conference at the Ontario Science Centre in Don Mills, Lennon announced that a two-day peace festival would be held at Mosport Park in July 1970. Although fans were excluded from this media-only event, Yorke reported that "the vibes were beautiful." The $30-million showcase for science and technology had opened in North York in the fall. As usual, Lennon did most of the talking, and Ono, who appeared nervous and chewed gum, was relatively silent. "We aim to make this the biggest music festival in history," John told reporters, "and we're going to be asking everybody who's anybody to play." They had chosen Canada because "there is still hope here." He also explained that "Canada talks to China" and that the country's "vibes are good." John defined peace as "no violence and everybody grooving" and (as the FBI dutifully noted) stated that they would love to take the festival to Czechoslovakia and Russia.[46] John, asked about the violence at the Altamont festival on December 6, described it as "a bad scene" that

Lennon and Ono arriving in a Rolls-Royce at the Ontario Science Centre in Toronto

may have been inspired by the image that the Rolling Stones projected. Queried about their leadership role in the peace movement, Lennon explained that he and Yoko distrusted leaders and wished for a decentralized, mass movement, propelled by the world's youth but assisted by straights such as Rabbi Feinberg, who was present. Appropriating a phrase associated with Nixon, he claimed that lovers of peace were the real "silent majority."[47]

At the press conference, Lennon spoke of a "peace committee" or council that included Feinberg and Stanley Burke, the former CBC news anchor who was active on the Biafra aid issue. The new organization could promote humanitarian missions such as aid to Biafra. Lennon claimed that he and Yoko had contemplated travelling to Biafra to promote peace but did not want to become "dead saints." Ono opined: "I think we did a lot of good for Biafra when John returned his MBE."[48] Lennon explained that the idea of the festival had originated with "Toronto people" and that "you must run things the way the Establishment does." The performers at Mosport would be paid, but any extra revenue would be used to start a "peace fund." How a free concert could generate revenue, or even cover basic costs, was not explained, and this would be the project's fatal flaw. Lastly, John explained how people would be given a chance to vote for war or peace via mail-in coupons and that when twenty million had been received, they would be sent to the "United States" (presumably to the government). Brower, who would help organize the peace festival, explained that Canada was a logical location for such an event because of its positive world reputation and open-minded politicians.[49] Once Lennon began to publicize these plans, he was placed on the radar of the RCMP Security Service. Ironically, despite interest by both the FBI and RCMP, the War Is Over campaign was dismissed as naïve and pointless by elements within the New Left and had no discernible connection to any Canadian peace, student or radical organization.

From Hawkins's farm south of Streetsville (or, as it was some-times called, "ranch"), the celebrities worked their media contacts. John was interviewed for WABC radio by *Village Voice* reporter Howard Smith and the Associated Press. On December 18, Nick Steed and Ken Cavanaugh conducted a CBC-TV interview. John and Yoko also benefited from national coverage on CTV. In a seg-ment on *W5*, the couple explained their peace mission, starting with the claim that Canada was the only place in the world where people attempted to help them as opposed to writing "begging letters" seeking assistance. John defined peace as "peace of mind . . . peace in the street . . . peace in your own home . . . and peace "throughout the world." He explained that as he was "not educated," he had to "talk in jingles" to promote his message. When pressed about his MBE, John insisted that when he had accepted it, he "was on the make" and that as "a socialist," this act of hypocrisy had always bothered him. The decision to return the medal had been made easy by Britain's role in the Biafra issue and its diplomatic support of the United States in Southeast Asia. The *W5* episode included a promotional film for the single "Cold Turkey," shot in Montreal by Ono's friend Jonas Mekas.[50]

Ritchie Yorke, Johnny Brower, Yoko and John at the Ontario Science Centre

The Toronto visit also involved a shopping expedition to the clothing store Le Chateau on Yonge Street. Yoko and John arrived in Hawkins's Rolls-Royce and in the space of thirty minutes managed to spend $800 on hats, jumpsuits and scarves, with Yoko selecting several blouses by Finnish designer Hans Metzen. (Over the years, more than one observer has referred to Ono's shopping therapy.) They had contacted the owner, who provided some privacy by locking the doors to the boutique, in advance. Word of the celebrity shoppers soon spread, and an excited crowd formed outside. The manager asked them to remain calm and allow the visitors to leave without being hassled. John spoke briefly to the spectators on the importance of peace, and the couple was driven away in the Rolls.[51]

At the Hawkins farm, the celebrities were visited by Dick Gregory, who was continuing his activism. Gregory, who had a large following among university students, was one of the possible performers at the peace festival.[52] Another visitor was Ralph Ginzburg, editor of the magazine *Avant Garde*, and his wife Shoshana. Ginzburg had been prosecuted under a federal law dealing with obscene advertising. In 1969 he had drawn the attention not only of Progressive Conservative MP John Diefenbaker, who described him as a "convicted pornographer," but also the *Canadian Intelligence Service Bulletin*, a right-wing publication edited by Ron Gostick.[53] Regarded as a pioneer of the sexual revolution and free speech, he was using his new publication to promote social causes such as peace. Ginzburg met with Lennon to discuss the publication of his erotic drawings based on his honeymoon. Shortly after the visit, *Avant Garde* published a feature on the lithographs, promoted on the cover as "Wedded Bliss." Lennon's fourteen-drawing series, entitled *Bag One*, had been printed as lithographs. Dan Richter described the drawings as "sexy, naïve, delightful."[54] The magazine issue described John as "master musician, promoter of peace and one of the Now Generation's most inspiring and kaleidoscopic figures."[55] In addition to putting three hundred sets of *Bag One* on the market for $1,000 each, Lennon planned to exhibit the originals in London in January and New York in February. According to Anthony Fawcett, organizing the *Bag One* project from Canada presented logistical challenges:

> The lithographs, which had been shipped to New York, were driven to Toronto by truck. They were held up at the border for twenty-four hours while officials impounded them as possibly obscene, until the publisher's lawyers managed to prove that they were original Fine Arts prints. They finally arrived in the middle of a snowstorm and were stacked up in the living room. It was a surreal sight to see the piles of lithographs almost reaching the ceiling. I wondered whether John would have second thoughts at having to sign every one, but he seemed happy and joked about it.[56]

Signing was tedious, but chatting about music and smoking hashish helped pass the time. Yorke claimed that during one of these sessions he confessed that he was not a big fan of the early Beatles and preferred the original versions of the cover songs they had recorded, most of which were by African-American artists. Lennon did not disagree.[57] The collection of drawings, aimed at the respectable art world, was another attempt to popularize John and Yoko's philosophy of Bagism and to show that John was an artist. Some of the images were explicit, and early in 1970, Scotland Yard would raid the London Art Gallery and seize several of the drawings. Kelly Jay, at the time keyboard player for Hawkins, claimed to have met Lennon and Ono when at the ranch. Years later, he still had, among his collection of rock memorabilia, a *Bag One* set, supposedly given to him by the British celebrity.[58]

The reaction to Lennon's explicit drawings was another example of the hip/square divide. One reality of the cultural upheaval of the 1960s was that traditional moral controls, either formal or informal, were being eroded. By 1967, for example, there were dozens of theatrical agents in Toronto booking exotic dancers — many described as ex-"go-go girls" — in bars across the province. According to the Liquor Control Board of Ontario (LCBO), they could not perform in the nude, but gradually more and more dancers began removing their tops and bottoms. For the most part, exotic dancers were associated with beer parlours catering to a working-class male audience, but nudity, for better or worse, was part of the sexual revolution, which is why pornography in the late 1960s could be seen as progressive and liberating. It was uncool to be "uptight" about nudity and sex in general. Movies were censored for sex and violence by provincial boards but with little consistency. In 1969, the Swedish film *I Am Curious (Yellow)*, a serious film about a young woman's life — including her love life, was exhibited in Montreal but not in Toronto. Sex was not the only problem for censors: movies such as *The Wild Bunch*, released in 1969, portrayed more realistic violence. Although prosecutions for obscenity under the

Criminal Code were becoming rare, they still happened. After the Toronto police successfully charged a theatrical director and three producers, they were emboldened to seize copies of the sexually-explicit American film *Can Heironymous Merkin Ever Forget Mercy Humppe and Find True Happiness?* (which was shown without incident in Montreal). Bookstores, artists and art galleries also challenged the moral code in the name of artistic freedom, individual morality and consumer choice. One sign that staid Toronto was losing its puritanical image was the announcement in 1969 that the hippie musical *Hair,* with its infamous mass nude scene, would play at the Royal Alexandra Theatre the following year.[59]

In the battle over censorship, one target of the authorities in this era was the underground press, an understudied manifestation of the counterculture in Canada. The alternative media, together with poets, novelists, artists and campus newspapers, challenged the status quo, especially in the area of sexual taboos. Most underground newspapers did not survive; others were bought out and went mainstream. The most sustained effort by police and municipal and provincial authorities against non-traditional journalists who challenged the status quo was in Vancouver, where the *Georgia Strait* faced prosecutions for criminal libel and obscenity and other forms of official harassment. The goal appeared to be to drive the newspaper, founded by several poets concerned with police brutality, out of business through excessive legal fees. This nasty and sustained campaign confirmed that there was considerable opposition to hippies in Vancouver.[60]

In December 1969 John Lennon was preoccupied by much more than the reaction to his drawings. British journalist Ray Connolly, who had interviewed the Beatles in the past as the pop music columnist for the London *Evening Standard,* was another visitor to the Hawkins farm. In 2016, he recalled that John had given him momentous news during the early winter visit to Canada. As a frequent guest at Apple headquarters, Connolly knew that all was not well. When speaking on the phone to Lennon about song lyrics, he was invited to Toronto. When he arrived at the Hawkins home, John ushered him into the bedroom he and Yoko were using. Lennon giggled with glee as he casually informed Connolly, "I've left the Beatles." At this time, *Abbey Road* was the top album in the world. Connolly was "devastated" but also realized that he had been given one of the biggest scoops in entertainment history. Yet Lennon, on the advice of Allen Klein, asked him to sit on the story so that news of the breakup would not jeopardize the forthcoming movie *Let It Be*. Later, the British journalist found out that McCartney was still wishing that John would change his mind about quitting. During the weekend in Canada, Connolly was told of the turbulent meeting of the Apple board when John had asked for "a divorce." At the time, he believed only two people in the world favoured the demise of the Beatles: John and Yoko.[61]

Two Gurus Meet

On Saturday, December 20, Yoko and John met with Marshall McLuhan of the Department of Culture and Technology at the University of Toronto. McLuhan has been described as "the best-known and most cited Canadian author in the world" but also as the most misunderstood.[62] His comments ("education is war") seemed best suited to provoking discussion than to providing definitive answers.[63] He was the author of several books, including the best-selling *The Medium Is the Message* (1967). Arguably Canada's first celebrity academic, McLuhan was in high demand as a consultant and speaker. In 1964, he advised Canada's PCs "to study the Beatle phenomenon and translate their image techniques into political persuasion."[64] Four years later, he treated Prime Minister Trudeau and a number of Liberal parliamentarians and party officials to a seminar on social trends and communicating with the citizenry.[65]

The encounter at the University of Toronto, filmed by CBS Television (an American network) for the program *60 Minutes*, featured the celebrities exchanging thoughts with their host on peace, music and modern communications. American television viewers would have been familiar with the fifty-eight-year-old McLuhan, who was also embraced by the counterculture and whose works were read by university students and younger academics.[66] For the young, a McLuhan event was a happening, where, like a rock concert or an acid trip, one's mind could be "blown."[67] In a *Rolling Stone* interview in 1969, he explained that television was "revolutionizing every political system in the Western world." It allowed for new political showmen such as John F. Kennedy, Cuban leader Fidel Castro and Nixon, who wore "masks" when in public. The generation gap was not just a divide by age but "cultures." Youthful society was not only alienated but becoming "retribalized," manifested by drugs, unisex fashions, long hair, rock music, open and guilt-free sexuality, couples cohabiting and groups of people living communally. Personally, McLuhan was not a fan of these changes and believed the United States, as a nation, was "doomed."[68] Canada, which had no single national identity, was "utopia" by comparison.[69]

Yorke described the forty-five-minute exchange as an intense experience, with the professor asking rapid-fire questions of the celebrities.[70] His speaking style, combined with Lennon's occasional tendency to talk in stream-of-consciousness fashion, meant that the dialogue with John and Yoko was difficult to follow. John explained that he had first been motivated to become a musician after he heard Elvis Presley. He spoke of the Beatles as having "turned into a museum, so they have to be scrapped or deformed or changed."[71] As he had in recent interviews, John continued to say positive things about Canada. He explained that violence was "everybody's responsibility" but cited "American paranoia" as an obstacle to international peace. Lennon explained his interest in "love and peace" as a natural outcome of meeting Ono.[72] The professor spoke of Canada as vulnerable to American influences. Lennon (who had spent less than two weeks in the country) disagreed and described his host nation as less Americanized than

Britain or Japan. According to Ritchie Yorke (who appeared to have recorded the full meeting), McLuhan spoke of the mass rock festival phenomenon, which he attributed to growing social frustration. He and John also discussed the potential of everyone to be creative.[73] In a post-meeting interview, Lennon expressed his Christmas message for peace as "No violence. No starving children. No violent minds, no violent households. No violence."[74]

Later that day, Yoko and John appeared on the Toronto-based *CBC Weekend*, a television current affairs program hosted by Lloyd Robertson. Lennon introduced the show and spoke of a possible "peace weekend" in Canada for 1970. The segment began with a television connection from the CBC studio in Winnipeg, featuring a representative of Manitoba's NDP government, which was planning the province's centennial. Manitoba had become Canada's fifth province in a controversial manner in 1870. In late 1869, Métis at Red River, led by Louis Riel, became alarmed over the pending takeover of the area, traditionally under the weak authority of the Hudson's Bay Company, by Canada. The Métis (a distinct people of mixed Indigenous and European ancestry) had armed themselves and proclaimed a provisional government. The political solution to this act of resistance was provincial status for Manitoba. Representative Russell Doern, MLA, read a letter from Premier Ed Schreyer conveying a request from the provincial centennial commission to contact the celebrity couple and invite them to Manitoba's 100th birthday celebrations.[75]

Lennon, surprised by the invitation, was gracious: "That's beautiful, and we'd like to thank you very much. And we can't give a date or anything now, but we'll be there definitely. And it's just . . . we're overwhelmed by that offer and we just don't know what to say. It's too much, you know."[76] Robertson, who opined that Canada had an inferiority complex, was intrigued by Lennon's flattering views on the country. During the interview, John explained that they originally had arrived in Canada by accident but found the country welcoming. Canada was also peaceful: "I don't want to be Mr. and

Mrs. Dead Saint of 1970." He alleged that British- supplied weapons in the hands of the Nigerian military were endangering Canadian volunteer relief pilots in Biafra. Rabbi Feinberg, also present for the interview, was asked if the peace campaign had any prospects of success. He responded: "It's intended to leap over the politicians and reach the people," especially young people.[77]

On Sunday, the visitors spent their last day at the Hawkins residence. "Rompin' Ronnie," now enlisted in the crusade, planned to accompany John and Yoko on the next stage of their mission, trips to Montreal and Ottawa. A Bag Productions letter indicated that John and Yoko had been holding telephone conversations since at least early December with Prime Minister Trudeau's staff regarding a meeting and had asked that Yorke, Johnny Brower and Richard Miller be involved in the planning.[78] The official meeting was confirmed on the understanding that the media could not be informed in advance (although rumours began to swirl). On December 22, the celebrities boarded a private glass-roofed observation train car at Toronto's Union Station. Their entourage included Anthony Fawcett, John Brower, Wanda and Ronnie Hawkins and Ritchie Yorke and his wife, Anne, who photographed the event. Heavy Andrews provided security. The CNR Rapido trip to Montreal took five hours. Embarking in two white limousines, the celebrities gave a press conference at the upscale Chateau Champlain, where they made it clear that the only topic of the day was peace. Photographers captured them in matching black jumpsuits, with John holding a red "laughing bag" that emitted the sound of human laughter. A *Montreal Star* reporter commented that Lennon, "a rich man and entertainer," was attempting to instruct the average person on how to work for peace by talking to "workmates," putting up posters and avoiding violence. One new detail was that the peace festival might include British actor Peter Sellers. Yoko, describing the couple as "citizens of the world" and "a think tank," reiterated her husband's comments on the welcoming nature of Canada, which contrasted with England.[79] John added: "We think this was a positive decade, not a depressing one. This is just the beginning. What we've got to do is keep hope alive, because without it we'll sink." Yorke reported that the press conference was successful, with no "cracks, no sarcasm, no dog shit" from reporters.[80]

Given recent events, many in the Montreal area would have been struck by the irony of the city being associated with an idealistic counterculture plea for global peace. On October 7, a wildcat strike by the Montreal police and firefighters had created a genuine public order crisis; the provincial government asked Ottawa to deploy troops in aid of the civil power. Aside from salaries, spokespersons for the thirty-nine hundred officers cited the strain of responding to continued demonstrations and separatist bombs. Over the course of the sixteen-hour walkout, there were reports in several neighbourhoods of fights, vandalism, bank robberies, looting, fire bombs, rioting and the carrying of weapons. Windows at the Queen Elizabeth Hotel, the site of the bed-in, were smashed. Members of a taxi drivers' union and supporters converged on the garage of a limousine company and gunfire broke out, killing a plainclothes Sûreté du Québec (SQ) officer. The provincial authorities quickly legislated the police back to work. For five and a half days, several hundred members of the Royal 22nd Regiment, armed with rifles and submachine guns, assisted the SQ, the RCMP and local police in patrolling the city. The presence of the troops fuelled wild rumours that the military was planning a major counterinsurgency operation with heavy weapons and paratroopers. The shooting at the garage remained unsolved. In the aftermath, the prime minister expressed sympathy with the Montreal police but warned that Canada's government would not tolerate "self-styled Robin Hoods and revolutionaries and romantics" who relied on violence.[81]

By 1969, anti-war demonstrations in Quebec were eclipsed by nationalist protests. On October 29, a fairly orderly demonstration by up to fifteen thousand mainly young people converged on City Hall in defiance of the provincial government and the civic authorities. Their main target was the Union nationale's Bill 63, an attempt

At the Montreal press conference with "War Is Over" campaign signs

to find a compromise on the language of education issue. The province-wide reaction included class boycotts by francophone university and junior college students. The Front de libération populaire (FLP), which called for a Cuban-style revolution in Quebec, organized the Montreal demonstration. It denounced not only "traitors" who failed to protect Quebec's language and culture but also "Anglo-Saxon capitalists" who exploited the people.[82]

The CYC, with its mandate of encouraging young people to help organize disadvantaged communities, had been criticized by local officials in various parts of Canada in the past. But the intense political climate in Quebec put the CYC under greater scrutiny. In late September, the secretary of state stated that the organization's young volunteers were permitted to assist minorities but not support "sedition," which, in his definition, included Quebec separatism. The Montreal municipal authorities had complained to the

RCMP in March about radicals infiltrating the organization. The disturbances of October led to more accusations that the organization was not only sheltering radicals and convicted criminals but also fomenting armed revolution. Three different police agencies investigated its connections to unrest during the police strike and links to the FLQ and FLP. One allegation was that a CYC office had copies of plans for making Molotov cocktails. One CYC-associated "agitator" named by Lucien Saulnier, a political ally of Mayor Drapeau, was Jacques Larue-Langlois, who had met Lennon and Ono at the Queen Elizabeth Hotel. Montreal's ruling Civic party was using all means at its disposal to hold on to power.[83]

Following vandalism in the financial district in early November during another FLP protest, the Montreal city government, on the recommendation of the police director, passed a controversial and possible illegal bylaw to control demonstrations. Under it, the city's executive committee was empowered to ban any demonstration by a group (two or more people) that endangered "public tranquility, peace or order." The penalty under Bylaw 3926 was up to two months in jail and a fine of up to $100. In response, Larue-Langlois, president of the Comité Vallières-Gagnon, explained that his group had co-operated with the police on the night of the parade and warned that the law was similar to the Nazi bans on demonstrations in the 1930s. The first test came in late November when members of the Front commun des Québécoises (Common Front of Quebec Women, a feminist organization) attempted to march to City Hall. Blocked by the police, they staged a sit-down protest, and more than one hundred and thirty women were arrested.[84] Despite pressure from civil liberties supporters and other political parties, the Trudeau government refused to intervene against the measure, which many viewed as unconstitutional.[85] The situation was so tense in Montreal in late 1969 that the Eaton's Christmas parade was cancelled because of fears for the safety of children and families.

John on Drugs

By the late 1960s, in addition to anti-war and student protests, many "square" Canadians were concerned about the illicit drugs becoming normalized among youth. It did not help that many pop idols were writing and singing songs that seemed to support drug use, were being arrested for drug possession, or speaking out against the criminalization of psychoactive substances. Canadians had been visibly reminded of this in May 1969 when flamboyant rock guitarist Jimi Hendrix was arrested for possession at the Toronto International Airport, two weeks into a two-month tour of North America. Customs officers had discovered heroin and hashish in a bottle in his luggage. *Rolling Stone* reported two suspicious circumstances: RCMP officers were waiting for the musician as he stepped off the plane, and Hendrix and entourage, rather than being searched and interviewed in private, were kept for an extended period in full view of the public. The population of Toronto was described as "very conservative," prone to looking "with suspicion upon anybody who looks or dresses a little different than themselves."[86] Hendrix was arrested but released on $10,000 bail with a promise to appear at a hearing in June. Music writer Ritchie Yorke appeared as a character witness. A Toronto drug squad officer later testified that the suspect's arms contained no needle marks. That evening, the Jimi Hendrix Experience delivered a high-powered performance to ten thousand fans at Maple Leaf Gardens.[87]

On December 8, 1969, Hendrix flew in from a gig in Detroit to stand trial for possession of narcotics. The stakes were high; a conviction, for which the maximum penalty was seven years in penitentiary, could have ruined his career. The star denied that he had any knowledge of what was in his luggage and would testify that a young woman in Beverly Hills, California, had given him a bottle containing some type of substance. Through his attorney, Hendrix admitted to having used marijuana, cocaine and LSD but denied ever trying heroin. The defence attempted to show that rock musicians attracted many fans, some of whom insisted on providing performers with drugs. In the end, Hendrix was acquitted by an all-male jury and expressed no ill will against the authorities. "Some of my best friends," he told reporters, "are Canadians." Hendrix described his acquittal as "the best Christmas present Canada has given me".[88]

By late 1969, John Lennon had spoken to the media about drugs many times. At the Ontario Science Centre, he had explained that "hope" was the best antidote for "drug taking and liquor" and that the Beatles had searched in vain for happiness, first through LSD and then the Maharishi.[89] After the press conference in Montreal, the party returned to its private railcar at the CNR station, where special phone lines allowed them to carry out more interviews. According to Yorke's account in Rolling Stone, Ralph Miller, research director for the Le Dain Commission, had approached Lennon to seek his views on illicit drugs.[90] In 1976, Fawcett wrote of a "secret meeting . . . set up at the rear of Platform 18 for John and Ono."[91] Yorke reported that senior research associate Charles Farmilo and commissioners Dr. Heinze Lehman and Ian Campbell took part. Psychiatrist Lehman was the director of Montreal's Douglas Hospital, and Campbell was dean of arts at Sir George Williams University.[92]

Contradicting his reporting at the time, in 2015 Yorke wrote that Gerald Le Dain, chair of the commission, and a colleague visited the observation car to discuss drug policy and that Lennon had asked them if they had ever tried marijuana. When told no, he allegedly insisted that they smoke a joint, which they did, in the privacy of the sleeping compartment. Brower has also insisted that someone from the commission indulged.[93] The meeting supposedly took five hours, two of them in the middle of the night when the train was travelling from Montreal to Ottawa.[94] Both celebrities gave their views; years later, the transcript of Lennon's remarks was declassified, but Ono's will remain unavailable while she is alive. The reports of the Le Dain Commission, whose main focus was on the possible decriminalization of cannabis, made no mention of Lennon or Yoko, possibly because their names were too controversial with conservative Canadians in the early 1970s. Yet it is fascinating that members of the commission, to try to better understand youth culture, including drug use, interviewed pop music celebrities with counterculture credentials. In late 1969, possibly the most famous of those opinion moulders was in a Montreal train station planning to meet Pierre Trudeau the next day.

In terms of the drug scene, Canada was similar to the United States and Britain. During the 1950s, cannabis was rarely mentioned in police reports or the media. In 1967, only 437 Canadians had been arrested for simple possession. Three years later, the number had exploded to 5,339 and by 1971 to 8,389. The Le Dain Commission had been appointed to examine not only the issue of cannabis use but also wider drug problems, particularly as they involved young people and the law. The growing incidence of marijuana smoking by teenagers and young adults had become a

Lennon, Ono, Anthony Fawcett, Johnny Brower, Wanda Hawkins, Ronnie Hawkins and Ritchie Yorke on board the observation car, travelling from Montreal to Ottawa, December 1969

major issue for lawmakers, educators, police and judges and was both a symbol and a vivid manifestation of the generation gap. The media covered the issue in detail. Another reason why social scientists turned to rock musicians when studying the impact of drugs on society was because those with liberal opinions saw drug abuse not as an individual moral failing but as the product of an affluent society, where people had more money and leisure time.[95]

The Le Dain Commission opened its Toronto hearings in October 1969. The first witness was a senior RCMP officer who claimed that cannabis was a moral and social threat that had to be contained and brushed aside concerns about large numbers of young people acquiring criminal records. The RCMP, he explained, actually wanted to save young Canadians from drug abuse. Earlier in the year, a national magazine had reported that most marijuana smokers were urban, educated, articulate individuals in their twenties and thirties who looked down on hippies. According to *Maclean's*, the police, by focusing almost exclusively on youthful deviancy, were in denial about the true extent and nature of the marijuana phenomenon.[96]

John Lennon was no addictions researcher or medical expert, but he had personal experience with illegal drugs and had been convicted of possessing cannabis. More importantly, he exerted an immense influence on global youth culture. In the past, there had been criticism of drug messages and other allegedly objectionable lines in Beatles lyrics; in 1967, the BBC banned "A Day in the Life" on the grounds that it promoted drug use. The Beatles had used "uppers" (amphetamine pills) during their German club years. According to Lennon's first wife Cynthia, Bob Dylan introduced the group to marijuana when they first visited the United States in 1964. LSD came soon after, and many Beatles compositions were linked to the hallucinogen.[97] Many young people in the mid- to late 1960s believed that the group's music was best appreciated when under the influence. According to Wayne Hampton, "the Beatles' psychedelic sound was meant to be listened to when one was stoned, and the combination of drugs and music was supposed to lead the listener to a new sense of awareness."[98] Other than commenting on the Vietnam War, the Beatles as a group shied away from politics, but in 1968, they and other celebrities had purchased a full-page advertisement in the *London Times* in support of decriminalizing cannabis possession and use.[99]

By many accounts, drugs became a problem for John sometime after 1965, and it is not clear exactly when in the next decade he gave them up. John and Yoko began snorting heroin in 1968 and were probably using in 1969 when they launched their peace crusade. In his autobiography, Keith Richards of the Rolling Stones recalled an "acid-fuelled road trip" with Lennon. According to Richards: "It was one of those cases of John wanting to do more drugs than me. Huge bag of weed, hash and acid."[100] For better or worse, Lennon was regarded, in Establishment circles, as an apostle of the drug culture, and his shoulder-length long hair and avant-garde lifestyle were offensive to many.[101]

By the time he reached Montreal, Lennon was already on record as a supporter of decriminalizing soft drugs and an opponent of hard drugs. Given that he was an occasional heroin user and had ingested either cocaine or speed before taking the stage at the Toronto Rock 'n' Roll Revival, the latter opinion was ironic, but it did fit the views of many progressive people at the time. In his recent Toronto press conference, he had pointed out that alcohol was more damaging to society than illegal drugs.[102] In his private testimony to the Le Dain Commission, Lennon supported the decriminalization of cannabis and argued that it could be a source of government revenue; his comments on LSD were more ambivalent. At times, he claimed it expanded consciousness; at other points, he admitted its drawbacks. Although he was either still using heroin or suffering from heroin withdrawal, he strongly opposed hard drugs and viewed them as a threat to youth. Lennon linked the decriminalization of soft drugs to a more peaceful world and argued that marijuana users were non-violent and creative (two characteristics highly valued within the counterculture). John praised Canada's political culture as more tolerant than that of Britain and the United States and expressed hope that its objective examination of drug use would lead to realistic policies that could be emulated by other nations. When the meeting ended and the commissioners and staff prepared to leave the train, Lennon promised he would give them his "hotline" contact information in case they needed to follow up with further questions.[103] The "secret" testimony of John and Yoko was no secret to those who read *Rolling Stone* at the time.[104] In late 1969, before the celebrities returned to Canada, Yorke penned a short article in the magazine in which he claimed that "heads" (competent drug users) were sensing that the Trudeau government would relax the law on marijuana as it was realizing that deterrence did not work.[105]

John, Yoko and Pierre

On their third visit to Canada in the 1960s, Lennon and Ono would succeed in meeting its hip leader. Decades later, Hugh Segal, who had met John and Yoko in Ottawa in June 1969, was not above partisanship when recalling Trudeau's alleged pandering to the permissive society: "Appealing to a self-indulgent, youth-focused society's desire to have their "bedroom freedoms" elevated to the national agenda by a trendy politico was far more politically astute than trying to deal with grinding but dull problems of poverty or income disparity."[106]

Yet not all of Trudeau's attitudes and policies were trendy by the standards of 1969. As mentioned above, his plans for Canada's Status Indians were starkly assimilationist. In response, Alberta Cree Harold Cardinal wrote *The Unjust Society*, an indictment of the Canadian state's policies of coercion and neglect. The Indian Association of Alberta issued a red paper demanding that Status Indians not be assimilated but treated as "citizens plus." Trudeau and his Indian Affairs minister, Jean Chrétien, attempted to

Pierre Elliott Trudeau meeting with Ono and Lennon, Ottawa, December 1969

defend the document, but later it was withdrawn and a more conciliatory approach adopted. Although the government's insensitive handling of this issue did not directly affect Canada's Métis and Inuit populations, it also helped establish a new era of organizing and activism among these groups.[107]

On the morning of December 23, John and Yoko were driven to the Parliament Building by Allan Rock, who had organized their June visit to Ottawa. What *London Times* correspondent Hilary Brigstocke dubbed the "flower power summit" in a nod to Lennon's counterculture credentials was made possible when a meeting with Privy Council clerk Gordon Robertson and Trudeau's principal secretary Marc Lalonde was cancelled.[108] Brigstocke exaggerated when she claimed that although visiting British prime ministers were not always granted an audience with Canada's leader, the celebrities were given nearly an hour. Trudeau had learned the power of media images during his leadership bid and the 1968 national election, which may explain why he insisted that only photographers and television camera crews, not reporters, be present. This was a photo opportunity, not a press conference. The media was given a twenty-minute warning.

John and Yoko, continuing with their unisex theme, wore floppy hats and long, dark cloaks outside the prime minister's office. They may have purchased them on their recent shopping trip to Herschel Segal's rue Sainte-Catherine store, Le Chateau.[109] About twenty photographers were on hand. The informal encounter, planned for ten minutes, lasted much longer.[110] Trudeau shook Lennon's hand and hugged Ono. Photos of the meeting show a shaggy Lennon uncharacteristically in a sports jacket and tie. In 2014, Segal spoke of the significance of one photo, which he claimed was "the first picture of Prime Minister Trudeau to go global around the world." He continued:

> This is before Twitter and before e-mails. That photo spoke to millions because he was the first NATO leader to associate himself with the "Give Peace a Chance Tour." It is fascinating for me to look back on that and realize that I had been a part of a piece of history that set Trudeau on the trajectory to becoming known as one of the most different kinds of Prime Minister out there at that tumultuous time.[111]

Lennon and Ono were aware of Trudeau the celebrity but likely knew little about Canadian politics and the Liberal prime minister's complicated relationship with the young and people on the Left. On the other hand, they were television and newspaper addicts and may have picked up some recent knowledge of Canada's public affairs. Trudeau remarked that John was attracting more media attention than a visiting ambassador. His welcoming attitude contrasted with the Nixon administration's later crusade against Lennon. By 1969, John had soured on Britain's Labour government, particularly because of its foreign policy. In contrast, Canada was non threatening and Trudeau was friendly and respectful and spoke of the importance of "spanning the generations."[112] Anthony Fawcett recalled that Trudeau asked John about his books and poetry, "which he said he enjoyed." Then they spoke of youth culture, music and peace. The prime minister supposedly was interested in the planned peace festival and, according to Fawcett, pledged his government's support. Next Trudeau reminisced about visiting China (he had co-written a book on his experiences) and asked John if "he had any private life." This question was probably prompted by Trudeau's growing frustration with the media, which continued to delve into his private life. The meeting concluded with the prime minister stating that he was optimistic about the future of young people and their potential for advancing the cause of peace.[113] According to John Wiener, Trudeau, along with Israel's Golda Meir, was the only world leader to plant the peace acorns the couple had sent him.[114]

Speaking to reporters outside the meeting, Lennon described Trudeau as "beautiful," and Ono, who confessed that she had harboured doubts about the meeting, agreed that the prime minister was "more beautiful than we expected." Her spouse declared that Canada's leader could contribute to world peace. "You don't know how lucky you are," John told Canadians via reporters. "If there were more leaders like Mr. Trudeau, the world would have peace." The *Montreal Star* opined that the meeting of Lennon, Ono and Trudeau was "not likely to hurt the prime minister's future," especially when the Liberal government lowered the voting age to eighteen.[115] According to a correspondent from the *New York Times*, "Trudeau found himself fascinated by Lennon's personality and effort to change an image from a pop ideal into a serious figure: there was something of a parallel with his own case."[116] The same journalist continued:

> One or two commentators condemned Trudeau
> for granting so much time when, for instance,
> the Mennonites had long been attempting

unsuccessfully to make an appointment on a
similar mission of peace. Some of the dinosaurs in
the Civil Service even wondered if it was proper
for a Prime Minister to associate with a Beatle.
But, as Trudeau himself remarked, informally, he
was worried whether it would be bad for Lennon's
image to call on a Prime Minister.[117]

As one historian has written, "It did not strike anyone as
incongruous that Canada's middle-aged prime minister would be
consorting with one of the Beatles."[118]

Following the media scrum, John and Yoko and the reporters
wished each other Merry Christmas. They next met with federal
Health Minister John Munro. Munro was not part of Trudeau's
inner circle but had been made a cabinet minister in 1968 and
was in charge of what was arguably the highest-profile domestic
department, National Health and Welfare. A labour lawyer from
the industrial city of Hamilton, he was first elected MP in 1962
after serving in municipal government. One journalist described
him as hardworking and compassionate but with "little charm
and no discernible wit."[119] His major preoccupation in the late
1960s was the rolling out of medicare, a major cost-sharing program between Ottawa and the provinces. This put him in conflict
with the powerful Canadian Medical Association, which saw
medicare as a threat to the autonomy of doctors.[120] Munro was
also in charge of the Liberal government's cautious but evolving
response to a new public health threat: smoking. Tobacco companies were still denying any scientific link between smoking and
poor health; Munro (a smoker) was on record as favouring a ban
on tobacco advertising and promotion, and the government was
signalling a tougher response.

Munro was best known to the public in this period because
of his department's work on the non-medical use of drugs and
the Le Dain Commission. A far from flashy or trendy politician,

he appeared to become more appreciative of the generation gap. Speaking to a pharmaceutical industry meeting in May, he warned that for many youth, marijuana was becoming "a symbol of persecution of their generation."[121] In 1968, he suggested that the Liberal government was considering liberalizing the law of simple possession. Munro not only relied on advisors for information on drug use, he also "learned firsthand from heads, speed freaks, dealers, rock musicians and street level workers" in places like Yorkville, making him one of the best-informed politicians on the subject in Canada.[122] During his meeting with Munro, Lennon explained that they were planning a peace festival for Mosport in July 1970 and wanted to "keep it healthy," in other words, to reduce the danger of drugs.[123] Fawcett recalled that federal health officials "didn't want the problem covered up" and that John repeated his support for legalizing soft drugs and opposition to hard drugs. Munro supposedly asked the Beatle for advice on dealing with young people who tended to protest with "placards, posters and catch phrases."[124]

On the flight back to Toronto, Ronnie Hawkins noticed Lester Pearson, the former prime minister and winner of the Nobel Peace Prize. John sent him a congratulatory note on the back of a War Is Over handbill. Pearson sent back his thanks and regards.[125] Yorke later claimed that "representatives of spy agencies" such as the RCMP or FBI were also on the flight.[126] Before they departed for London, John spoke of "the maturity of the Canadian people," which was impressive given the relative newness of the country. He reiterated that Canada's immigration authorities had treated them well compared to "other countries I could mention." Lennon (or Yorke embellishing on his behalf) praised Canada's "attitudes towards Vietnam, China and NATO." He continued: "Everything points to Canada being one of the key countries in the race for survival." Lennon mentioned the arms race and the space race; now was the time for the "peace race."[127] John and Yoko were happy to have had direct contact with the Establishment and to have spent so much time with "a national leader."[128] Yorke claimed that John regarded the visit to Canada as "the best trip [they'd] ever had." He added, "We got more done for peace that week than in our whole lives."[129]

For the most part, the Canadian media reported on the War Is Over campaign in a neutral or respectful manner. Editorials could be different; one Alberta newspaper dismissed the campaign's tactics as naïve and futile but speculated that Lennon may be using it to "manufacture credentials" as a political leader of "the Now Generation."[130] A December 23 Canadian Press story was entitled "Smile, Clap Hands and Hope and the World Will Find Peace." CBC Television broadcast an interview with the couple on Christmas Day where John reiterated his interest in promoting peace and in staging a peace festival "near Mosport Park" that would be a positive contrast to the violence at Altamont.[131] Lennon continued to flatter Canada, but his real motivation, according to Wiener, was to mobilize public opinion against Nixon.[132]

Professor James Eayrs, an expert on Canada's foreign policy, wrote of Yoko and John as "two splendid if slightly spooky" people and, in terms of the broader peace movement of the era, described them as utopian optimists. Their theory of peace rested on "a cultural revolution à la Woodstock," with the under-twenty-five generation exerting its social power as opposed to getting involved in politics. In fact, according to Eayrs, Lennon's peace message clashed with the more activist approach of the Vietnam moratorium. He believed the couple's crusade was actually a sign that the anti-war movement was being weakened by factionalism, although he did speculate that the youth of 1969 could carry their idealism into their thirties and forties, when their views would dominate the nation's agenda. On the other hand, they could also turn into the conservative "silent majority" of the future.[133] Less restrained, *Rolling Stone* interpreted the meeting with Trudeau as a good omen for peace, speculating that a private conversation between Lennon and President Nixon "would be a more significant summit than any Geneva Summit between the USA and Russia."[134]

Promotion of the campaign and planned festival continued, with ongoing coverage in the media, including *Rolling Stone*, which reminded readers that the proposed Toronto event would take place in the following summer. In addition to authorizing the media and billboard campaign, John appointed Ritchie Yorke and Ronnie Hawkins roving peace emissaries (their travels are discussed in the next chapter.[135] Other than media coverage, it is difficult to assess the actual impact of this stage of the peace campaign. It certainly added to John's peacenik image, but that would soon be clouded by his shifting associations with more radical causes. The War Is Over campaign also lacked the tangible results of George Harrison's 1971 effort to raise funds for humanitarian relief in Bangladesh, the breakaway province of Pakistan. In contrast, Lennon was associated with "bed-ins, bagism and myriad woolly gestures of the age which generated lots of heat but very little light."[136]

Aftermath

John and Yoko's return to Britain capped the end of a turbulent year for Canada. Recently, a number of historians have suggested that 1969 was Canada's equivalent of the global turning point of 1968.[137] One sign of turbulence was a backlash against the counterculture and youth culture in general as events in the United States, as they had in the past, intruded into Canadian life. One was a misleading but influential media narrative linked to the murder of several people by members of the Charles Manson cult in California that associated hippies with violence. On December 8, Manson and three followers were indicted for the murders of actress Sharon Tate and three others. Another was pushback against the Black Power movement and civil rights in general, epitomized in police harassment and violence against the Black Panthers. Tensions over politically motivated violence were evident in Quebec, where in December FLQ intellectual Pierre Vallières was sentenced to two and a half years in connection with the 1966 bombing death of a woman at a Montreal shoe factory. At the sentencing hearing, Jacques Larue-Langlois allegedly led a sit-in protest and was later fined.

Pierre Trudeau ended his political year with another round of constitutional talks with the premiers in early December. Quebec stood alone in demanding that the federal government remove itself from all social spending in that province. This was not a new idea, but it carried added intensity given the growing support for sovereignty in Quebec and the feeling in much of English Canada that the Trudeau government somehow favoured that province. At a press conference in December, the prime minister mused that in the future Canada might end its formal ties with the British monarchy, although his envisioned constitutional reforms would maintain that connection. The "values of the present generation," he argued, were leading Canada in new directions. To conservatives, any slight to the monarchy, such as replacing the Queen's likeness on the $5 bill, was "creeping republicanism."[138]

John and Yoko returned to Britain on December 24, where, accompanied by Dick Gregory, they planned to take part in a fundraiser at Rochester Cathedral for the homeless. Not wanting to overshadow the event with their celebrity status, they returned to Tittenhurst Park. A few days later, the couple flew to Denmark for a private visit. In the last several weeks of 1969, television programs, newspapers and magazines around the world explored not only the usual "year in review" themes but also the significance of the decade of the 1960s. In these stories, the Beatles — and John Lennon — often had a place of prominence, further underscoring for Canadians the significance of the visits of May–June, September and December 1969. Many were now anticipating John and Yoko's next Canadian project: their festival for peace.

Chapter 4

From Peace Festival to Strawberry Fields

The Aquarian Age, like Swinging London, turns out to be an invention of Time Inc.

— Dennis Duffy, University of Toronto, 1970

From Denmark, John and Yoko started 1970 — "Year One A.P. (After Peace)" — by announcing that in the future, all royalties from their music would go toward "promoting peace on earth." Lennon predicted that the 1970s would be a decade of peace.[1] Peace was definitely a powerful branding concept for both non-governmental organizations and capitalist enterprise by 1970. After John and Yoko's third visit to Toronto, a peace centre was established at Rochdale College that planned to blend the ideals of Lennon, the Hare Krishna movement and the "free" philosophy of Abbie Hoffman. In March 1970, it hosted an event that included chanting by Hare Krishna devotees and performances by local rockers Luke and the Apostles and upcoming folk singer Bruce Cockburn.[2]

For several months in 1970, Canada remained a major focus in the international pop music world because of the possible peace festival associated with Lennon. It was expected that John and Yoko would make their fourth trip to Canada and that the festival would carry on the positive mood established at Woodstock. An official visit to Manitoba was also still possible. The celebrities would never return to Canada as a couple, and as Lennon distanced himself from the peace festival, it morphed into the nation's first major outdoor pop festival, organized by hip entrepreneurs. The story of the Strawberry Fields Festival goes to the heart of an intense debate at the time over the very soul of rock culture. In the wake of Woodstock, idealists such as Lennon envisioned a future communal pop music scene devoid of the profit motive, a concept that elements of the New Left exploited. Pragmatists insisted that rock was, and always had been, a business. The Strawberry Fields Festival was also a vivid example of Canada's intolerance of the counterculture.

The celebrities spent most of January 1970 at a farmhouse in Ellidsbølvej, Denmark, hosted by Ono's ex-husband and his partner. During their sojourn, John and Yoko's long locks were shorn, an event that made headlines. When they returned to Britain, he went into the Abbey Road studio with Klaus Voormann, Alan White and a keyboardist to record a new single, "Instant Karma." It was released as a Plastic Ono Band song, not a Beatles song.[3] Although his activism was often criticized in Britain, John continued to have many admirers. Early in 1970, Jann Wenner proclaimed him *Rolling Stone*'s "Man of the Year." In addition to praising his contribution to music, art and activism, the editor admired John for "speaking openly" about the Beatles and "admitting mistakes." Wenner also expressed the generational fear that the beloved and trend-setting group might dissolve.[4] In a December 1969 interview with Ritchie Yorke in Toronto (published in the same issue of *Rolling Stone*), John explained that the Beatles were "competing with each other" and that working within the group was limiting. As part of his ongoing revisionism, he opined that he and McCartney had written "a lot of rubbish." Lennon was impatient and wanted to get his solo songs on record as soon as possible, which was why he was excited by the Plastic Ono Band.[5]

The Peace Festival in Jeopardy

Song writers, performers, publishing and record companies, radio stations, promoters and venue owners knew that rock and capitalism were not antithetical and that not all of pop culture, despite its counterculture trappings, was ideological. Yet Lennon, who had been linking the idea of a large music gathering to his War Is Over campaign, remained hopeful that the proposed festival in Canada could be a free event. It was a natural outgrowth of Ono and Lennon's two bed-ins and their War Is Over campaign. Yet as the year progressed, they became involved with other causes and distracted by personal issues, such as their heroin addiction. This was also the year that the Beatles ceased functioning as a music group if not a business entity. Another complication was entanglement with eccentric personalities from the emerging subculture, which was eventually dubbed "New Age." In Denmark, he met Don Hamrick, a California resident with whom he shared a belief in UFOs. Hamrick, who claimed to have been abducted by aliens, headed an organization called Frontiers of Science, which by this time had a presence in Peterborough, Ontario. When visiting John and Yoko at the Danish farmhouse, Johnny Brower met Hamrick, who claimed to be building "a city in the clouds." In his book on Lennon's peace campaign, Ritchie Yorke wrote that Lennon was under the influence of Hamrick, but in a 1970 *Rolling Stone* interview, John explained that he met with the American in the hope that he could help him quit "ciggies" through hypnosis. The people in Harbinger, the commune/UFO cult associated with Hamrick, were, according to Lennon in 1970, "obviously all insane."[6] The insanity, as discussed below, included a design for an "air car," a flying vehicle powered by "psychic energy," which supposedly would be premiered at the peace festival.

Although Lennon initially seemed keen on working with Allen Klein despite his hefty fees, he appeared not to trust his American manager completely and asked Ritchie Yorke to gather music industry intelligence on him from people such as Jann Wenner of *Rolling Stone* and Morris Levy of Roulette Records. According to Brower, Klein "did not want the festival to happen" and hoped he could convince the Beatles to go on tour.[7] Klein's public stance was that the festival should be free, as his client insisted. Yorke, who later described Klein as "a hustler of epic proportions," wrote that the report on Klein was not favourable and that he and Brower, when they visited the farmhouse in Denmark, delivered it with reluctance as the American was present. This was before Yorke left on his peace junket with Ronnie Hawkins. Lennon judged their report "crap" and allowed Klein to read it. The outcome was that Klein, Brower and Yorke were instructed to co-operate on the peace festival project. After a subsequent meeting in New York with Klein, Brower was convinced that Lennon's agent was not on board. Exactly who was in charge of planning the Canadian festival was not clear, and available sources offer little help with this question.[8]

Another publicity-seeking event that kept the Lennon-Ono peace mission in the public eye was a colourful promotional tour by Ronnie Hawkins and Ritchie Yorke in early 1970, apparently organized and paid for by "the peace festival folks."[9] Hawkins's career had revived after his 1969 *Rolling Stone* interview, and having John and Yoko as house guests did his image no harm. Similarly, Yorke had benefited from being the couple's chief Canadian contact. The pair was sent on a roving peace mission in service of the War Is Over campaign, which Hawkins also used to promote his new album.[10] The first stop was Australia, where Yorke spoke on behalf of John and Yoko at the Pilgrimage for Pop Festival at Ourimbah, considered Australia's first rock festival. In Japan, Yorke recorded an anti-Vietnam War message for a pirate radio station. Their most dramatic adventure occurred during their Hong Kong stop, where a local journalist convinced them to take John and Yoko's message to nearby Communist territory. In his memoir, Yorke described the dramatic journey to the frontier of the Peoples' Republic of China and a hair-raising encounter with armed border guards at Lok Ma Chau. The publicity stunt, in the company of Hong Kong journalists, was captured in a photograph depicting Yorke holding a "War Is Over If You Want It" sign in Chinese. From Bangkok, they flew to Rome via New Delhi, Tehran and Tel Aviv. Following a press conference in Paris, they pushed on to Holland, Denmark and Sweden. Finally reaching London, they booked a suite in the Playboy Club, endured an epic party and promoted Hawkins's record. By this time, Yorke had been picking up rumours that the Canadian peace festival might be a dud.[11]

For a number of reasons, the festival envisioned by John and Yoko never materialized. As Jon Wiener explained, Lennon had never been strong on organization and had a short attention span. His new agent was adept at dealing with record companies but was not experienced with organizing live events.[12] It fell to Johnny Brower and his associates to keep the project — or a project with different attributes — in the public eye. The Mosport racetrack,

Ritchie Yorke and Ronnie Hawkins at the Chinese border with "War Is Over" campaign signs, 1970

located in Ontario's rural Clarke Township eighty kilometres east of Toronto, remained the ideal location for what was still being described as John Lennon's peace festival. The immediate impediment was a zoning bylaw passed by the township council that limited the use of the facility to car and motorcycle races. Interviewed in January 1970, the reeve of the township explained that many residents were apprehensive about 250,000 or more young people flooding into the area and confirmed that neither promoters nor the Mosport track had made any contact.[13] Karma Productions spokesperson Brian Gilhooley announced that the promoters were exploring their options. He explained that the event would not be simply a music festival but would include a symposium on ecology, the arts and technology and "seminars in psychic survival in post-industrial society."[14] At this point, the working dates for the festival were July 3–5.

The already strange Harbinger-Lennon connection took a stranger twist in February and embarrassed almost everyone involved in the peace festival. Johnny Brower travelled to California to shore up support and appeared at a press conference in San Francisco at the mansion of Jefferson Airplane. Even by the standards of Aquarian-Age counterculture, things became bizarre when two Canadian disciples of Don Hamrick, who purported to be Lennon's representatives in Canada, spoke to the reporters present and announced that "interplanetary brothers" — extraterrestrials — would appear at the peace conference.[15] Brower, who had tolerated the Harbinger types out of deference to Lennon, immediately parted ways with them. But the damage had been done. At some point in February, pressured by an embarrassed *Rolling Stone* after the San Francisco event, Yorke quit working with Karma Productions, but he remained supportive of the festival. More criticism — and resulting uncertainty — arose with a *Village Voice* article, "Canada & the New Age: Peacemaker to the World," which examined the struggling festival project and Karma Productions.[16]

Backlash in Manitoba

By the late 1960s, John Lennon was not the only celebrity attempting to use star power to advance social causes. But for the young,
he was the most influential exponent of the global counterculture.
J. Patrick Boyer, a young PC activist, wrote that Lennon's lyrics,
and the evolving musical expression of the Beatles, exerted greater
social and cultural impact than Canada's political elites.[17] Yet much
like there was no consensus on the role of drugs such as marijuana,
not everyone agreed that idols of youth such as Lennon were positive role models. The young and those of liberal opinions saw his
beliefs and lifestyle as within the realm of acceptable debate, but
squares or straights viewed them as deviant and therefore a threat
to the status quo. These conflicting viewpoints came into sharp
focus during a controversy that erupted in Manitoba in late 1969
over the province's centennial celebrations.

Under young leader Ed Schreyer, voters elected Canada's first
NDP government in 1969, ending eleven years of Conservative
rule. The NDP was described as socialist in its philosophy, but
Schreyer was more interested in "democratizing the provincial
power structure and extending civil liberties" than in restructuring
the economy.[18] First elected an MP at age 22, he described himself
as a social democrat and a great admirer of Scandinavian policy
making that combined social planning and social justice with capitalism. He wanted to attract investment to the province and update
its somewhat bland image. Although a new brand of politician who
sported sideburns and suits of non-traditional hues, he shied away
from the radical anti-Americanism of the Waffle movement within
his national party.[19]

Winnipeg, which decades earlier was Canada's most dynamic
city, had its progressive side in the late 1960s, as evident with the
Committee Representing Youth Problems Today (CRYPT). In late
1969, prior to the formation of the Winnipeg Committee to Assist
War Objectors, CRYPT had helped two hundred draft dodgers

and one hundred military deserters with temporary housing and information on American draft rules and Canadian immigration regulations.[20] The city also had a Vietnam Mobilization Committee, which, much to the anger of conservative politicians such as Alderman A.E. Brotman, planned a protest march for April 1970. Brotman was convinced that the organization was a "Communist front."[21] The prairie city also had its hip side; the "swinging set" (aged 16–25) patronized community dances and all-ages discotheques where DJs and bands supplied the music.[22] Winnipeg had long been part of North America's touring circuit for live acts and had its own thriving music scene, which produced performers such as Neil Young and the Guess Who. After a failed British tour, the latter became the house band on the Winnipeg segment of the CBC-TV program *Let's Go*. Its 1970 album *Wheatfield Soul* produced the number one single in Canada and the United States, "These Eyes." Later that year came the group's signature hit, "American Woman," whose lyrics, guitarist Randy Bachman remembered, were a protest against the Vietnam War.

Like other provinces, Manitoba had taken part in Canada's 1967 centennial celebrations, which produced a series of useful public facilities such as parks, libraries and hockey and curling rinks. The year 1970 was both the centennial of the province and the 300th anniversary of the firm that had dominated so much of western and northern Canada, the Hudson's Bay Company. According to George Manuel, president of the National Indian Brotherhood, the company had brought "misery, deprivation and exploitation of Canada's indigenous people."[23] Manitoba's celebrations consisted of arts, cultural and heritage events that emphasized the province's multicultural fabric. Because of this confluence of anniversaries, it was expected that major dignitaries would be invited to Manitoba. In the end, they included Queen Elizabeth and her husband, Prince Phillip, and their children, Princess Anne and Prince Charles. When the Royal family reached Winnipeg in July, it attracted a huge crowd.[24]

In early February, the *Winnipeg Free Press* reported that a centennial rock festival would probably take place on August 7 and 8. The festival idea, part of programming for youth, was a new addition to centennial planning, and the chosen site was the Winnipeg Stadium. The organizers hoped to book well-known performers but explained that Manitoba talent would be given first priority.[25] The same issue of the newspaper carried a story about a growing backlash against the NDP government's invitation in December to Lennon and Ono. Premier Schreyer, whose letter had been read over national television, now explained that inviting "the Beatle-peace prophet" had not been his idea. Lennon had been contacted on behalf of the Centennial Corporation, and it was not clear if the celebrities would take part in the festival or even come to the province. The mayor of North Kildonan, adjacent to Winnipeg, personally opposed Lennon's participation but understood that young people may have other views.[26]

Sixties nostalgia notwithstanding, in 1969 and 1970 many Canadians held conservative views on youth, the counterculture and the New Left.[27] Cold War attitudes died hard. In 1969 at a workshop on dissent, PC party delegates were advised that student unrest was largely the work of "outside Communist agitators" who took advantage of naïve or immature students. The meeting was held a month after the events at Sir George Williams University, and many PC delegates equated dissent with the destruction of property and blamed the press for exaggerating any act of protest or civil disobedience. One Saskatchewan Tory opined that students should "consider themselves lucky to have the opportunity to go to university." Voices of tolerance were present, but those who advocated a stronger hand received the most applause.[28] For those on the right, admitting draft dodgers and foreign activists, allowing dissent on campus, liberalizing drug laws and increasing individual freedoms were not advances in democracy but threats to it.

Publications such as *Saturday Night* and *Maclean's*, which appealed to educated, middle-class urbanites, often promoted positive or at least ambivalent portrayals of youth and youth culture. But more Canadians consumed local newspapers such as the *Vancouver Sun* and listened to local radio, which could be quite conservative and hostile to the hippies and the counterculture.[29] The fault line over the prospect of Lennon and Ono coming to Manitoba appeared to coincide with the generation gap. Resistance began in late 1969 when angry citizens responded to an editorial by Winnipeg radio phone-in show host John (Heidman) Harvard, later a well-known TV personality and lieutenant governor of Manitoba.[30] Talk radio, then mainly local in focus, was popular daytime programming that was fertile ground for conservative opinion. Harvard described Lennon as a "creep" and "alien to Manitoba." He continued: "Can you imagine anything more hypocritical than a man who supposedly believes in peace lying in bed with his wife? Inviting John Lennon is tantamount to inviting Ho Chi Minh! He's a kooky-looking character, and I don't like him!"[31]

Deputy Speaker Russ Doern, who had invited Lennon and Ono on behalf of Schreyer, explained that centennial organizers could handle the large crowds that would turn out to see the celebrities and that Manitoba would not become a magnet for hippies. As in other parts of Canada, the local media often expressed negative or sensationalist views of the counterculture, student activism and drugs. In February of 1969, for example, the *Winnipeg Free Press* dismissed activist students at SFU, McGill University, Sir George Williams University and the Université de Moncton as "extremists," in contrast to moderate student leaders at the University of Manitoba.[32] The debate in Manitoba may have been influenced by lingering media coverage of the Manson family murders in California and controversies with the CYC.

The debate over the most controversial Beatle became more intense after entrepreneur Lech Fulmyk paid for mail-in coupons for those who opposed the visit to be published in local newspapers; by late February, nearly twenty thousand had been forwarded to the premier. On the yes side were five thousand mail-in coupons promoted by Youthbeat, a popular column in the *Winnipeg Tribune*, thousands of letters and the Council of the University of Manitoba Students Union. The Union of Manitoba Municipalities warned that if Lennon came to the province, it could become "a hippie haven." Conservative religious leaders also expressed alarm. In a late February interview, John explained that he and Yoko had received no formal invitation, but the Centennial Corporation confirmed that it would be issuing one in the future. Lennon added: "If they don't want us, well we haven't even had the letter yet. And we don't want to disturb the peace."[33]

The Toronto Peace Festival Adrift

Wiener concluded that the collapse of the Toronto Peace Festival was one of John Lennon's "most significant political failures."[34] Yet the Beatle's level of commitment to this utopian project, which died in stages, is not clear. On March 11, Johnny Brower announced from Los Angeles that Karma Productions and Lennon had parted ways. The Ontario Municipal Board had refused to strike down the local bylaw that blocked use of the Mosport facility, and the provincial government was demanding substantial advance guarantees to cover the costs of policing, medical services and water and sewage. Without sizable donations from benefactors, organizers needed to charge admission to cover basic costs. In a telegram to Brower, Lennon, seemingly oblivious to these basic logistical and legal realities, complained that the young Canadian entrepreneur hadn't kept his promise: "You said it would be free. We want nothing to do with the festival. Please do not use our name or our ideas or symbols."[35] The situation became more confusing when Lennon's agent issued a press statement explaining that although the Beatle had not kept "artistic control" of the event, he and Ono still wanted to be involved, a sentiment that Brower encouraged. Klein insisted that the festival was still Lennon's and that all acts would be paid.[36]

In April, perceptive Toronto journalist Melinda McCracken described peace as a "commodity" for promoters, especially when associated with John Lennon. As noted elsewhere in this book, this trend, expertly documented by Thomas Frank in *The Conquest of Cool: Business Culture, Counterculture, and the Rise of Hip Consumerism*, was hardly a unique situation in the entertainment industry in the counterculture age. McCracken speculated that a conflict with Festival Express, a rival festival, had forced Brower to move his tentative date to August, close to the anniversary of Woodstock.[37]

April was also the month that Lennon song-writing partner Paul McCartney, who had released a solo album, publicly explained that he was not sure if he would be recording again with the group. This was not quite the same as saying that the Beatles had split, but that is how the press interpreted it, and McCartney, in the words of journalist Ray Connolly, "became the most hated man in the world." The irony was that Lennon, not his bandmate, had been the most insistent about the dissolution. John was displeased that Paul had gone public before him and chided Connolly for not divulging the news to the world when they had spoken in Canada before Christmas. In early May, the last Beatles album, *Let It Be*, was released. The documentary with the same name followed. Although the news would not fully sink in until 1971, a major era in pop culture was ending.[38]

While it did not attract the same media coverage as the future of the Beatles or the Canadian peace festival, Lennon and Ono's possible official visit to Manitoba that summer remained unresolved. If a formal invitation had been sent, the celebrities appear not to have responded, at least according to proceedings in the Manitoba legislature on April 23. The NDP minister of cultural affairs, when summarizing the centennial plans, made no mention of "the Lennons," but the issue surfaced in debate. Jacob Froese, the Social Credit MLA for Rhineland, read a petition from his constituents that took no issue with the Beatle's views on peace, or even drugs, but criticized his promotion of sex, most recently in a series of "sex photos for sale." This was a reference to the *Bag One* lithographs signed at Ronnie Hawkins's home that included explicit drawings of John and Yoko. The portfolios, displayed for sale at a Toronto galley a month later, were considered pornographic by many. The petitioners claimed that Lennon was too controversial and that his presence would be an affront to other official guests, who included British royals. The leader of the Liberal party warned that the presence of Yoko and John would attract "every hippie in the west side of North America" to Manitoba.[39]

For young people, according to the Canadian Secretary of State's Committee on Youth, criticisms of and resistance to pop festivals by police and government officials were a form of "anti-youth discrimination."[40] In 1970, pop festivals were of interest to national security agencies. In April, the RCMP Security and Intelligence branch, relying on open sources, sent a report on Canada's planned "youth oriented rock festival" that mentioned Brower and Yorke to the FBI via the U.S. Embassy in Ottawa. The FBI offices in Los Angeles, using informants whose names were redacted in the declassified file, reported on Lennon's activities in California. The subject on the file was "New Left — Foreign Influences — Canada."[41] In 2018, Brower explained that the authorities in Ontario feared John's "political influence," but the immediate problem in early 1970 was not Lennon himself but the political backlash caused by the large numbers of young people associated with the counterculture lifestyle that a festival could attract.

The Government of Ontario and rural municipalities were pressured by the Ontario Provincial Police (OPP), which opposed Mosport for a variety of reasons, the most prominent being its potential as a precedent. There was also a "not-in-my-backyard" effect at work. The OPP, relatively new to drug enforcement, had film footage depicting anti-social behaviour at Woodstock, which they showed to officials in rural municipalities. The OPP assigned a senior officer the task of educating municipal officials about the perils of hippies and pop music. Chief Superintendent Lawrence Gartner denied that he was trying to stop these events, but that was the result of his visits to several townships. In addition to the New York State Police film on Woodstock, he was armed with photographs and a copy of *Bag One*, John's erotic drawings. Although Lennon was no longer formally associated with any Canadian festival, his counterculture notoriety was useful for the Establishment. Gartner also travelled to California to gather information on the controversial Altamont festival.[42]

The OPP campaign, together with resistance from rural residents, added to Karma Production's problems. In April, a Chicago journalist expressed disappointment that the Canadian festival had reached another impasse in Parkhill, Middlesex County. The "Woodstock Nation" needed some hope after the Altamont disaster, but things looked grim. One resident who leased land to Karma Productions supposedly had a barn torched by vigilantes. Mike Lang, one of the producers of Woodstock, was disassociating himself from the Canadian peace festival, as was a *Los Angeles Free Press* editor who had been co-ordinating things in the United States. The article mentioned "peace caravans" that were planned from Detroit and New York and concluded that the backlash against rock music was proof that Canada "was no haven."[43]

On April 16, *Rolling Stone* published an extensive piece by Lennon explaining why the celebrity couple had pulled out of the "Toronto Peace Festival." The rambling article endorsed the concept of a free festival and alluded to the 1967 global broadcast of "All You Need Is Love":

> Can you imagine what we could do together in one spot...thinking, singing and praying for peace ... one million souls apart from any TV link-ups, etc. to the rest of the planet. If we can be together for one reason, we could make it together. We need help! It is out of our control. All we have is

our name. We are sorry for the confusion, it is
bigger than both of us. We are doing our best for
all our sakes . . . we still believe. Pray for us.[44]

Lennon provided his own version of the festival's progress, or
lack of, to date, explaining that the idea had originated in late
1969 with Brower and Yorke and giving the reasons why he and
Yoko wanted a free event. He called their report on Klein "hearsay
crap." The multimillionaire who lived in a mansion and travelled
by limousine also criticized the "bread hangup scene" (desire to
make money) of the young Canadian organizers. He claimed that
he and Ono still wanted to attend the festival and mused about a
mass chanting of Hare Krishna to "change the balance of enemy
power."[45] The following month, having won the temporary right
to enter the United States, Lennon and Yoko travelled to California
and stayed with record producer Phil Spector. FBI Director J. Edgar
Hoover sent a message to the Los Angeles FBI office stating that,
despite the absence of any actual evidence, Lennon had "shown
a propensity to become involved in violent anti-war demonstrations." But the real reason for the California trip was to start primal
therapy with its creator, Arthur Janov. John and Yoko would spend
five months in therapy, which was based on the idea that childhood
trauma could be exorcised through screaming. This was another
attempt to kick their heroin and methadone addiction.[46]

In Toronto, meanwhile, Brower and his colleagues hoped to
salvage what was still being called the Toronto Peace Festival.
A Toronto investor, lawyer Bill Graham, advanced the producers $30,000. American advertising expert Bruce Ballister advised
Karma Productions on publicity and advertising as the festival
morphed from a free Lennon/Ono counterculture event to a
Canadian version of Woodstock guided by the profit motive. In
Denmark, Lennon had given Brower a piece of paper with the
words "John Lennon Peace Festival" and "free (1 dollar)." John
had forgotten that Woodstock had been planned with profits in

mind and that nearly two hundred thousand tickets had been sold. Karma Productions' Hugh Curry (a former CHUM DJ) later described Lennon's free ticket concept as "bull shit." Despite his professional advice and contributions to the evolving project, Ballister claimed that he was never compensated for his services.[47]

Like the Toronto Pop Festival and Rock 'n' Roll Revival, the planned event required a major investment. According to the OPP, the Mosport venture's chief financial backer was Colin William "Willie" Webster of Don Mills. In 2018, Brower explained that Willie Webster had a "trust fund" as a member of the wealthy Webster family of Montreal and Toronto[48] (R. Howard Webster had been sole proprietor of the *Globe and Mail* for a decade starting in 1955). In 1970, Willie Webster, together with American producer David Briggs, opened a recording studio, Thunder Sound, on Toronto's Davenport Road. Its first manager was Moses Znaimer. In 1971, Columbia Records released the LP *The Family*, which Quebec group Mashmakhan recorded at the studio. Thunder Road, the first studio in Canada to acquire a twenty-four-track mixer, also recorded early Bruce Cockburn albums and did work for television programs. Another investor associated with the festival organizers was Jerry Hebscher of Malton, just north of Toronto.

Year One in Canada

In Toronto in 1969, Lennon, possibly inspired by French revolutionists who wanted to restart the clock on world history, had spoken of 1970 as "Year One, A.P. (After Peace)." Many activists admired Lennon's humanitarian philosophy of peace and watched as he became more involved with specific issues in Britain, such as anti-Black racism, but they believed that political and social change derived not from positive thoughts and sound bites but action. Canada in 1970 would experience protests and other types of mobilizations by feminists, especially in the cause of abortion rights, and environmentalists. The Abortion Caravan protestors disrupted Parliament in May 1970, complaining that Canada's 1969 abortion law, which placed power in the hands of male-dominated hospital committees and not women, was discriminatory. Later that month, young feminists confronted Trudeau in Vancouver as he returned from his Pacific tour. He was brusque and argumentative but promised to look into their complaints. Feminists also began to complain about beauty contests, especially on university campuses. Earth Day was first celebrated in April 1970, and provincial governments were beginning to regulate pollution. Chafing under anti-inflation wage controls, a new generation of labour activists was engaging in more militant action. Mobilized against the 1969 white paper, younger Indigenous leaders, many survivors of residential schools, were building their organizations to address treaty and Aboriginal rights and the often-dire socio-economic conditions in their communities.[49] And Black Canadians, inspired by the civil rights movement and Black Power ideology south of the border, were also more active. There were small victories, such as when Halifax activists launched a successful campaign against the hiring of an American as city manager who they insisted was anti-union and prejudiced toward minorities. And there were setbacks, such as in March when an all-white jury in Montreal convicted eight of the "Trinidad Ten," West Indian students arrested after the Sir George Williams University incident.[50]

Lennon's hope that the world would give up war in 1970 proved to be unrealistic in a year when the conflict in Southeast Asia not only continued but expanded geographically. Based on its activities and statements, Canada's anti-war movement felt it required more than John and Yoko's slogan and billboards. Participants in the "Enough Village," an anti-war protest camp on Parliament Hill, were frustrated that Trudeau, who had issued a pro-peace message at Christmas, would discuss peace only with visiting celebrities.[51] One was Claire Culhane, a former Communist and a labour activist whose RCMP file extended back to 1940, who had helped establish a hospital in South Vietnam in 1967. In early April, an orderly anti-war march converged on Parliament Hill in Ottawa as part of a pan-Canadian peace weekend. The organizers demanded complete removal of American forces from Vietnam, changes to immigration regulations to encourage more war resisters to enter Canada and an end to military equipment exports to the United States. Maoists, who supported an escalation of the "people's war," interrupted the proceedings, leading to shoving matches and fist fights. The NDP leader, sixty-five-year-old Tommy Douglas, a former boxer, landed a few punches on a Maoist interloper who was pushing a young woman. Maoists, like Trotskyists, were direct-action radicals within the New Left who denounced social democrats and other leftists as "social fascists." They admired both China and Mao Zedong and were critical of Soviet Communism. A Montreal Maoist accused the McGill Moratorium Committee of being a counterrevolutionary agent of "English Canadian colonialism." RCMP who guarded Parliament Hill did little to stop the fracas.[52] Later in the month, a second anti-war demonstration on Parliament Hill proceeded without incident. This time, Ottawa police clashed with Maoists near the U.S. Embassy, making sixteen arrests, all people in their twenties. Maoists disrupted a smaller march in Vancouver and were also a presence in Winnipeg when anti-war protestors were addressed by economist Mel Watkins, one of the authors of the Waffle manifesto. At an Edmonton demonstration, Indigenous activist Art Manuel compared the treatment of Canada's Indigenous peoples to the treatment of the Vietnamese by the American military.[53]

This widening of military operations in Southeast Asia produced a student strike in the United States, which led to the killing of four Kent State University students and the wounding of nine by the National Guard on May 4, 1970. This led to another massive round of protests; hundreds of college campuses closed, and the National Guard was called out. On May 6, several youths were arrested at a series of small spontaneous demonstrations near the U.S. Consulate in Toronto against the Kent State killings. A few days later, an authorized march organized by Toronto's Vietnam Mobilization Committee and other leftist organizations attracted five thousand. There was fighting with pro-war protestors (the Edmund Burke Society) outside the U.S. Consulate, rocks and bottles were hurled and the police were called "pigs" and "fascists." Police on horseback and foot broke up the demonstration, arresting nearly one hundred, despite the fact that the marchers, for the most part, were orderly and kept to the sidewalk. Although this was described as the city's most violent demonstration since the 1930s, few were injured. Among the arrested for obstructing police were lawyer and activist Clayton Ruby and "superhippie" and activist David DePoe. In Ottawa, demonstrators burned effigies of Nixon and Trudeau, and police in Montreal arrested twenty people outside the U.S. Consulate. The reaction to the Kent State killings produced a new leftist group in Toronto, one that would become a critic of pop festivals promoted by hip capitalists. At a press conference at Rochdale College, representatives of the May 4th Movement described the Toronto police as an oppressive force. Mayor Dennison suggested that the protest at the consulate had been orchestrated by Americans.[54]

In Quebec, students and other young people were increasingly drawn to nationalist issues. In April, leftists were disappointed when three-quarters of voters supported "bourgeois" parties in the provincial election, notably the victorious Liberals. But almost one vote in four had been captured by the PQ, the social democratic separatist party. Many youth regarded jailed FLQ activists as heroes. Soon after the election, a Montreal post office was bombed, presumably by the FLQ. This was followed in June by the bombing of the Montreal Board of Trade and four private residences in Westmount, the Montreal area municipality associated with Anglo-Canadian corporate privilege. On Saint-Jean-Baptiste Day, the FLQ struck at the nation's capital with a bomb at the headquarters of the Department of National Defence, which killed a female civilian employee and injured three others. Montreal's Anti-Terrorism Squad made arrests and seized explosives and detonators, firearms, ammunition, cash from armed robberies and revolutionary literature, including copies of an urban guerrilla warfare pamphlet supposedly translated into French by Jacques Larue-Langlois. Quebec's justice minister claimed that terrorist activity in the province was confined to fifteen or twenty young militants, who could not be rehabilitated through the justice system. Ominously — in terms of the October Crisis of 1970 — two of the arrested supposedly had been plotting to kidnap an Israeli diplomat. By 1970, one question within police, government and media circles was whether urban guerrillas in Quebec would develop ties with like-minded radicals in English Canada, who would then launch bank robbery and bombing campaigns similar to those of the Weather Underground Organization (also known as the Weathermen), a radical offshoot of the New Left, in the United States.[55]

Despite the city's anti-demonstration bylaw, Montreal activists continued to publicize nationalist causes such as the defence of the French language and separatism. On May 12, police in riot gear used steel barricades to disperse an unauthorized march to the Montreal Stock Exchange to protest the detention of FLQ "political prisoners." The administration of the l'Université Laval in Quebec City attempted to tamp down leftist and nationalist dissent on campus by banning unauthorized meetings, posters and literature and the occupation of buildings. After the Kent State incident, students in Quebec City marched on the U.S. Consulate, denouncing American imperialism and Quebec's legal assault on the FLQ. On Dominion Day, Montreal police dispersed 200 separatist youth planning a march against Confederation and Quebec's high unemployment rate. Organized by the FLP, the aborted demonstration included literature and signs revolutionary in tone.[56]

Rescuing the Festival

While Canadian politicians, police, university officials and journalists in 1970 reacted to anti-war, student and separatist protests, the music business followed its own agenda Much romanticism followed in the wake of Woodstock. In his book *Woodstock Nation*, in which he cited Marshall McLuhan, Abbie Hoffman described the festival as "a trip to our future," a site of "liberated land" that facilitated a creative "gathering of the tribes."[57] Because of the hype, promoters, musicians, fans and journalists tried hard to recreate the now legendary festival. Commercial motives were paramount, with film producers and record companies hoping to cash in on the new trend; performers in the post-Woodstock era also demanded increased fees. The informal outdoor setting, where many of the audience members slept in tents or in the open, shared food and drugs and were relatively free from police surveillance, added to a festival's "sense of community."[58] Despite rock's profit motive, the genre's lyrics and sounds and the various sites of performance — radio, recordings, television shows, clubs and festivals — assumed a communal and political significance in the late 1960s.[59] Festivals also were influenced by the new "acid or psychedelic" rock emanating out of San Francisco in 1966 and 1967 and by the hippie movement's sense of public theatre. In the aftermath of Woodstock, journalists portrayed the mass rock concert as another manifestation of the youth-focused counterculture, similar to underground newspapers, transiency and communal living.[60]

At festivals in Canada, Canadian bands sometimes shared billings with higher-profile American and British acts. Except for rare groups such as Winnipeg's the Guess Who, who enjoyed airplay and tours in the United States, most Canadian acts were confined to local or regional circuits. Some served as warm-up acts for better-known American and British bands. In March 1970, Whiskey Howl took part in the Toronto Rock Festival, but most fans were there to see and hear the Zombies, the Amboy Dukes, the Small Faces and Canned Heat.[61] Yet Canadian rock was on the rise, and one of its most passionate advocates was Ritchie Yorke. In April 1970, he appeared at CRTC hearings in support of Canadian content regulations for AM radio, arguing that Canadian record companies required an incentive for taking risks with Canadian artists. Lighthouse drummer Skip Prokop also supported the CRTC's proposal, explaining that it would help singers and bands known regionally develop a national profile, promote recording studios and create a critical mass for advancing Canada's cultural sector.[62]

Johnny Brower was not the only Toronto promoter planning something big for 1970. In late April, as the Mosport peace festival seemed to reach a dead end, former partner Kenny Walker, together with the Eatons, made a major announcement. They had organized a four-city tour by major American and Canadian rock and folk acts, starting in Montreal and ending in Calgary. Striking a deep chord with Canadian history and identity, the musicians and their gear would travel by train. Festival Express was an attempt by agents, performers and promoters to exploit fan interest in large, multi-band rock shows. In a way, it was related to the buzz created by Lennon's anticipated Canadian festival and possibly the continued struggles to get that event off the ground. Despite a logo that featured a dove (a symbol of peace) and the counterculture aura of the hip performers engaged, Festival Express was not "political." This, it turned out, would prompt a response from the New Left.

The partners hoped to sell two hundred thousand tickets. The imaginative cross-country venture, with advance fees of $500,000, required deep pockets, and the promoters were joined by the Canadian communications/publishing company Maclean-Hunter, publisher of *Maclean's*. Executive Vice-President J. Lin Craig, who was neither young nor hip, explained that his company was a sponsor of the tour. A dedicated CNR train included two lounge cars for jamming musicians, one dedicated to blues and rock and the other to country and folk, and a dining car. Walker claimed to have used family connections to hire the train (CNR was a Crown corporation until it was privatized in the 1990s). Local acts were engaged for each city, and Walker explained that stadia had been booked as they were safer and more secure. The promoters, no doubt inspired by the profitable movies *Monterey Pop* and *Woodstock*, hired film producer Willem Poolman, director Frank Cvitanovich and cinematographer Peter Biziou to document the trip and music. Much of the footage, valuable social history, later disappeared. Fortunately, some of it was saved in the National Archives of Canada, and in 2004, the ninety-minute documentary *Festival Express* was released.[63]

In the end, the train rolled not from Montreal to Vancouver (the original route of the Canadian Pacific Railway) but from Toronto to Calgary. Montreal authorities were concerned about public unrest connected with left-wing Quebec separatism and especially worried about the planned date for the concert at Expo's Autostade, June 24. Saint-Jean-Baptiste Day in 1968 and 1969 had been associated with politically motivated violence. Even worse, by June 1970, Montreal was enduring a new FLQ bombing campaign. Fans with tickets for Montreal were transported in buses to Toronto.[64] The official excuse for the cancellation of the Vancouver concert was the need to protect stadium Astroturf, but opposition from hippie-fearing local officials such as Mayor Campbell cannot be discounted. Conservative opinion in Vancouver was bolstered by ongoing anxieties about drugs and organized crime. In July, more than two dozen young people were arrested during an unauthorized protest march that followed conflict with police in the English Bay area. The Vancouver Liberation Front demanded the mayor's resignation, legal aid, the abolition of bail, free use of beaches and hostels with meals and medical care. Ominously, the Vancouver city council had recently voted to equip the local police with sixty-six-centimetre long riot sticks.[65] Campbell urged the Canadian government to close the country's borders to American hippies and draft dodgers and opposed a proposal to use a local armoury as a temporary shelter for young transients, fearing it would help create a "hippie road" to Vancouver.[66]

Festival Express, later described as "the greatest and longest non-stop party in the history of rock and roll," was launched in Toronto on June 27.[67] At Exhibition Stadium, fans were entertained by Mountain, Traffic, Janis Joplin and the Full Tilt Boogie Band, blues guitarist Buddy Guy, the Band, the Grateful Dead, Ten Years After, Phil Ochs and Ian and Sylvia and their band Great Speckled Bird. Four hundred people were treated on site for adverse reactions to drugs by Queen Street Mental Health Centre. Typically, this consisted of a dose of Valium and rest on a cot. The May 4th Movement demanded that part of the box office be redistributed to various social causes and encouraged youth to force their way into the event. For some reason, they accused promoters, not performers, of "rip-offs."[68] The activists appeared to be based in Rochdale College, and one, David Frank, was editor of the University of Toronto's student paper *The Varsity*. The names of Frank and other activists were on a list of so-called revolutionaries in "Academe and Subversion," a RCMP Security Service report to the federal cabinet later in the year. Protestors and gate crashers did turn up in Toronto, but there were relatively few arrests given that ten police officers were injured and more than ten thousand supposedly attended. Jerry Garcia and the Grateful Dead and other performers agreed with the protest in part and, at the suggestion of a Metropolitan Toronto Police inspector, performed a free concert in Toronto's Coronation Park, which several thousand people enjoyed.[69]

The Winnipeg concert at Red River Stadium on July 1 was less successful, selling only forty-six hundred tickets. Instead of a "crash-in," it appeared that the Manitoba stop was affected by a boycott, either political or economic. Those who did have the foresight to attend missed a memorial experience, with performances by many of the acts noted above, as well as Southern rockers Delaney and Bonnie and Friends, Robert Charlebois and James and the Good Brothers. Joplin, who earlier had visited local "freaks" hanging out in a city park, was in good form, and so was the Band.[70] Sylvia Tyson remembered musicians on the train partying with alcohol, marijuana and LSD but believed that Joplin, in contrast to her hard-living image, was more in control of the situation than it appeared.[71]

Calgary's performances, scheduled for July 5 and 6 at McMahon Stadium, were also shrouded in controversy, complicated by a quarrel between a conservative police chief and Mayor Rod Sykes. The local May 4th Movement also demanded free admission for "the people." Now a major metropolis by Canadian standards, Calgary in the late 1960s was viewed as culturally deprived. According to Sykes's biographer, the event was still remembered with excitement four decades later. The medical officer of health, warning that "music love-in festivals are generally only attended by hippies and the oddballs of society," advised against permitting the concerts. Mayor Sykes, who sympathized with youth, saw no legitimate reason to deny the permit. The mayor's office viewed the event as a chance to demonstrate that the Alberta city could be progressive. The police department, fearing civil unrest, spoke of enlisting the militia or the armed forces in case of an emergency and invited the RCMP to provide a riot squad. More than twenty thousand were drawn to the stadium to hear Joplin, New Riders of the Purple Sage, Tom Rush, Eric Anderson, Ten Years After, Traffic and other internationally known performers, as well as Ian and Sylvia, Mashmakhan and James and the Good Brothers. As in Toronto, a free alternative concert was organized, in this case at Prince's Island.[72] Festival Express assumed legendary status among musicians, but, according to organizers, poor ticket sales, exacerbated by anti-capitalist activists, made it a business failure, with a possible loss of $500,000.[73]

The Strawberry Fields Festival

In late July and early August, Quebec was the focus of its own rock festival controversy, the Festival Pop de Manseau, located in a small rural area near Quebec City. Billed as a second Woodstock, this event promised not only Québécois rock groups and chansonniers but also major acts, such as Hendrix.[74] Promoters promised three days of "peace and love."[75] Area residents were so apprehensive that the local bank closed and removed all of its cash deposits.[76] The negative publicity began when the authorities arrested three of the organizers for fraud.[77]

The festival was poorly organized and the facilities makeshift. Between eight and ten thousand people attended. Many youths criticized the uncertainty over the lineup and the high ticket prices, and many entered without paying for tickets. The organizers at Manseau supposedly had agreed with the SQ to cut the power to the public address system if any performers started "inciting the crowd politically." With three hundred officers stationed nearby, the SQ appeared to be more concerned about threatened disruptions by anti-capitalist protestors such as the Comité culturel du Québec than by drugs.[78] After private security walked off the job, the organizers opened the gates. A number of acts failed to show because their deposits had not been paid or they were offered lower fees. Five hundred people were treated for drug-related medical issues.[79] The Quebec government ended up blocking a festival planned for Sainte-Croix de Lotbinière later that summer, citing illegal drug use, public nudity and the Manseau fiasco. The second festival, which was supposed to feature major acts such as Joe Cocker and Led Zeppelin, sold nearly three thousand advance tickets. The organizers, who claimed to have lost money after their permit was cancelled, spoke out on behalf of "the youth of the province."[80] For Ritchie Yorke writing in Billboard, the Manseau and Sainte-Croix controversies, and the attitude of the New Brunswick government, were proof that the Canadian pop festival scene was "bleak."[81]

Rebuffed at Mosport in March, in May the Toronto promoters purchased several hundred acres of rural land in Cardwell Township north of Toronto and obtained permission from local officials to stage an event that, according to Ritchie Yorke in Billboard, could attract two hundred thousand.[82] Writing in Maclean's, a youthful columnist concluded that the "sharp, hip young entrepreneurs" were actually allies of the Establishment.[83] The venture certainly

Strawberry Fields Festival stage, August 1970, at Mosport Park in Bowmanville, Ontario, now called the Canadian Tire Motorsport Park

required Establishment-level funding and legal advice. In the final arrangements, the provincial government required bonds totalling $2.5 million for the cost of medical, sanitation and water services. There was also the cost of a field hospital and nearly $1 million for police services outside the venue site. Chief Superintendent Gartner, who, bizarrely, had become a leading Canadian expert on pop festivals, estimated that the promoters would gross $15 million and net $5 million.[84] By early June, Karma Productions, which owed money to investors, faced another obstacle when Cardwell Township officials, supposedly in reaction to OPP scare tactics, withdrew from the agreement. Brower claimed that someone (presumably police) had placed a tap on his home phone. The Cardwell issue was litigated, but without success. Clearly frustrated, the young Toronto promoter described John and Yoko as "phoney" and claimed to have been misled by their "press side" or public image as opposed to their "power side." At this point, he pronounced the peace festival dead. Brower, however, kept at it, negotiating with the Chippewa First Nation on Georgina Island on Lake Simcoe in case their reserve could host a festival.[85]

That summer, the squares also appeared to be winning in Manitoba, despite the desire of young people for John Lennon and Yoko Ono to visit their province. As late as June 3, 1970, a tourism-slanted newspaper article by Evelyn Bowen promoting Manitoba's celebrations to a national audience explained that John and Yoko, along with President Nixon and "the moon astronauts," had been invited as special dignitaries.[86] The pop stars never reached the "Keystone province," but Canada's political celebrity did. On Dominion Day, Trudeau spoke at an official event in Winnipeg, accompanied by several cabinet ministers. The prime minister dismissed a small number of protestors on the fringe of the event as "gripers," to the applause of the crowd. Their griping was about poverty, Canada's complicity in Vietnam and the Liberal government's opposition to Quebec's self-determination.[87] The backlash in Manitoba indicates that for many middle-aged and older citizens, John Lennon was not a positive symbol of peace, individualism, healthy pleasure-seeking and self-fulfillment but of a permissive society that was catering to the young and possibly planting the seeds of its own destruction. For the young, the outcome was a reminder of the hang-ups of adult society, the same attitude that opposed pop festivals.

A July profile in *Maclean's* of the struggle to make Brower's festival a reality included a critical view of the organizers and a somewhat judgmental take on the new rock scene, evidenced by a recent concert at Toronto's Varsity Arena: "The music is heavier, the drugs harder and the colour faded." Bob Bossin (himself an accomplished folk musician) wrote that the peace aspect for the planned event was now "a liability," but the Toronto organizers continued to promise things such as a peace magazine, support for a healthy food franchise and free food at the event itself. Free food, according to Brower, had the potential to "cool out revolutionary types." Bossin described Brower musing about making a B movie during the festival, possibly with a motorcycle gang, and explaining that he was not "anti establishment."[88]

The organizers next looked eastward to New Brunswick. Louis J. Robichaud, elected Liberal premier of New Brunswick

in 1960, is remembered as the architect of a modernizing equal
opportunity program and builder of a more equitable society. He
stood up to the powerful industrialist K.C. Irving, who introduced official bilingualism and faced a bitter backlash for his
taxation, centralization and linguistic polices that was fuelled in
part by anti-Acadian bigotry.[89] One of Robichaud's last decisions
prior to being defeated by Richard Hatfield's PCs in the fall of
1970 was banning Brower's newest attempt to save his festival.
In July, the organizers had settled on land at Barrachois, on the
Northumberland Strait near Shediac. Permission was granted to
Par Productions, Webster's company, and the advertised dates
were August 6th through the 9th. The name of the reborn festival, Strawberry Fields, appeared to be an attempt to connect, for
commercial purposes, with the Beatles brand and the idealism
of Lennon's peace offensive. But it was inspired not by Lennon's
song, according to Brower, but a local strawberry farm. This coin-
cidence, real or concocted, did not hurt marketing of the event,
which was expected to attract hundreds of thousands.[90]

Promotion of the festival south of the border played on American
stereotypes of Canada as a rural, unpolluted and scenic wilderness.
The older view of the healing and redemptive powers of unspoiled
nature fit easily into counterculture imagery. The counterculture
had produced a romanticized back-to-the-land movement that
encouraged idealistic youth to abandon movement politics such as
anti-war or student activism and commune with nature.[91] This anti-
modernist view of Canada as a nation with an unspoiled natural
environment also appealed to Canadian nationalism.[92] Advertising
also hinged on the counterculture notion of Canada as "unoccupied
territory" — in the words of John Lennon, "American without being
American." The event was organized in the wake of the American
invasion of Cambodia and the new wave of anti-war protests. Advertising for the Strawberry Fields Festival invited young Americans to
visit "Free North America: Canada."[93] This implied a land free of
Nixon, the military-industrial complex and the draft.

On July 22, the New Brunswick government reneged on its decision to allow the festival to go ahead. Hundreds of youth took part in two protest meetings at nearby Moncton. Teenagers interviewed by the press in Fredericton were also disappointed. Robichaud explained that his government had examined the issue in great detail and had ruled that the promoters could not "meet the standards of security, hygiene, water and services which the province would require for an assembly of the site forecast."[94] At least one anonymous letter writer, who opposed the decision, suggested that Robichaud, who was facing an election, wanted to be seen as standing up to "the long-hair, drug-crazy, Communist-inspired, sexual pervert hippie."[95] A number of young Americans who had bought advance tickets found out about the cancellation only after they arrived in the province.[96] As recently as July 26, an ad in the *New York Times* had promoted the Strawberry Fields event as "three days of love, sun and sound in Moncton, New Brunswick, Canada."[97]

The reaction to rock festivals was also related to current anxieties in the media and political spheres over the possible decriminalization of marijuana and fears that the drug was a gateway to LSD and heroin. The message of the Council on Drug Abuse, founded by the pharmaceutical industry and funded by business donors, was that illegal drugs were a menace for youth that could be ended only by abstinence. This was a decidedly unhip approach by the standards of the day. The interim report of the Le Dain Commission, released in June 1970, advocated making simple possession of cannabis punishable by a fine only, placing marijuana under the *Food and Drug Act* and not the *Narcotic Control Act* and destroying criminal records of persons convicted for simple possession after two years of good behaviour.[98] A running theme in the report, some of which was leaked to the media before official publication, was that police responses were "reactionary, uniformed and counterproductive." The use of undercover officers and "buy-and-bust" techniques was a particular sore spot.[99] Few had worried about these issues in earlier decades when the public perception of the typical drug user was a lower-class junkie, but drugs were now a middle-class issue capturing national media attention. The commissioners recognized that all drugs were potentially harmful and recommended a program of non-judgmental public education. But they also argued that using criminal law against those smoking hashish and cannabis was disproportionate to the actual social harm. The report also broke new ground by disputing the traditional view that drug use was connected to abnormal personalities.[100]

Reactions to the interim report were predictably mixed, and there was much speculation before its release that the federal cabinet was divided on its recommendations. Ontario's Addiction Research Foundation (ARF) appreciated the scientific tone of the document and supported most of its recommendations. It agreed that full legalization, given the lack of research on the actual effects of cannabis consumption, was premature. There was criticism of the proposal to make possession of heroin akin to possessing marijuana, punishable by fine. Not all provincial governments were opposed to aspects of decriminalization, but there was unease over full legalization of marijuana.[101] As they continued to gather more feedback from interest groups and the public and the findings of research studies, the Le Dain commissioners prepared for a further round of public hearings to begin in the fall. The Trudeau government explained that it would enact no changes to narcotics control legislation until after the commission's final report. Speaking to students in Whitehorse, the prime minister explained that he viewed smoking marijuana as unhealthy escapism but no worse than drinking alcohol.[102]

Following the setback in New Brunswick, the promoters of Strawberry Fields announced that they were examining another potential site close to the Canada–U.S. border, and their legal counsel explained that they had spent money on advertising and on deposits for talent.[103] New York attorney Jerrold Kushnick, Brower's booking agent, complained that the Robichaud government had not divulged any criteria in advance. Planning included securing insurance coverage and the provision of medical care, free food to be distributed by Yorkville's Penny Farthing coffee house, security and sanitation. The decision to block the event was made by the provincial cabinet following consultations with health and justice officials. At a meeting with representatives of the promoters, officials had asked for a guarantee that there would be no "riots or drug abuse." Kushnick pointed out the irony of New Brunswick spending considerable resources to attract American tourists during the summer months while at the same time seeking to prevent their arrival, possibly out of fear over drugs and hippies: "These people may be the hippies or subculture of the youth of today, but they are the Establishment of tomorrow."[104]

Transient youth was not a totally new social issue as communities across Canada were already providing, or planning to provide, drug information centres and summer youth hostels for growing numbers of hitchhikers, whose idealistic counterculture adventures were subsidized by the federal government. According to historian Linda Mahood, restless travellers were also influenced by pop music.[105] One Ontario journalist predicted that a hundred thousand youth —summer residents, Americans and "freaks" — would head to or settle in Toronto in the summer of 1970.[106] With panic about invading hordes of youth on the rise, governments across North America responded with injunctions and strict enforcement of health and sanitation regulations to discourage large-scale rock festivals.[107] Several days after Robichaud's government blocked the Barrachois event, the Nova Scotia government declined a licence application for a large-scale festival at the small coastal community of Port Howe. This was another attempt by Karma Productions to salvage its investment; residents and local officials objected to the scale of the proposed event. The local member of parliament declared that Manseau had shown that rock festivals were "bad news" and that the people of Cumberland County needed to be protected from drugs.[108]

With sixteen hundred advanced tickets sold and thousands of youthful rock music fans potentially heading north from the United States, the promoters of Strawberry Fields renewed their attempt to secure their initial venue, Mosport, which featured camping grounds. The reconstituted event was billed as motorcycle races accompanied by live music. Les Productions Sportives Ville-Marie Inc., a new entity based in Quebec, managed to rent the Mosport facilities for a race event. Its executive officers were Webster, Jerry Hebscher and Brower's wife, Michelle. In turn, that company engaged Par Productions of Toronto to hire rock bands for entertainment. Brower was the manager for the music side of the event.[109] The Montreal production company had not told the manager of the Mosport track all the details in advance. The Canadian Motorcycle Association, which initially supported the event, changed its mind as negative publicity arose but feared legal action if it withdrew its support. By early August, local residents, who had pressured the township officials in March to block the festival, once again became concerned. This time, the Ontario government intervened by attempting to block the event through the courts.[110]

On August 6, on the eve of the Strawberry Fields Cup motorcycle races, several thousand fans were camped at Mosport, most of them reportedly Americans and many veterans of festivals such as Woodstock. There were fears that the event would be cancelled at the last minute, as had recently happened at Powder Ridge, Connecticut. Manseau was also on their minds.[111] The Mosport festival had been heavily promoted on radio stations and in newspapers in the American northeast not as motorcycle races but as "a giant love-in," an obvious tactic to capitalize on the Woodstock myth.[112] Top international acts had been advertised, but the final lineup for Mosport was uncertain. One reason was performers, like fans, had difficulties crossing borders. New York folk singer and Woodstock veteran Melanie was strip-searched for drugs at the Toronto airport en route to Mosport. According to Brower, the British supergroup

Admiring a chopper at the Strawberry Fields Festival, 1970

Led Zeppelin had accepted a large deposit on its fee, but when the venue changed, it could not or would not agree to perform.[113]

Ontario's PC government instructed the attorney general to secure a court injunction to prohibit Strawberry Fields on public health and safety grounds. On August 6, the day before the musical acts were scheduled to begin, Justice D.A. Keith of the Ontario Supreme Court refused to grant the injunction, declaring that "it had not been proved that mischief would occur at the park."[114] He also commented that money had gone into the event and that the plans of large numbers of people would be disrupted if it were cancelled. Brower and his colleagues, who held a press conference to explain their hope that all the advertised groups would appear, had won a last-minute reprieve. Assistant OPP Commissioner E.W. Miller commented that large rock festivals "just don't bring any good." He continued: "Now that the injunction has been refused, we'll police it like any other event. I just hope the hell that we can police it." The OPP set up a "command centre" three kilometres from the Mosport track.[115] An OPP official reported that

(Above) Van advertising Harbinger, *an underground newspaper*

(Left) Free food at the festival

although many of the young people arriving at the festival were "high on drugs," the police would not interfere if they remained within the grounds. As the attorney general of Saskatchewan had explained at the federal-provincial drug conference earlier that summer, consuming drugs at rock concerts was similar to drinking beer at football games. Both acts were technically illegal, but police were forced to use discretion to maintain general order and goodwill. Nevertheless, the scale of drug use at large pop festivals, according to the attorney general of Ontario, added to the cost of staging these events.[116]

The lineup at Strawberry Fields included a number of acts that had appeared at Woodstock, and the promoters hoped to benefit from the publicity and optimism of that festival. Delaney and Bonnie and Friends, who included keyboardist Leon Russell, were highly regarded by other musicians such as Eric Clapton and George Harrison.[117] A highlight for many was the appearance of the energetic San Francisco-based soul act Sly and the Family Stone, who closed the festival.[118] Canadian balladeer Leonard Cohen, who had been featured in some advertising, did not show up. American/British groups or solo performers included Procol Harum, Mountain, Jose Feliciano, Alice Cooper, the Youngbloods, Ten Years After, and Grand Funk Railroad, some of whom had performed at past Brower-managed events. Hog Heaven consisted of former members of Tommy James and The Shondells. Typical of the macho world of rock in 1970, the stage was heavily laden with testosterone; aside from Bonnie Bramlett, female members of the Family Stone and Melanie, women were absent. The Canadian groups or solo performers were Luke and the Apostles, Crowbar with King Biscuit Boy, Lighthouse, Fat Chance, Freedom Express and James Leroy.[119] The psychedelic band Leigh Ashford from Toronto opened the festival at 4:30 p.m. on August 7. Toronto journalist James Bawden reported that the "filler acts" were amateurish — an uncharitable assertion if one listens to the records made by a number of these groups.[120]

Most media accounts of rock festivals stressed youthful hedonism and ritualized behaviour, with the music being of secondary importance.[121] People at Mosport sheltered in tents, plastic lean-tos, VW campers or open fields. Press accounts of the first day described young people smoking pot, swimming in the nude, listening to local bands and watching motorcycle races. The races were soon called off for safety and insurance liability reasons.[122] Drug and alcohol use aside, the crowd generally was well behaved. Explicit manifestations of New Left politics were minimal, with most people focusing on having a good time, although Toronto's underground journal Harbinger had a presence. Many vehicles with American licence plates were new, and many of the camp-

Festival goers

Listening to a band at the festival

ers, despite hippie garb, seemed too prosperous to accept free food, suggesting a middle-class audience. Press accounts noted the popularity of army surplus jackets with American flags sewn on the back.[123] A number of accounts stressed a nationalist theme, arguing that American youth were impressed by the forbearance and friendliness of the Canadian police compared to their American counterparts.[124] Despite Canada's welcoming image, immigration officials, possibly under instructions from Ottawa, had turned back thousands of young Americans who had tried to enter the country at border crossings such as Niagara Falls. At this time, the Nixon administration had also stepped up its anti-drug border security, particularly on routes that led to Quebec.[125]

The ARF, provincial emergency medical services and three youth agencies provided clinical, nursing and counselling services. At least three thousand people sought on-site treatment, with one hundred fifty requiring a trip to local hospitals. Most sought help for minor injuries and sunburn; serious drug overdoses were limited in number. Marijuana reportedly sold for $20 an ounce (accounting for inflation, this was less expensive than today's more potent varieties) and hits of acid for $1.50–2.00. Promoters viewed engaging ARF as proof of due diligence, but there were tensions over planning and provision of services at a profit-making event.[126]

According to New York security expert Arthur Kassel, the four hundred private security guards working for the festival would share information with police on drug dealing. Relations with the police were possibly strained by the discovery of telephone taps in the festival office. Plainclothes OPP officers took photographs of drug dealing and made notes but made no arrests on site. The RCMP also had twenty undercover officers inside the grounds.

Going natural at the festival

Despite all the media hype about LSD and cannabis, alcohol was the drug of choice. In the end, only twelve people, ten of them Americans, were arrested — outside the fence — for bootlegging and drug trafficking. The entire operation, which cost the OPP $100,000, involved three-hundred-fifty officers, two spotter airplanes and a helicopter.[127]

Many in the audience were still in high school. Sean Gadon was a Toronto teen who heard of the concert on FM radio the day before it began. He hitchhiked to Mosport with friends and decades later still had positive memories of the three-day event, insisting that there had been a positive vibe of peace and love.[128] As photos attest, children were present. Bronny Davis attended with her husband, their young son and three friends. In 2014, she recalled: "We camped up near the corn field but staked out an area closer to the stage to go hear the bands. We were right next to a motorcycle gang who looked scary but were actually really nice." Sonny Marciano travelled from Rhode Island with twenty-five other people in a U-Haul truck. He remembers people getting rid of their drugs as they approached the Canadian border. Chris Messum, who hitchhiked from Toronto with her boyfriend to check out the bands, "got stuck doling out water all night." Bruce Wedlock, a veteran of the Atlantic City Pop festival, drove from Pennsylvania in a "psychedelic VW bus." Jean Oliver, attending with her boyfriend, had a psychoactive experience after ingesting a "Purple Haze" pill. Her strongest memory of Strawberry Fields was "seeing people of all ages, color and arriving from all corners of the U.S.A. and Canada. And getting along and helping people." Another attendee recalled that the lineup consisted of bands "that rocked the earth" in 1970.[129]

New York filmmaker Jeff Lieberman and his future wife flew into Toronto to attend the festival. Once on site, he kept hearing an announcement asking Jeff Lieberman to report to the stage area. Thinking it was for another person with the same name, he ignored it. Later, he found out that a colleague who was present at

Festival goers helping someone in distress

Strawberry Fields had wanted him to take over directing the film-ing of the festival. One of the lessons of Woodstock was that there was money to be made from pop festival movies and soundtracks. Later Lieberman and his colleague visited promoter Willie Webster in Toronto to view footage and discuss the prospects of a docu-mentary. The problem was that the filming and audio recording were not synchronized and were carried out by amateurs, whereas Woodstock had been filmed by professionals. In addition, no one had thought to secure the music and film clearances from perform-ers. In 2020, Lieberman speculated that it was possible that raw 16-mm footage of the festival still existed someplace.[130]

Readers of *Billboard* were provided with a positive report by an enthusiastic Ritchie Yorke, who credited Brower with organizing "a winner" that attracted between seventy-five and one hundred thousand people; the *Toronto Daily Star* estimates were between fifty and fifty-five thousand.[131] There was no reliable estimate of revenues or profits. The sound system broadcast a report that the organizers had lost money, with an appeal for people to make donations to help cover costs.[132] Following the Mosport festival, the press reported some negative aspects, including rumours that two women had been sexually assaulted and telephone lines had been damaged. In addition, the promoters supposedly were now "hard to find." There were also allegations regarding the lack of professionalism of Powder Ridge 2, a group of medical volunteers assisting with drug overdose cases.[133] Some press accounts of garbage and abandoned tents and equipment clashed with the idealistic "pro-nature" promotion of the festival, but others pointed out that bigger messes were left behind after automobile races. Gartner, the OPP's "rock festival specialist," exacted his revenge in the media by suggesting that the organizers could be charged with perjury for misrepresenting the truth in affidavits and by threatening to ask the provincial government to force organizers to pay the full cost of policing the event. He also reported, darkly, that the police had "photographed key figures behind the event."[134]

Following a drug raid at Toronto's Rochdale College, "the largest countercultural space in Toronto,"[135] one hundred fifty American transients, supposedly veterans of Mosport, were evicted. By this point, the experimental student-run college was in trouble. Months earlier, its governing council had urged that the building — designed to house eight hundred fifty — be sold. Although most so-called "speed freaks" (the term at the time for people regularly injecting amphetamines) had been expelled, only half of the residents, who included transients and students at other institutions, were paying rent, the facilities were being damaged and drug sales and use remained a problem. Rochdale's financial situation improved by the summer of 1970, but the bad press continued as municipal authorities expressed concern about health and safety issues. At a time when Toronto and other cities were attracting large numbers of restless young hitchhikers who were putting pressure on hostels and shelters, this narrative contributed to public perceptions of "the dirty hippie" and echoed the Yorkville hepatitis scare of 1968.[136]

Aftermath

Aside from the murky question of profits versus losses, Johnny Brower, once again assisted by inherited wealth from the Canadian elite, had beaten the odds and given birth to "Canada's Woodstock." In addition to financial challenges, bad press, personality differences, interference from the OPP, the opposition of three provincial governments, the hostility of rural residents, the vacillation of municipal officials and bad vibes from John Lennon and much of the rock press, Strawberry Fields, featuring some of the major pop acts of the day, had arisen out of the ashes of the Toronto Peace Festival. Within the music industry and among young pop music fans, the anticipated peace festival, which was associated with John Lennon well into 1970, was a big deal. One rumour in August was that Lennon would make an appearance at Mosport. There is no record of him making a public comment on what he had hoped would be "John Lennon's Peace Festival." At the time and for months to come, there were few Lennon stories in the media, although Beatles news, such as McCartney's August clarification that the group had ended and controversies over the impact of their song "Helter Skelter" on indicted murderer Charles Manson, persisted. Although Strawberry Fields never captured the imagination of participants, the media and the public like Woodstock did, neither was it another Altamont. It was only a tenth of the size of the New York festival, and there was no legacy soundtrack or film to promote it to a larger audience. The reaction of local communities and politicians suggests that suspicion of and resistance to large outdoor pop festivals were part of an ongoing backlash against youth and counterculture, the same force that ultimately led to the Trudeau government's refusal to reform the *Narcotic Control Act* after the final report of the Le Dain Commission in 1972.

Brower's determination, war chest and luck aside, Strawberry Fields would not have taken place without John Lennon, who by March had turned into a major obstacle to a Canadian event that did not meet his demands. In two of his Canadian trips in 1969, he had been self-deprecating, open-minded and good-humoured, attempting to convince young people to jettison violent rhetoric and action and convince straights that a peaceful world was possible. The lure of a peace festival had helped bring John and Yoko back to Canada in December 1969 and added lustre to their War Is Over campaign. The year 1970 was a transition period for the celebrity couple as they drifted from a number of radical causes in Britain to therapy in the United States and endured the bitterness of the breakup of the Beatles. The evidence above suggests that Lennon's erratic involvement with the Canadian peace festival was driven more by celebrity ego than activism: an unrealistic dream of a second Woodstock associated with the personal views of John and Yoko. When he did not get his way, Canada, the nation he had flattered many times in 1969, was no longer important to his plans. Although free to do so starting in 1976 when he received permanent resident status in the United States, Lennon would never visit Canada again, despite living several hundred kilometres from Montreal for much of the last decade of his life.

Conclusion

Several weeks after the Strawberry Fields Festival, Canada was jolted into reality by the dramatic situation in Quebec. Within New Left circles, political rhetoric by 1970 was heating up. Fears of a breakdown in social order were not confined to social conservatives; in the spring, the prime minister remarked that Canada was not immune to the type of social unrest sweeping the United States. Events such as the disorder at Sir George Williams University, ongoing FLQ bombing and the Montreal police strike suggested that, in the words of a 1969 magazine story, "It can happen here."[1] Optimism for the future was also undermined by an economic recession, which meant fewer jobs for baby boomers, who had heightened expectations. Public perceptions continued to be influenced by developments in the United States, where large protests against the Vietnam War continued and the Weather Underground Organization began a bombing campaign to protest war and racism.

According to one historian, "Canada's 1960s lost momentum" with the 1970 October Crisis in Quebec.[2] Another interpretation is that it lost its innocence. The forces unleashed in that province in the 1960s continued to inspire nationalists and frighten federalists and middle-aged citizens. The tactics of the FLQ, which consisted of a small number of radicalized nationalists, did not represent the larger sovereignty movement, which was driven by union leaders, intellectuals, students, artists, musicians and young Québécois.[3] Yet there was some support for the FLQ's goals, and when its members resorted to violence, the heavy-handed response of the state created sympathy among left-wing nationalists and young people predisposed to be attracted to romantic nationalism. The election of a Liberal government under Robert Bourassa in April 1970 confirmed the belief of militant sovereigntists that the liberation of Quebec could be achieved not by the ballot box but by direct action.

In October, two Montreal cells of the FLQ kidnapped James Cross, a British diplomat, and Pierre Laporte, Quebec's minister of labour. By this time, a number of FLQ members were in prison for various offences, and the kidnappings were designed to pressure the authorities into releasing them. The youthful terrorists, to use the words of John Lennon during the Montreal bed-in, were putting "twelfth-century thinking" into practice, employing violence for political ends. A reality of the twentieth century was that national liberation often depended on military action. But even the more radical Lennon of the early 1970s would not have condoned political kidnapping and an ideology partly built on ethnic chauvinism. As the police hunted for the terrorists and their captives, the Trudeau government agreed to send military units to Montreal and Quebec City to aid the civil power and to invoke the *War Measures Act*, which allowed the authorities to ignore usual due process. Trudeau justified the suspension of civil liberties with the need to preserve order and protect democracy. Hundreds, many of them students and activists, were swept up in police raids; most were released without being charged. The response of the Quebec and Canadian governments created much sympathy for the FLQ, especially before the discovery of the body of Laporte, who had been murdered supposedly in an escape attempt. His body was discovered the day after the *War Measures Act* was proclaimed.

At the University of Ottawa, in the city visited by John and Yoko ten months earlier in the interest of peace, troops and an armoured personnel carrier supposedly protected students and faculty against violent separatists. Hugh Segal recalled how police entered the student union building and seized the records of the PQ club, ignoring the other student political organizations.[4] Several thousand troops with rifles, bayonets and machine guns were deployed to Montreal, visited by Lennon and Ono less than a year earlier. For several years, Canadians had watched news clips of U.S. Army and National Guard troops squaring off against demonstrators and rioters in cities and on campuses. Peaceful and complacent

Canada — or at least Montreal — like the United States and Northern Ireland, now required heavily armed troops to preserve order. Children were warned that if they scribbled "FLQ" on the school wall, they could go to jail.

The crisis continued for nearly three months. After police tracked down the hideout of his kidnappers in early December, Cross was freed and his abductors permitted to flee to Cuba; the suspected killers of Laporte were captured in a farmhouse later in the month. The military was withdrawn in early 1971, but federal emergency legislation was in place until late April 1971. For better or worse, the leader anointed by John and Yoko in 1960 as a model for the world had resorted to the iron fist not the velvet glove. Famously, when asked by CBC reporter Tim Ralfe in October 1970 how far he would go in using the military to enforce law and order, Trudeau had responded, "Well, just watch me." Trudeau's handling of the crisis in 1970 was approved by most of English and French Canada but in time was regarded by many as one of the most egregious violations of civil liberties in Canadian history. In addition, historians have suggested that the government's response was motivated more by politics than genuine security concerns.[5]

People arrested during the FLQ crisis could be detained for up to twenty-one days before appearing before a judge. Montreal bed-in visitor Jacques Larue-Langlois, lawyer Robert Lemieux, labour leader Michel Chartrand, Pierre Vallières and Charles Gagnon were indicted for seditious conspiracy. Larue-Langlois was also charged with assaulting a reporter. The indictment alleged that they had been conspiring since early 1968 to overthrow the Quebec and Canadian governments. Along with other young Québécois men and women, the "Montreal Five" were also charged with being members of an unlawful association.[6] Legal proceedings were often rowdy, partly because Vallières and his comrades regarded courtrooms as opportunities to expose the class struggle. The vocal FLQ supporters, who raised clenched fists Black Panther style and shouted revolutionary slogans, were now genuine celebrities, signing autographs and shaking hands with sympathizers. Larue-Langlois was later released after an appeal court quashed the charges but was re-arrested in 1971 and tried with Gagnon for seditious conspiracy. Prior to this, he spoke at Toronto and Ottawa meetings to raise funds for the legal defence of FLQ prisoners, where he denounced the Quebec and federal governments as "fascist" and the PQ as a right-wing party that welcomed American investment. At one point, he described the murder of Pierre Laporte as "not bad" from a tactical point of view as he represented "the enemy" of Quebec workers. In June 1971, Larue-Langlois was acquitted by a Montreal jury.[7]

On many levels, the October Crisis seemed to emphasize that for Canada, the 1960s — an era of optimism, experimentation, freedom and hedonism — had ended. Pop culture provided further evidence. In early October 1970, sixteen days after the death of Jimi Hendrix, Janis Joplin, who had toured Canada as part of Festival Express months earlier, died from a drug overdose.[8] At the time, these deaths were viewed as symbolic of the counterculture in decline. The other big story was the breakup of the Beatles, which assumed more certainty with the beginning of legal proceedings in late 1970 to dissolve their business entity. The group's legacy created unrealistic expectations of the solo careers of John Lennon and his bandmates, efforts that, despite some successes, "never equalled their collective work," according to Lennon biographer Jon Wiener.[9] This arguably overlooks the evolving reaction to Lennon's "Imagine," but most critics and fans would probably agree about the Beatles up to 1970 being the more dominant cultural force. In 2005, the CBC, based on a listener poll, declared "Imagine" the top song of the past century.[10]

Historians continue to debate the nature and impact of the 1960s counterculture. One argument is that it died, or at least fragmented, or that it was co-opted by the Establishment. Another is that it raised awareness of issues such as racism, patriarchy, homophobia and environmental degradation and that ideas, networks and organizations with roots in the 1960s influenced the next decade. American war resisters, for example, by virtue of their social class and education levels, continued to influence politics, social movements and arts and culture in Toronto through community organizations, higher education, theatre, the underground press and lesbian and gay liberation groups. In late 1970, the Royal Commission on the Status of Women issued its report, which called for increased access to abortion and daycare for working women.[11] Canada's commitment to multilateralism and disarmament and its growing interest in human rights were reflected in Trudeau's warning in late 1970 that continued British military support to the apartheid regime in South Africa was a serious threat to the Commonwealth. And in the early 1970s, building on the recent past, the country continued to move away from its historical "White Canada" immigration policy. Many newcomers from places such as the West Indies, India and Pakistan faced prejudice and discrimination, but their growing presence helped make multiculturalism a reality.[12]

By 1971, despite the assertion of one writer that John Lennon stood for "personal freedom, participatory democracy and cultural revolution,"[13] his views were confusing and contradictory. In controversial interviews, he freely admitted to having been addicted to heroin, criticized Beatlemania and classic Beatles songs (most of which he had co-written) and excoriated critics for not recognizing that he was a "genius." Lennon lashed out at people with long hair and peace signs who believed they had greater awareness and explained that he was fed up with "uptight maniacs" who purported to speak for youth. One phrase he used in an interview from this period, "the dream is over," captured the belief of many young people toward the unfulfilled promises of the 1960s. A key arbiter of cool seemed to be telling fans to grow up.

Despite his disavowal of peace-loving "maniacs," Lennon, under Ono's influence, began to write and record songs of a more political nature. One important contribution to his peacenik image was the song "Happy Christmas (War Is Over)," released in 1971. The single enjoyed greater popularity after Lennon was murdered and remains a staple on commercial radio stations at Christmas time. Before they left England, the couple made the film *Imagine* to help promote their album of the same name and document their life together. Their music and art continued the counterculture message of "rebellion and "tolerance."[14] In a sense, John and Yoko were still promoting their Canadian-launched War Is Over campaign but in an erratic and half-hearted way.[15]

In August 1971, John and Yoko left Britain for New York and "a new life of dwindling achievement and declining charm."[16] They interacted with the art and activist scenes and adopted more radical stances on social and political issues. The Lennon/Ono/Plastic Ono Band LP *Sometime in New York City* contained protest songs dealing with feminism, racism, Northern Ireland, prisoners' rights and drug prohibition.[17] In 1972, the Nixon administration, fearing Lennon's influence among young voters, targeted him for deportation; he was monitored by both the CIA and the FBI but fought back legally.[18] From the summer of 1973 until late 1974, John and Yoko were parted, and he lived a dissolute life in Los Angeles. After they were reunited, their son Sean was born, and Lennon appeared to give up music, living the quiet life of an involved father.[19]

The news of the murder of John Lennon in New York in December 1980 shocked many Canadians and ignited public displays of grief and a new round of commemoration of the Beatles in general and Lennon in particular. Radio stations gave both Lennon's solo songs and the music of the Beatles heavy coverage. But much of the mourning that swept the globe focused on Lennon the peace activist — the activist who came to Canada in 1969. In 2019, Gilles Gougeon, who as a Radio-Québec journalist had interviewed Yoko and John in Montreal in 1969, described December 8, 1980, as "the day somebody killed my youth."[20] According to one writer, the worldwide response to the celebrity's death was not simply grief over the loss of a revered individual but was a requiem for "lost dreams, ideals, hope and beliefs."[21] Torontonians did not wait for the Yoko Ono-sanctioned day of mass mourning, December 14. On the evening of December 10, 1980, an estimated thirty-five thousand people, many of them weeping openly, gathered in Nathan Phillips Square for a candlelight vigil. Like events in New York and elsewhere, the Toronto gathering was a mass counterculture gathering two decades after the counterculture had supposedly peaked.[22] In Ottawa four days later, the official mourning date, five thousand gathered near the Peace Tower on Parliament Hill, observed two minutes of silence and sang choruses of the peace anthem written and recorded in Montreal nearly a dozen years earlier. In the House of Commons, Trudeau, who had returned as prime minister earlier in the year after defeating the Progressive Conservative government, explained that he had written a personal sympathy letter to Yoko Ono.[23] The emotional reaction, and the frequent airplay of "Give Peace a Chance" and John's equally utopian "Imagine," helped reinforce the nostalgic view that the Beatles had mainly been about peace and love, the embodiment of the positive aspects of the 1960s counterculture.[24] "Give Peace a Chance," Lennon's Montreal composition, continued to be sung by Canadians at various demonstrations over the years, notably in the lead-up to the 1991 Gulf War, when Canada's participation in military operations against Iraq was opposed by many young people. Prime Minister Brian Mulroney sent Canadian air and naval units into combat for the first time since the Korean War, challenging the nation's peacekeeping image.[25]

On more than one occasion in 1969, Lennon told reporters in Canada that he had no wish to become a "dead saint." One close friend has pointed out the irony of the musician who saw himself as "a joker and a rebel," and who opposed the worship of "dead heroes," becoming a martyr in death and an inspirational global citizen.[26] Memorials and monuments were created in his honour in several countries (but not in Canada), and musicians too young to experience the Beatles and Lennon's solo years look up to him as a role model. Biographies, memoirs and investigative journalism in the years following his death, despite allegations of less than saintly attitudes and behaviour, have not really tarnished Lennon's overall image as a humanitarian and promoter of peace.[27]

Yoko Ono, never a big fan of the Beatles when they were together, in the years after her husband's death worked hard to maintain his legacy as a solo artist, celebrity activist and martyr to peace. Her focus was on the John and Yoko years, 1966 to 1980. Labouring to promote the positive image of her spouse, she spearheaded or supported a number of projects and events to commemorate this legacy, speaking out, for example, against gun violence. She continued to support various charities and maintained an active social media presence. By 2020, no doubt the hippest eighty-seven-year-old on the planet, Ono remained an active artist and activist.[28] She has benefited from Beatles-derived financial resources (an estimated $600 million) not available to the average artist, as well as celebrity status.[29] Ono has also continued a music career. In 2017, she received credit as co-writer of "Imagine," John's most famous solo song.

In her ongoing quest to make art and stay connected with her husband's peace brand, Lennon's widow has not forgotten Canada. She remained a friend of Ritchie Yorke, a major contributor to John and Yoko's image in Canada, until his death in 2017. In 2012, her exhibition "Add Colour" was displayed at a museum in Kitchener, Ontario. In keeping with her conceptual and participatory approach, visitors to the gallery were invited to add images or words to a white canvas that was part of the exhibit's central piece.[30] Six years later, a visual arts reporter covering her exhibit at Toronto's Gardiner Museum described Yoko as "the godmother of conceptual arts, a charter member of the Fluxus movement . . . a minimalist composer, an experimental filmmaker, a globetrotting peace activist and . . . likely still the world's most famous widow."[31]

For the Yoko Ono version of the John Lennon story (which is the John and Yoko story), Montreal has become more important over time. In 2009, on the fortieth anniversary of the bed-in, Yoko staged an exhibit at the Montreal Museum of Fine Arts: "Imagine: The Peace Ballad of John and Yoko." Two years later, she released a new documentary on YouTube, *Imagine Peace*, a chronicle of the Montreal bed-in. On a webpage about the making of the film, she wrote: "In 1969, John and I were so naïve to think that doing the Bed-in would help change the world." She continued: "There are things that we said then in the film, which give some encouragement and inspiration to the activists of today."[32] In 2019 (the fiftieth anniversary of the bed-in), the PHI Foundation for Contemporary Art in Montreal hosted Liberté Conquérante/Growing Freedom, an extensive exhibit of the artwork of Ono and Lennon that adopted a historical, archival approach. Housed on four floors, it included recreations of some of Ono's participatory art from the London years when she met Lennon and a film of "Cut Piece," the 1964 happening where audience members used scissors to cut off pieces of the artist's clothes. There was also a recreation of *Ceiling Painting*, also known as *Yes Painting*, which is central to the lore of how John and Yoko met and became a couple. In May 2019, the author participated in some of these works and even crawled into a bag in order to experience Bagism, part of the stage show at the Toronto Rock 'n' Roll Revival. He also had a glimpse of the room on the seventeenth floor of the Queen Elizabeth Hotel, which had hosted the bed-in (the hotel promoted the fiftieth anniversary of the event with an exhibit). The PHI interactive exhibit ran from April 25 to September 15. There were twelve hundred people at the opening, and the free exhibit ended up drawing twenty thousand people. A separate building housed a multimedia historical exhibit dedicated to the Montreal bed-in. The foundation also sponsored a panel discussion (posted to YouTube) that included Jerry Levitan and Minnie Yorke, widow of Ritchie.[33] The exhibit guide for Growing Freedom explained that the artist "has consistently espoused opening the mind up against all prejudice. The lyrics she penned with her husband to "Give Peace A Chance" in 1969 serve as a sort of *reductio ad absurdum* against any '-ism' one could dream up."[34]

John and Yoko's three visits to Canada in 1969 turned out to be footnotes in the larger history of pop culture and had little lasting impact on the nation, but its media has commemorated them, especially the Montreal bed-in, as reflecting the spirit of the age. In 2000, the CBC released the documentary *John & Yoko's Year of Peace.* In it, Allan Rock remembered Lennon:

> My deep impression of him is of a man who was kind, and gentle, thoughtful, with deep convictions which he expressed sometimes in a very...naive way or over-simplified way. But they were all so positive and all so humanitarian that you really couldn't find fault with the energy that he put into this cause that he believed in so deeply.[35]

Jerry Levitan's 2009 book *I Met the Walrus*, which included his 1969 Lennon interview on DVD, described his subject as "one of the most important figures of the twentieth century."[36] In 2008, Levitan's short animated film of the same name was nominated for an Academy Award. John Lennon and Pierre Trudeau (who, coincidentally, also embarked on a quixotic peace crusade[37]) were two of Levitan's heroes. The fortieth anniversary of the bed-in was also commemorated by Joan Athey and Paul McGrath's edited book of photos by Gerry Deiter, which included essays by Yoko Ono and others. *Give Peace a Chance: John and Yoko's Bed-in for Peace* was a respectful and overwhelmingly positive contribution to the post-1980 Lennon image. A decade later the Canadian Mint issued a $99.99 silver coin commemorating the bed-in and Folk Arts International filmed a number of musicians, including Canada's Susan Aglukark, Stephen Fearing, Connie Kaldor and Shakura S'Aida, singing "Give Peace a Chance" in the hotel suite made famous in 1969.[38]

Ritchie Yorke's insider account of John's 1969 peace quest, framed against nationalist stereotypes about Canada in the late 1960s as a kinder, gentler version of both the United States and Britain, was another brick in the wall of the Lennon myth. As Minnie Yorke explained in Montreal in 2019, her husband had a passion for social justice and viewed Lennon's music as a force for positive good. The quest for social justice continues. As Canadians are increasingly recognizing, their nation has its own problems of racism, exclusion and poverty and a record of internal colonialism against Indigenous peoples. Lennon was a symbol of the counterculture and youth at a time when there was widespread fear and disapproval of young people by adults.[39] Nothing symbolized this better than the backlash in Manitoba against an official Lennon and Ono visit. These views were not unique to Canada; a British poll in 1969 suggested that 99 per cent of those surveyed disapproved of Lennon being named "Man of the Decade" by a media personality. Another indicated that John's involvement with Yoko was also unpopular with many Britons, including young people.[40] For Canada, 1969, Lennon and Yoko's "year of peace" was actually one of the most turbulent periods since Confederation. In the decade of the 1960s, cool had an edge. The following year, associated with Lennon's ill-fated peace festival, was even more dramatic. Yet there is no debating that Canada in 1969 and early 1970 was a different and more dynamic and exciting place than it had been a decade earlier. That cool factor, if not appreciated by all citizens, owed much to the three visits of John and Yoko.

Acknowledgements

The idea for this book came a few years ago when I came across a newspaper article explaining that Led Zeppelin almost performed at a rock festival in New Brunswick in 1970. Investigating that story led me to John Lennon, Yoko Ono and other people discussed in this study. Completing a book during the Covid-19 crisis, with libraries and archives closed and offices not always accessible, presented a number of challenges. I wish to thank Johnny Brower, Allan Rock, Jeff Lieberman, Joan Athey, Minnie Yorke, Scott Cisco, Robert Whitney, Dann Downes, Berkely Flemming, Mike Mendelson, Bronny Davis, George MacLean, Ray Small, Fondation PHI pour l'artcontemporain and the University of New Brunswick Saint John Dean of Arts and Department of History and Politics for their help with this project. The staff at the University of New Brunswick Public Libraries and York University Libraries were of immeasurable assistance. The support and hard work of James Lorimer, David Gray-Donald and Ashley Bernicky at James Lorimer & Company and Holly Dickinson is gratefully acknowledged. Finally, the role of my 'invisible author,' my wife Donna, has to be recognized. Over the last six years, four books (plus two updated editions of one of these books) have been produced in our house, mostly at the kitchen table. She is now an expert on John Lennon and Yoko Ono.

Endnotes

Introduction

1. Catherine Carstairs, "'Roots' Nationalism: Branding English Canada Cool in the 1980s and 1990s," *Histoire sociale/Social History*, vol. 39 (77) (2006): 235–55.
2. Wayne Hampton, *Guerrilla Minstrels: John Lennon, Joe Hill, Woody Guthrie, Bob Dylan* (Knoxville: University of Tennessee Press, 1986), 4.
3. Joel Dinerstein, "American Cool: An Introduction," in Joel Dinerstein and Frank H. Goodyear III, *American Cool* (New York: Delmonico Books-Prestel, National Portrait Gallery, 2014), 10.
4. Pierre Berton, *1967: The Last Good Year* (Toronto: Doubleday Canada, 1997).
5. Ian Milligan, *Rebel Youth: 1960s Labour Unrest, Young Workers, and New Leftists in English Canada* (Vancouver: UBC Press, 2014), 3.
6. Berton, *1967*, 14.
7. Canada was not at war, but it was involved in United Nations peacekeeping missions. Dozens of Canadian armed forces personnel have died in these missions over the years.
8. Berton, *1967*, 17.
9. Meaghan Elizabeth Beaton, *The Centennial Cure: Commemoration, Identity and Cultural Capital in Nova Scotia during Canada's 1967 Centennial Celebrations* (Toronto: University of Toronto Press, 2017).
10. For details on the Centennial, see Berton, *1967*.
11. "Toronto Celebrates Canada's Centennial," July 1, 1967, CBC Archives: https://www.cbc.ca/archives/entry/toronto-celebrates-canadas-centennial.
12. Paul Litt, *Trudeaumania* (Vancouver: University of British Columbia Press, 2016), 100.
13. John English, *Citizen of the World: The Life of Pierre Elliot Trudeau: Volume 1: 1919–1968* (Toronto: Alfred Knopf, 2006), 439.
14. "Interview with Piers Hemmingsen," Q, CBC Radio, June 1, 2017.
15. The 2017–20 exhibit was an interactive audiovisual record based on many interviews of people who experienced Expo 67 as children or youth.
16. "Opinion poll favours bilingualism," *Globe and Mail*, Dec. 6, 1967, 9.
17. Harold Troper, *The Defining Decade: Identity, Politics and the Canadian Jewish Community in the 1960s* (Toronto: University of Toronto Press, 2010), 219.
18. Berton, *1967*.
19. *Ibid.*
20. *Canadian News Facts*, Volume 2, (Toronto: MPL, 1968) 151.
21. Don Macpherson, "Don Macpherson: The Parti Québécois seems to be dying off with the baby boomers," *Montreal Gazette*, Sept. 19, 2016: https://montrealgazette.com/opinion/columnists/don-macpherson-the-parti-quebecois-could-end-up-a-destabilized-party.
22. Steve Turner, *Beatles '66: The Revolutionary Year* (New York: Ecco, 2016), 289.
23. "Our World: 1967 TV experiment links five continents by satellite," June 25, 1967, CBC Digital Archives: https://www.cbc.ca/archives/entry/our-world-five-continents-linked-via-satellite.
24. Blair Foster and Alex Gibney directors *Rolling Stone: Stories from the Edge* Episode 1 (Shout Factory, 2017; Martha Bari, "Taking It to the Streets: John Lennon and Yoko Ono's 1969 War Is Over! Campaign," in Eric J. Schruers and Kristina Olson, eds. *Social Practice Art in Turbulent Times: The Revolution Will Be Live* (New York: Routledge, 2020), 34. The BBC refused to broadcast *The War Game*, but it played at film festivals and won an Academy Award.
25. Dan Richter, *The Dream Is Over: London in the '60s, Heroin and John and Yoko* (London: Quartet Books, 2012), 77–78.
26. L.B. Kuffert, *A Great Duty: Canadian Responses to Modern Life and Mass Culture in Canada, 1939–1967* (Montreal: McGill-Queen's University Press, 2003), ch. 5.
27. Jeff Sallot, "Trudeau's cabinet divided in 1969," *Globe and Mail*, Feb. 5, 2000, A4.

28.   Victor Levant, *Quiet Complicity: Canadian Involvement in the Vietnam War* (Toronto: Between the Lines, 1986).

Chapter 1
1.   Linda Bohnen, "Beatle flies to Toronto, detained at airport," *Globe and Mail*, May 26, 1969, 1.
2.   *Ibid.*
3.   *Ibid.*
4.   Ritchie Yorke, "Pop Scene: Lennon and Ono bring message for youth to Canada," *Globe and Mail*, May 27, 1969, 13.
5.   John Lennon and Yoko Ono directors, *Bed Peace* (Bag Productions, 1969).
6.   Paul McGrath director, *John & Yoko's Year of Peace* (Chatsworth, CA: Image Entertainment, 2002).
7.   Litt, *Trudeaumania*, 183–84; 187.
8.   English, *Citizen of the World,*, 472.
9.   Canadian Press, "Trudeau marries Vancouver girl, 21," *Globe and Mail*, March 5, 1971, 1.
10.   Litt, *Trudeaumania*, 10–11.
11.   John English, *Just Watch Me: The Life of Pierre Elliot Trudeau 1968-2000* (Toronto: Alfred A. Knopf Canada 2009), 2–3.
12.   Litt, *Trudeaumania*, 91.
13.   *Ibid.*, 295.
14.   English, *Just Watch Me*, 115.
15.   Canadian Press, "Champion of women's rights finds fault with Canadian women," *Globe and Mail*, Feb. 14, 1969, 11.
16.   English, *Just Watch Me*, 16.
17.   *Ibid.*
18.   English, *Just Watch Me*, 4-5; Edith Iglauer, "Prime Minister/Premier Ministre," *New Yorker*, July 5, 1969, 5. See also: Edith Iglauer, "The Prime Minister Accepts," GEIST: https://www.geist.com/fact/dispatches/prime-minister-accepts.
19.   Michael B. Stein and Janice Gross Stein, "From Swinger to Statesman: Canada Comes of Age in the Era of Pierre Elliot Trudeau," *Policy Options*, (June 1, 2003); http://policyoptions.irpp.org/magazines/the-best-pms-in-the-past-50-years/from-swinger-to-statesman-canada-comes-of-age-in-the-time-of-pierre-elliott-trudeau.
20.   English, *Just Watch Me*, 7–9.
21.   *Canadian News Facts*, Volume 2, 109.
22.   *Ibid.*, 27–30.
23.   George Bain, "What right do we have to presume to give answers? Don't shrug off," *Globe and Mail*, Jan. 10, 1969, 4; "Riel unveiling ceremony: students mob Trudeau to protest loan policy," *Globe and Mail*, Oct. 3, 1968, 1.
24.   "Riel unveiling ceremony," *Globe and Mail*, Oct. 3, 1968, 1.
25.   Ronald Lebel, "Trudeau crosses sound barrier in plane and poverty line on a train," *Globe and Mail*, May 19, 1969, 1.
26.   Donald Newman, "Trudeau is heckled just once, replies 'Relax Buster . . . this is a fun day,'" *Globe and Mail*, July 7, 1970, 9.
27.   Beverly Mitchell, "What's the good of being Miss Canada if I can't sit with Pierre?" *Montreal Star*, Dec. 2, 1969, 14.
28   English, *Just Watch Me*, 56.
29.   John Kennair, *A Forgotten Legacy: Canadian Leadership in the Commonwealth* (Bloomington, Indiana: Trafford Publishing, 2011), 111.
30.   "Angry Trudeau flays 'crummy behaviour' of prying reporters," *Globe and Mail*, Jan. 16, 1969, 1.
31.   Scott MacDonald and Yoko Ono, "Yoko Ono: Ideas on Film: Interview/Scripts," *Film Quarterly*, Vol. 43, No. 1 (Autumn, 1989), 2–23.
32.   Yorke, "Pop Scene: Lennon and Ono."
33.   Lennon and Ono directors, *Bed Peace*; Ritchie Yorke, "Boosting Peace: John and Yoko in Canada," *Rolling Stone*, June 28, 1969, 1.

34. Leroy Adams, "John and Yoko: Life in a 'Fish Bowl,'" *Washington Post*, May 27, 1969, 13.
35. Barry Miles, *Paul McCartney: Many Years from Now* (New York: Holt Paperbacks, 1998), 566.
36. Yorke, "Pop Scene: Lennon and Ono."
37. Bradley Scott, "Ritchie Yorke on Rock and Roll," *Vice*, Dec. 2, 2013: https//www.vice.com/en_us/article/znwxmx/Ritchie-yorke-on-rock-n-roll.
38. Joyce Carter, "Mod Squire," *Globe and Mail*, Oct. 12, 1968, A20.
39. Ritchie Yorke, *Christ You Know It Ain't Easy: John and Yoko's Battle for Peace* (Middleton, Delaware: Ritchie Yorke Publishing, 2015).
40. Ritchie Yorke, "Beatlemania and the bed-ins: When John and Yoko came to Canada," *Toronto Daily Star*, Oct. 10, 2015: https://www.thestar.com/news/insight/2015/10/10/beatlemania-and-bed-ins-when-john-and-yoko-came-to-canada.html.
41. Ken Hull, "Beatle John Lennon Asks Trudeau to Peace Bed-In," *Toronto Daily Star*, May 26, 1969, 1.
42. William Cameron, "The City: Waiting for John: Behind Police Lines at the King Edward Hotel," *Toronto Daily Star*, May 27, 1969, 3.
43. Jo Carson, "Jacqueline Susann calls criticism of books 'sour grapes,'" *Globe and Mail*, May 27, 1969, 12.
44. Jerry Levitan, *I Met the Walrus: How One Day with John Lennon Changed My Life Forever* (Toronto: Harper Design, 2009), 31.
45. *Ibid.*, 58–71.
46. *Ibid.*, 80–88.
47. Ritchie Yorke, "Fans ambush Beatle, outward bound," *Globe and Mail*, May 27, 1969, 13.
48. *Ibid.*
49. Yorke, "Boosting Peace," 6
50. Yorke, "Beatlemania and bed-ins."
51. Yorke, "Boosting Peace," 8.
52. Pop music fans outside of Canada were exposed to these views through *Rolling Stone*, founded in San Francisco in 1967. The magazine covered the Beatles in great detail: Michael R. Frontani, "'Beatlepeople': Gramsci, the Beatles and 'Rolling Stone' Magazine," *American Journalism*, Vol. 19 (2) (July 2002): 39-61.
53. McGrath director, *John & Yoko's Year of Peace.*
54. Mark Kurlansky, *1968, The Year That Rocked the World* (New York: Random House, 2005), xvii.
55. Pat Smart, "Queen's University History Department and the Birth of the Waffle Movement," in M. Athena Paleologu, ed. *The Sixties in Canada: A Turbulent and Creative Decade* (Vancouver: University of British Columbia Press, 2009), 314.
56. "Won't appear at U of T festival: Yippie leader Abbie Hoffman cancels visit," *Globe and Mail*, Sept. 21, 1970, 5.
57. Litt, *Trudeaumania*, 245.
58. "Poll Finds Canadians Back U.S. Stance," *Globe and Mail*, Nov. 23, 1962, 5.
59. Bryan D. Palmer, "New Left Liberations: The Poetics, Praxis and Politics of Youth Radicalism," in Palaeologu, ed. *The Sixties in Canada*, 79–93.
60. Douglas A. Ross, *In the Interests of Peace: Canada and Vietnam, 1954–73* (Toronto: University of Toronto Press, 1984), 309, 317.
61. Ryan Goldworthy, "The Canadian Way: The Case of Canadian Vietnam War Veterans," National Defence and the Canadian Armed Forces: http://www.journal.forces.gc.ca/vol15/no3/page48-eng.asp.
62. Ross H. Munro, "Nine arrested during demonstrations on Vietnam," *Globe and Mail*, April 29, 1969, 17.
63. Ross H. Munro, "Arrival of Vietnamese delegates helps save Montreal conference," *Globe and Mail*, Nov. 3, 1968, 10.
64. Ross H. Munro, "The Violent Death of a Peace Meeting," *Globe and Mail*, Dec. 5, 1968, 7; Ross H. Munro; "Conference backs Quebec fight against U.S. imperialism," *Globe and Mail*, Dec. 2, 1968, 9.
65. Josephine Matyas, "You say you want a reservation," *Toronto Daily Star*, March 27, 2009: https://www.thestar.com/life/travel/2009/03/27/upo_say_you_want_a_reservation.html.

66.   *Ibid*; Beverley Mitchell, "Kyoko: number one flower child," *Montreal Star*, May 28, 1969, 85

67.   Yoko Ono, Liberté Conquérante/Growing Freedom exhibition, exhibited at Fondation PHI pour l'art contemporain, Montreal, 2019.

68.   Yorke, "Pop Scene: Lennon and Ono."

69.   Sean Mills, "Democracy, Dissent and the City: Cross-Cultural Encounters in Sixties Montreal," in Palaelogu, ed. *The Sixties in Canada*, 150.

70.   Ronald Lebel, "Police director wants Ottawa to bar entry of 'red rabble rousers,'" *Globe and Mail*, Nov. 12, 1968, 1.

71.   Mills, "Democracy," 151.

72.   Sean Mills, *The Empire Within: Postcolonial Thought and Political Activism in Sixties Montreal* (Montreal: McGill-Queen's University Press, 2010), 13.

73.   Nick Auf der Maur, *Quebec: A Chronicle: 1968–1972* (Toronto: James Lorimer, 1972).

74.   "Militant is Hanged in Trinidad after Long Fight for Clemency," *New York Times*, May 17, 1975, 4. When de Freitas was arrested for extortion in 1971, Lennon provided his bail money. John also paid for a defence lawyer when Michael X was charged with the murder of two people on his Trinidad commune. John and Yoko were convinced of his innocence, but he was convicted of one death and was hanged in 1975.

75.   Canadian Press, "U Students Go Beserk," *Winnipeg Free Press*, Feb. 12, 1969, 1.

76.   Ronald Lebel, "Riot suspects denied bail, defence counsel protests," *Globe and Mail*, Feb. 19, 1969, 1; Doug Owram, *Born at the Right Time: A History of the Baby Boom Generation* (Toronto: University of Toronto Press, 1997), 287–89.

77.   Mina Shum director, *The Ninth Floor* (National Film Board, 2015).

78.   "Importunate Guests," *Winnipeg Free Press*, Feb. 3, 1969, 3.

79.   Paul Williams, "Crawdaddy! Founder on His Experience at the Bed-in for Peace," Paste Music, July 20, 2011: https://www.pastemagazine.com/blogs/crawdaddy/2011/07/crawdaddy-founder-on-his-experience-at-the-bed-in-for-peace.html.

80.   Yorke, "Beatlemania and bed-ins."

81.   Alison Gordon, "Those Strange Few Days," in Joan Athey, Paul McGrath and Gerry Deiter, eds. *Give Peace a Chance: John and Yoko's Bed-In for Peace* (Ottawa: John Wiley & Sons, 2009), 15.

82.   Mike Mendelson interview with author, June 4, 2019.

83.   One American guest invited by the CBC was New Yorker Nat Hentoff, the *Village Voice* contributor and jazz music expert who also wrote for the *Washington Post* and other publications; John W. Whitehead, "Impressions: People I Knew: An Interview with Nat Hentoff," The Rutherford Institute, March 5, 2012: https://www.rutherford.org/publications_resources/oldspeak/impressions_people_i_knew_an_interview_with_nat_hentoff.

84.   Ritchie Yorke, "Festival success 'due to the police,'" *Globe and Mail*, June 24, 1969, 12.

85.   David Ellis, *Evolution of the Canadian Broadcasting System: Objectives and Realities, 1928–1968* (Ottawa: Minister of Supply and Services Canada, 1979), 83.

86.   Johanna Bertin, *Don Messer: The Man Behind the Music* (Fredericton: Goose Lane Editions, 2009).

87.   Bill Biroux, "This Hour Has Seven Days was part of Canadian TV's 'golden age,'" *Toronto Daily Star*, Nov. 28, 2014: https://www.thestar.com/entertainment/television/2014/11/28/this_hour_has_seven_days_was_part_of_canadian_tvs_golden_age.html.

88.   Gordon, "Those Strange Few Days," 15; McGrath director, *John & Yoko's Year of Peace*.

89.   Leslie Millin, "In this corner, CBC, in that corner, CTV: the public affairs battle awaits the gong," *Globe and Mail*, Sept. 7, 1968, 23; John Dafoe, "CBC takes roasting in Commons during debate on broadcast act," *Globe and Mail*, Jan. 23, 1968, 8; John C. Winn, *That Magic Feeling: The Beatles' Recorded Legacy, Volume Two, 1966–1970* (New York: Three Rivers Press, 2009), 300.

90.   Beverley Mitchell, "Kyoko: number one flower child," *Montreal Star*, May 28, 1969, 85.

91.   Mark Reid, "Come Together," *Canada's History*, Vol. 93 (2) (April/May 2013): 20–27.

92.   Canadian Press, "Press elbow about peace bed-in," *Globe and Mail*, May 28, 1969, 14.

93.   Dave Bist, "All we are say-ying," *Montreal Gazette*, May 30, 1999: https://montrealgazette.

com/news/local-news/from-the-archive-all-we-are-say-y-ying.

94. Jack Batten, "Jack Rabinovitch and Doris Giller: the love story behind Canada's most prestigious book award, *Toronto Life*, Aug. 8, 2017: https://torontolife.com/from-the-archives/for-doris-jack-rabinovitch.

95. Anthony Fawcett, *John Lennon: One Day at a Time* (New York: Evergreen, 1976), 53–54.

96. Winn, *That Magic Feeling*, 291.

97. Jon Wiener, *Come Together: John Lennon in His Time* (Champaign: University of Illinois Press, 1991), 92–93.

98. Charles Childs, "Selling peace," in Athey, McGrath and Deiter, eds. *Give Peace a Chance*, 40; "News in Brief," *The Times*, [London] June 3, 1969, 5.

99. Gordon, "Those Strange Few Days," 15.

100. Alain Martineau, "Il y a 40 ans, John Lennon et Yoko Ono signaient une page d'histoire en commençant un bed-in qui durera huit jours dans la suite 1742 de l'hôtel Reine-Élizabeth, à Montréal," *La Presse*, 25 mai 2009: https://www.lapresse.ca/arts/musique/200905/25/01-859724-le-bed-in-de-john-lennon-et-yoko-oni-a-40-ans.php.

101. Paul McGrath, "1969 Bed-In for Peace," in Athey, McGrath and Deiter, eds. *Give Peace a Chance*, 5.

102. Reid, "Come Together."

103. Chuck Chandler, "My John Lennon Story," in Athey, McGrath, Deiter, eds. *Give Peace a Chance*, 27; McGrath director, *John & Yoko's Year of Peace*.

104. Reuters, "Lennon invitation," *The Times* [London], May 28, 1969, 5.

105. Canadian Press, "Bed-in interview no joke to Lesage," *Globe and Mail*, May 30, 1969, 12; Susan Altschull and Dominique Clift, "'Bed-in' widens rift in NU ranks," *Montreal Star*, May 30, 1969, 1.

106. Winn, *That Magic Feeling*, 293–94; Wiener, *Come Together*, 93–94.

107. *Ibid.*

108. Winn, *That Magic Feeling*, 294.

109. David James O'Kane, "Canadian Public Opinion and the War in Vietnam, 1954–1973" (MA thesis: University of British Columbia, 1995).

110. Mark Satin, *Manual for Draft-Age Immigrants to Canada* (Toronto: Toronto Anti-Draft Committee/House of Anansi, 1968), 2.

111. Levant, *Quiet Complicity*, 207–209.

112. Robert Stall, "U.S. wasn't consulted on deserters policy," *Montreal Star*, May 23, 1969, 1; Dick Cotterill, My Difficult Decision to Desert, Canadian Museum of Immigration at Pier 21: https://pier21.ca/dick-cotterill-my-difficult-decision-to-desert.

113. Philip Winslow, "Bed-in Beatle Sells Peace Like Soap," *Montreal Star*, May 28, 1969, 11.

114. "Erects tipi outside City Hall," *Globe and Mail*, May 31, 1969, 4.

115. Lillian Shirt, Corinne George and Sarah Carter, "Lillian Piché Shirt, John Lennon and a Cree Grandmother's Inspiration for the Song 'Imagine,'" *Active History*, December 5, 2015: http://activehistory.ca/2016/12/lillian-piche-shirt-john-lennon-and-a-cree-grandmothers-inspiration-for-the-song-imagine. Neither Lennon nor Ono ever mentioned any connection with the 1969 conversation, and no tape of the interview survived; Geoff McMaster, "Was John Lennon's 'Imagine' inspired by an Alberta Cree grandmother?" *Folio*, December 7, 2018: https://www.folio.ca/was-john-lennons-imagine-inspired-by-an-alberta-cree-grandmother.

116. "Les Montréalais accueillent John et Yoko," Archives de radio-canada, 26 mai 1969.

117. Bronwyn Chester, "McGill français and Quebec society," *McGill Reporter*, April 8, 1999: http://www.reporter-archive.mcgill.ca/Rep/r3114/x3114.html.

118. Athey, McGrath, Deiter, eds. *Give Peace a Chance*, 93.

119. CBC, "A Bed-Time Story, *The Way It Is*, June 8, 1969. Larue-Langlois may have been echoing a famous line from a 1964 speech by American Black Power activist Malcom X.

120. Charles Childs, "Penthouse Interview: John Lennon and Yoko Ono," *Penthouse*, Oct. 1969, 29, 34.

121. Dennis McLellan, "Dick Gregory, who rose from poverty to become a groundbreaking comedian and civil rights activist, dies at 84," *Los Angeles Times*, Oct. 27, 2016: https://www.latimes.com/local/obituaries/la-me-dick-gregory-20170819-story.html.

122. Canadian Press, "Eight of 10 West Indians are found guilty of conspiracy in Sir Georges

Williams Trial," *Globe and Mail*, March 13, 1970, 1; Lawrence Hill, "How Harper Lee helped Canadians ignore racism in their own backyard," *Globe and Mail*, Feb. 19, 2016: https://www.theglobeandmail.com/news/national/how-harper-lee-helped-canadians-ignore-racism-in-our-own-backyard/article28826254.

123.   Winn, *That Magic Feeling*, 295.

124.   Lennon and Ono directors, *Bed Peace*.

125.   *Ibid.*

126.   Canadian Press, "Fredericton offered as peace site," *Toronto Daily Star*, June 5, 1969, 56.

127.   Dennis McLellan, "Rosemary W. Leary, 66; Ex-Wife of 1960s Psychedelic Guru," *Los Angeles Times*, Feb. 9, 2002: https://www.latimes.com/archives/la-xpm-2002-feb-09-me-leary9-story.html.

128.   CBC, "Timothy Leary on the possibilities of LSD," *Document*, April 24, 1966, CBC Digital Archives: http://www.cbc.ca/archives/entry/timothy-leary-on-the-possibilities-of-lsd.

129.   Robert Greenfield, *Timothy Leary: A Biography* (Toronto: Harcourt, 2006), 282.

130.   Williams, "Crawdaddy! Founder."

131.   Greenfield, *Timothy Leary.*

132.   Tony Thomson interview with Jim Morrison, June 27, 1970, *CBC Rewind.*

133.   "This Week in History: 1967," *Vancouver Sun*, March 24, 2017: http://vancouversun.com/news/local-news/this-week-in-history-1967-a-hairy-horde-descends-on-stanley-park-for-an-easter-be-in.

134.   For Yorkville, see Stuart Henderson, *Making the Scene: Yorkville and Hip Toronto in the 1960s* (Toronto: University of Toronto Press, 2011).

135.   Wally Dennison, "Drug Abuse Surges," *Winnipeg Free Press*, Feb. 8, 1969, 1–2.

136.   Jess Stern, "The Seekers," *Winnipeg Free Press*, March 4, 1969, 2.

137.   Greenfield, *Timothy Leary*, 370.

138.   "Never Before Published Transcript of a Conversation Between John Lennon, Yoko Ono, Timothy Leary and Rosemary Leary — at the Montreal Bed-In," May 1969, Timothy Leary Archives: http://www.timothylearyarchives.org/never-before-published-transcript-of-a-conversation-between-john-lennon-yoko-ono-timothy-leary-and-rosemary-leary-%E2%80%93-at-the-montreal-bed-in-may-1969.

139.   Paul Williams, "Doing the Bed-In for Peace," in Athey, McGrath Deiter, eds. *Give Peace a Chance*, 31.

140.   *Ibid.*

141.   Christopher William Powell, "Vietnam: 'It's Our War Too'": The Antiwar Movement in Canada: 1963–1975" (PhD thesis: University of New Brunswick, 2010), 245.

142.   Abraham L. Feinberg, "Atomic Ages Needs God's Discipline," *Globe and Mail*, April 30, 1960, 8.

143.   Abraham L. Feinberg, "Death Penalty Is Threat to Country's Moral Fibre," *Toronto Daily Star*, March 5, 1960, 8. After he died, the RCMP gave his daughter Feinberg's national security file, which, although many documents were missing, extended to more than one thousand pages. See: Phil Girard, *Bora Laskin: Bringing Life to Law* (Toronto: University of Toronto Press, 2015), 582, endnote 25.

144.   Austin Clarke, "From sit-ins to love-ins, Austin Clarke recalls life in 1960s Toronto," *Toronto Daily Star*, Aug. 15, 2015: https://www.thestar.com/news/insight/2015/08/15/from-sit-ins-to-love-ins-austin-clarke-recalls-lifein-1960s-toronto.html.

145.   Abraham Feinberg, *Hanoi Diary* (New York: Longmans, 1968).

146.   Bryan Palmer, *Canada's 1960s: The Ironies of Identity in a Rebellious Era* (Toronto: University of Toronto Press, 2009), 70–73.

147.   Feinberg, *Hanoi Diary.*

148.   McGrath director, *John & Yoko's Year of Peace.*

149.   Rabbi A.L. Feinberg, "Rabbi tells why we should join John, Yoko's bed-in," *Toronto Daily Star*, June 7, 1969, 4.

150.   "Let Vietnam turn Red if it must, Feinberg says," *Toronto Daily Star*, July 7, 1969, 22.

151.   Ritchie Yorke, "Pop Scene: Integration or No Show is Rascals' Ultimatum," *Globe and Mail*, Jan. 8, 1969, 10.

152. Leslie Millin, "Tom prefers to be Smothers, not stilled," *Globe and Mail*, 1969, 21.

153. CBS dropping Smothers Brothers," *Globe and Mail*, April 5, 1969, 16; "Canadian News Report," *Billboard*, April 19, 1969, 68.

154. Lennon and Ono directors, *Bed Peace*.

155. *Ibid.*

156. Michael Cragg, "Petula Clark: 'John Lennon gave me some advice that I can't repeat,'" *The Guardian*, Feb. 20, 2013: https://www.theguardian.com.music/2013/feb/20/30-minutes-with-petula-clark.

157. Greenfield, *Timothy Leary*, 358. Exactly who was in the room, and sang on the recording, is not clear.

158. Wiener, *Come Together*, 98.

159. Gordon, "Those Strange Few Days," 16.

160. Donald Tarlton, "Nothing Will Ever Rival that Moment," in Athey, McGrath, Deiter, eds. *Give Peace a Chance*, 19-20.

161. André Perry, "A Most Difficult Recording," in Athey, McGrath, Deiter, eds. *Give Peace a Chance*, 35.

162. "A black sheep among the singing separatists," *Maclean's*, April 1, 1969, 4.

163. Elizabeth Ménard, "La vraie histoire de Give Peace a Chance," *Le Journal de Montreal*, 23 mai 2014: https://www.journaldemontreal.com/2014/05/23/la-vraie-histoire-de-igive-peace-a-chance. Author's translation.

164. Perry, "A Most Difficult Recording," 35.

165. Bill Brownstein, "All They Were Saying . . ." *Montreal Gazette*, April 15, 2005, A15.

166. Phillip Norman, *Days in the Life: John Lennon Remembered* (New York: Century, 1990), 608.

167. Greenfield, *Timothy Leary*, 358.

168. Gordon, "Those Strange Few Days," 15.

169. Steven Heller, "Just How Bitter, Petty, and Tragic," *The Atlantic*, Feb. 28, 2013: https://www.theatlantic.com/entertainment/archive/2013/02/just-how-bitter-petty-and-tragic-was-comic-strip-genius-al-capp/273595/.

170. Canadian Press, "Stick to LSD Capp told Lennon," *Toronto Daily Star*, June 2, 1969, 1.

171. Wiener, *Come Together*, 94–95.

172. Lennon and Ono, directors, *Bed Peace*; Wiener, *Come Together*, 95–96; McGrath, *John & Yoko's Year of Peace*.

173. Williams, "Crawdaddy! Founder."

174. In a 1970 speech to a business group in Toronto, Capp denounced draft dodgers in Canada as "refuse," student agitators as "demented punks," the far Left as "fascist" and homosexual organizations as "militant fags" and hinted that feminists were lesbians: "Far left is shifty, Capp tells sales club," *Globe and Mail*, Oct. 7, 1970, 5.

175. William Johnson, "Traditional role rejected: the wave of feminism opposes motherhood, marriage," *Globe and Mail*, May 1, 1969, W5.

176. Allan Rock, interview with author, June 19, 2017.

177. "Lennon urges plugging of peace," *Globe and Mail*, June 4, 1969, 13. See Levitan, *I Met the Walrus*.

178. Allan Rock, interview with author, June 19, 2017.

179. "Students occupy faculty quarters at University of Ottawa," *Globe and Mail*, Nov. 21, 1968, 39; "Students end occupation in Ottawa," *Globe and Mail*, Nov. 28, 1968, 9.

180. John Burns, "Student-power issue simmers at crowded universities," *Globe and Mail*, Sept. 4, 1968, 5.

181. Milligan, *Rebel Youth*.

182. Clair Balfour, "70 McGill students occupy staff offices, plan to stay away from classes today," *Globe and Mail*, Nov. 26, 1968, 8.

183. John Burns, "Radicals clash with academics," *Globe and Mail*, Nov. 8, 1968, 8. The Union général des étudiants du Québec represented Quebec student councils that opposed federal support of post-secondary education and was not part of the Canadian Union of Students.

184. "U Chancellor labels student issues 'phoney,'" *Winnipeg Free Press*, Feb. 20, 1969, 10.

185. Canadian Press, "RCMP links campus troubles to U.S. agitators," *Toronto Daily Star*, May 7, 1969, 1.

186.   "CUS demise leaves vacuum," *Globe and Mail*, Dec. 8, 1969, 1.
187.   Kaleem Hawa, "Old Politics for a New Age," *Salterrae*, November 2014, 7–8.
188.   J.L. Granatstein and Robert Bothwell, *Pirouette: Pierre Trudeau and Canadian Foreign Policy* (Toronto: University of Toronto Press, 1990), 121–22.
189.   Allan Rock, interview with author.
190.   McGrath director, *John & Yoko's Year of Peace*.
191.   Allan Rock, interview with author.
192.   Judy Barrie, "'Gimmick — Yes. U of O gets a peace of the Lennon action," *Ottawa Citizen*, June 4, 1969 (transcribed in The Ballad of John and Yoko in Canada: http://beatles.ncf.ca/ca/proofs.html).
193.   Ian Milligan, "Coming Off the Mountain: Forging an Outward-Looking New Left at Simon Fraser University," *BC Studies*, No. 171 (Autumn 2001): 69–91.
194.   CBC, "Cold War-era gov't feared radical's 'disciples,'" CBC News, Oct. 15, 2010: https://www.cbc.ca/news/canada/cold-war-era-gov-t-feared-radical-s-disciples-1.953061.
195.   Barrie, "Gimmick — Yes."
196.   "Lennon urges plugging of peace."
197.   Wiener, *Come Together*, 93.
198.   Yorke, "Boosting Peace."
199.   Williams, "Doing the Bed-In"; Wiener, *Come Together*, xvii.
200.   Ritchie Yorke, "A quiet day in Lennon's life," *Globe and Mail*, June 5, 1969, 11.
201.   McGrath director, *John & Yoko's Year of Peace*.
202.   Allan Rock, interview with author.
203.   Allan Rock, "You can say that I'm a dreamer," *Globe and Mail*, Dec. 8, 2000, R9.
204.   Yorke, "A quiet day.'"
205.   Yorke, "Boosting Peace."
206.   Ritchie Yorke, "Lennon passes up visa, flies home," *Globe and Mail*, June 6, 1969, 13.
207.   The episode was directed by Carl Charlson.
208.   Owram, *Born at the Right Time*, 159.
209.   Letter to editor, Rev. G.H. Clement, *Toronto Daily Star*, Dec. 19, 1969, 6.
210.   Associated Press, "Should fight: welcome of draft dodgers is wrong, ex-PM says," *Globe and Mail*, July 2, 1969. 2.
211.   David Crane, "Dief wants revolutionaries kept out," *Globe and Mail*, Feb. 15, 1969, 55; Frances Russell, "Yippie's entry to Canada raised in the House of Commons," *Globe and Mail*, March 4, 1969, 3.
212.   English, *Just Watch Me*, 2.
213.   Yorke, "Pop Scene: John and Yoko."
214.   Jann Wenner, "John Lennon, Man of the Year," *Rolling Stone*, Feb. 7, 1970, 24.
215.   Wiener, *Come Together*, xvii.
216.   *Ibid.*, 96.
217.   *Ibid.*, 97.
218.   "The Peace Anthem," *Newsweek*, Dec. 1, 1969, 102.
219.   "To bid Hair fond farewell," *Globe and Mail*, Jan. 4, 1971, 13; Yoko, "Give Peace a Chance," in Athey, McGrath, Deiter, eds. *Give Peace a Chance*, 117.
220.   Perry, "A Most Difficult Recording."

Chapter 2
1.   Johnny Brower interview with author, Aug. 1, 2018.
2.   Richard Needham, "The real wealth of Toronto," *Globe and Mail*, March 3, 1966, 3.
3.   James Lorimer, "The politicians' attitude toward citizen participation," *Globe and Mail*, July 20, 1970, 7.
4.   For hip consumerism, see Thomas Frank, *The Conquest of Cool: Business Culture, Counterculture, and the Rise of Hip Consumerism* (Chicago: University of Chicago Press, 1998).
5.   Simon Frith, *Sound Effects: Youth, Leisure and the Politics of Rock and Roll* (New York: Pantheon Books, 1981), 11.
6.   Oliver Clausen, "The Sixties: A Personal Journey," *Globe and Mail*, Dec. 27, 1969, A5.

7.   Owram, *Born at the Right Time*, 156.
8.   Ryan Edwardson, *Canuck Rock: A History of Canadian Popular Music* (Toronto: University of Toronto Press, 2009), 9. See also: Larry Starr, Christopher Waterman, Jay Hodgson, *Rock: A Canadian Perspective* (Don Mills: Oxford University Press, 2009).
9.   Dwight MacDonald, "A Caste, a Culture, a Market II," *The New Yorker*, Nov. 29, 1958, 29.
10. "Photos: the Day Bill Haley and the Comets Rocked Vancouver," *Vancouver Sun*, July 26, 2013: http://vancouversun.com/entertainment/photos+bill+haley+comets+rocked+Vancouver/8583754/story.html.
11. Kevin Plummer, "Historicist: Elvis in Toronto in 1957," *Torontoist*, April 6, 2013: torontoist.com/2013/04histiricust-elvis-in-toronto-1957.
12. June Callwood, "Why do Canadian youngsters worship Elvis Presley?" *Chatelaine*, June 1957, 13.
13. Michael Valpy, "Youth at the Crossroads: Live It Up They Are Urged — Then They're Punished If They Do," *Globe and Mail*, April 17, 1973, 7.
14. Andrew Merey, "The man who brought rock and roll to Canada," *Whitby This Week*, April 9, 2014: https://www.durhamregion.com/whatson-story/4441532-the-man-who-brought-rock-n-roll-to-canada/.
15. 1964 Caravan of Stars Summer — Part Two, A Rock n' Roll Historian: http://rnrhistorian.blogspot.com/2014/03/1964-caravan-of-stars-summer-part-two.html.
16. Jason Schneider, *Whispering Pines: The Northern Roots of American Music . . . from Hank Snow to The Band* (Toronto: ECW Press, 2009), 53.
17. *Ibid.*, 72.
18. David Clayton-Thomas, *Blood, Sweat and Tears* (Toronto: Virgin Canada, 2010), 37.
19. 1964 Caravan of Stars Summer — Part Two, A Rock n' Roll Historian: http://rnrhistorian.blogspot.com/2014/03/1964-caravan-of-stars-summer-part-two.html.
20. Hugh Thomson, "Rolling Stones Bring Bedlam to Toronto," *Globe and Mail*, April 26, 1965, 13.
21. Canadian Press, "Investigation planned after Stones concert," *Globe and Mail*, July 21, 1966, 10.
22. Ritchie Yorke, "RCA Beacon on Toronto's Lighthouse," *Globe and Mail*, Oct. 25, 1969, A18; Canadian National Exhibition Grandstand Performers from 1948–1994: http://www.world-theatres.com/CNE.html.
23. Jean-Nicolas De Surmont, "les États-Unis: Chansoniers vs yé yé,'" *Cap-aux-Diamants*, 89 (printemps 2007): 21–24; A.J.B. Johnson, *Kings of Friday Night: The Lincolns* (Halifax: Nimbus Publishing, 2020).
24. Ritchie Yorke, *Axes, Chops and Hot Licks: Maple Rock* (Rock 'n Roo, 2015).
25. Scott Piroth, "Popular Music and Identity in Quebec," *American Review of Canadian Studies*, 38 (2) (2008), 148.
26. Neil Young, *Waging Heavy Peace: A Hippie Dream* (New York: Blue Rider Press, 2012), 72–73; 277.
27. Robert Cochran, "Long on Nerve: An Interview with Ronnie Hawkins," *The Arkansas Historical Quarterly*, Vol. LXV (2) (Summer 2008), 114.
28. Clayton-Thomas, *Blood, Sweat and Tears*, 37.
29. Enn Raudsepp, "The Mandala: a soul-full sound with shrieks and flashing lights," *Globe and Mail*, Sept. 17, 1969, 13.
30. The Paupers: http://www.canadianbands.com/Paupers.html.
31. 1050 CHUM Memorial Blog: http://wp1050chumto.blogspot.com/p/chum-chart-history.html.
32. Eric Spaulding, "Turning Point: The Origins of Canadian Content Requirements for Commercial Radio," *Journal of Canadian Studies*, Vol. 50 (3), (Fall 2016): 673–76.
33. Philip H. Ennis, *The Seventh Stream: The Emergence of Rock n' Roll in American Popular Music* (Hanover: Wesleyan University Press, 1992), 350.
34. Beverley Mitchell, "Manseau pop festival still awaits permit," *Montreal Star*, July 16, 1970, 3.
35. Robert Santelli, *Aquarius Rising: The Rock Festival Years* (New York: Dell Publishing, 1980).
36. John Kraglund, "Mariposa," *Globe and Mail*, July 29, 1969, 21.

37. Melinda McCracken, "Baez workshop almost reverent experience," *Globe and Mail,* July 28, 1969, 12.
38. Jim Beebe, "Mariposa was a carnival of musical delight," *Toronto Daily Star,* July 18, 1970, 15; Dick MacDonald, "Mariposa folk festival crashing success," *Montreal Star,* July 27, 1970, 6; Robert Martin, "Dylan surprise Mariposa visitor," *Globe and Mail,* July 15, 1972, 1, 11.
39. Ritchie Yorke, "A Toronto recording Revolution," *Globe and Mail,* Feb. 26, 1969, 11.
40. Ritchie Yorke, "Rock Pile: new heap on the music scene," *Globe and Mail,* Sept. 24, 1968, 12.
41. Yorke, "Pop Scene: Integration"; Johnny Brower interview with the author, Aug. 1, 2018.
42. Led Zeppelin timeline: http://www.ledzeppelin.com/show/february-2-1969.
43. Juliette Jagger, "The Domino Effect: How One of Toronto's Most Iconic Rock Concerts Almost Never Happened," *Vice,* April 13, 2015: https://vice.com/en_ca/article/6e4x4n/the-domino-effect-how-one-of-torontos-most-iconic-rock-concerts-almost-never-happened; Melinda McCracken, "The Beatles TV tour badly made, edited, yet full of fun," *Globe and Mail,* Jan. 3, 1969, 9.
44. Jagger, "The Domino Effect."
45. Johnny Brower interview with author, Aug. 1, 2018.
46. *Ibid.*
47. Urjo Kareda, "There's no business like show business," *Globe and Mail,* July 22, 1967, 11.
48. Promotional blurb for *The Canadian Establishment,* by Peter C. Newman: https://www.penguinrandomhouse.ca/books/121171/the-canadian-establishment-by-peter-c-newman/9781551996905.x.
49. Barbara Moon, "Inside real Toronto Society: Who's who in Toronto," *Globe and Mail,* June 25, 1966, A5.
50. *Ibid.*; Barbara Moon, "Inside Toronto Society," *Globe and Mail,* June 18, 1966, A5.
51. "Unions stray from initial idea, says Lady Eaton in address," *Globe and Mail,* Oct. 5, 1961, 14.
52. Alexander Ross, "What it's Like to Live in Toyland," *Maclean's,* June 1968, 14.
53. Joyce Carter, "Hailed as anti-establishment, fall look is a compendium of parts," *Globe and Mail,* Sept. 3, 1969, 9.
54. "Eaton retires, top job goes to non-Eaton," *Globe and Mail,* Aug. 7, 1969, 1.
55. Daniel Durcholz and Gary Graff, *Neil Young: Long May You Run: The Illustrated History* (Minneapolis: Voyageur Press, 2010), 48.
56. Jack Batten, "Why a promoter tapped his phone," *Toronto Daily Star,* June 21, 1969, 28.
57. *The Eatons,* 142. Thor's record distribution company, Grand Entertainment Corp., a partnership with Kenny Walker, later represented Greek singer Nana Mouskouri.
58. Zena Cherry, "After a Fashion," *Globe and Mail,* Aug. 22, 1966, 17.
59. "Record lineup in Mosport race," *Globe and Mail,* Aug. 22, 1969, 26; Ron White, "Eaton wins $50,000 in Can-Am series," *Globe and Mail,* Nov. 11, 1969, 25.
60. James Adams, "The tracks of his tears," *Globe and Mail,* July 24, 2004, R1.
61. "Toronto: 40,000 to see Pop Festival," *Billboard,* April 26, 1969, 73.
62. Batten, "Why a promoter tapped his phone."
63. Johnny Brower interview with author, Aug. 1, 2018.
64. Ritchie Yorke, "With the crowds, the stars and the amplifiers at Varsity Stadium," *Globe and Mail,* June 21, 1969, 27.
65. Ritchie Yorke, "Pop goes Toronto in two frantic, furry days of rock," *Globe and Mail,* June 23, 1969, 16.
66. *Ibid.* Hanley's crew was hassled at the border by Customs agents looking for drugs.
67. Yorke, "With the crowds."
68. *Billboard* had a regular feature "From the music capitals of the world," with Toronto news usually included.
69. Yorke, "Pop goes Toronto."
70. Clayton-Thomas, *Blood, Sweat and Tears,* 100.
71. *Ibid.,* 112–13.
72. Yorke, "Pop goes Toronto."
73. David Hepworth, *Never a Dull Moment: Rock's Golden Year* (New York: Bantam, 2016),

206.
74.   Johnny Brower interview with author, Aug. 7, 2018.
75.   Yorke, "Pop goes Toronto."
76.   Margaret Daly, "Toronto Pop Festival," *Toronto Daily Star*, June 23, 1969, 27.
77.   Yorke, "With the crowds."
78.   "Investigate use of public funds for Rochdale, grant jury urges," *Globe and Mail*, April 25, 1970, 4; "College head blames RCMP officers," *Globe and Mail*, Aug. 17, 1970, 5.
79.   Ian Porter, "Need tough laws to restrict hippies, controllers decide," *Globe and Mail*, Aug. 15, 1968, 1; "Teen-age girls shout obscenities at Yorkville arrests," *Globe and Mail*, July 13, 1868, 5.
80.   "Hippies will destroy Canada," CBC video, https://www.cbc.ca/player/play/2192814203.
81.   Marcel Marcel, "'They smell bad, have diseases and are lazy': RCMP Officers Reporting on Hippies in the Late Sixties," *Canadian Historical Review*, 90, no. 2 (June 2009): 215–45.
82.   "Drug probe taken on grass roots tour," *Globe and Mail*, Oct. 18, 1969, 5.
83.   "Chief says police can't enforce law against marijuana," *Globe and Mail*, Aug. 19, 1970, 1.
84.   Harvey Shepherd, "Criticizes freedom at universities," *Globe and Mail*, June 2, 1970, 5.
85.   Michael Valpy, "Toronto's freak-out team finds answers for blown-out minds," *Globe and Mail*, July 30, 1968, 5.
86.   Richard Goldstein, "But They Had No Patriotism!" *Toronto Daily Star*, June 23, 1969, 27.
87.   Ritchie Yorke, "Ulcers and serenity give pop a boost," *Globe and Mail*, June 14, 1969, A2.
88.   Ritchie Yorke, "Festival success 'due to the police,'" *Globe and Mail*, June 24, 1969, 12.
89.   *Ibid.*
90.   "At policy convention," *Globe and Mail*, Sept. 8, 1969, 5; "Let's not make another Yorkville: fear hepatitis will follow," *Globe and Mail*, Aug. 14, 1968, 1.
91.   Letter to editor by William Kilbourn, *Globe and Mail*, Oct. 13, 1971, 7. An opponent of the Eaton Centre, Dennison was a supporter of the Spadina Expressway, which the provincial government killed in 1971.
92.   Johnny Brower interview with author, Aug. 7, 2018.
93.   Ronald Lebel, "Mob upsets float, breaks windows after Baptiste parade," *Globe and Mail*, June 25, 1969, 1.
94.   New York Times Service, "Telling it like it was at the big rock festival," *Globe and Mail*, Aug. 27, 1969, 7.
95.   Ben Urish, *The Words and Music of John Lennon* (Westport, CT: Greenwood Publishing Group, 2007), 11.
96.   Clayton-Thomas, *Blood, Sweat and Tears,* chapter 11; Yorke, "Boosting Peace," 8.
97.   Robbie Robertson, "Woodstock Remembered: Robbie Robertson on Feeling 'Proud' to Be Part of Woodstock," *Rolling Stone*, Aug. 11, 2019: https://www.rollingstone.com/music/music-features/woodstock-the-band-robbie-robertson-856370. For The Band, see Steven Davis, *This Wheel's On Fire: Levon Helm and the Story of The Band* (Chicago: Chicago Review Press, 2013).
98.   Young, *Waging Heavy Peace*, 235.
99.   "Chief says buses turned back because passengers had drugs," *Globe and Mail*, Aug. 19, 1969, 5.
100. Geoff Pevere, "How Woodstock Affected Six Canadians," *Toronto Daily Star*, Aug. 1, 2009: https://www.the star.com/entertainment/2009/08/01/how_woodstock_affected_six_canadians.html.
101. Roger Ebert, "Woodstock," Great Movie Reviews, May 22, 2005, at: rogerebert.com. See also: Abbie Hoffman, *Woodstock Nation A Talk-Rock Album* (New York: Vantage, 1969).
102. "Why the kids are turning from revolution to a new lifestyle — and why they shouldn't," *Toronto Daily Star,* Sept. 11, 1969, 6.
103. Johnny Brower interview with author, Aug. 7, 2018.
104. *Ibid.*
105. Ritchie Yorke, "Toronto show commemorated by Ono band," *Globe and Mail*, Dec. 12, 1969, 15.
106. "Interview with Jim Morrison, by Tony Thomson, June 27, 1970," *CBC Rewind*: https://www.cbc.ca/radio/rewind/rewind-1.2822187.

107.   Winn, *That Magic Feeling*, 259, 262.
108.   Hepworth, *Never a Dull Moment*, 228.
109.   Rock 'n' Roll Revival advertisement, *Billboard*, Oct. 19, 1974, 23–26.
110.   Harvey Kubernick, "Kim Fowley: John Lennon & The Plastic Ono Band Live In Toronto '69," Cave Hollywood, Oct. 13, 2013: http://cavehollywood.com/kim-fowley-john-lennon-the-plastic-ono-band-live-in-toronto-69-by-harvey-kubernik-c-2009.
111.   Ritchie Yorke, "Pop scene: the credo of a hardline rock and roller: it's time to return to simplicity and unsubtle sex," *Globe and Mail*, Aug. 16, 1969, 25.
112.   Melinda McCracken, "Fowley All Round Promoter," *Globe and Mail*, Sept. 8, 1969, 14.
113.   Jack Batten, "They revived rock n' roll despite John Lennon's wife," *Toronto Daily Star*, Sept. 15, 1969, 20; Johnny Brower interview with author, Aug. 7, 2018.
114.   Yorke, *Christ You Know It Ain't Easy*, 48.
115.   *Ibid.*, 48–51.
116.   *Ibid.*, 53.
117.   In March 1968, Lennon had performed at one of Yoko's shows at Cambridge University, but his contribution had been limited to experimental guitar sounds.
118.   Johnny Brower interview with author, Aug. 7, 2018.
119.   Ritchie Yorke, "The Lennons and the Rock and Roll Revival," *Globe and Mail*, Sept. 20, 1969, 29.
120.   Fred Goodman, *Allen Klein: The Man Who Bailed Out the Beatles, Made the Stones, and Transformed Rock & Roll* (New York: Houghton, Mifflin Harcourt), 2015, 101.
121.   Norman, *Days in the Life*, 19.
122.   Johnny Brower interview with author, Aug. 1, 2018.
123.   *Eric Clapton: Life in Twelve Bars*, Lili Fini Zanuck director (Passion Pictures, 2017).
124.   Goodman, *Allen Klein*, 204.
125.   "Beatles roadie Mal Evans, article," Toronto Rock 'n' Roll Revival: http://torontorockrevival.blogspot.com. See also: Keith Badman, *The Beatles: Off the Record* (London: Omnibus Press, 2009).
126.   "Beatles roadie."
127.   Melinda McCracken, "Rock joy fully revived," *Globe and Mail*, Sept. 15, 1969, 14.
128.   *Ibid.*
129.   Greil Marcus, "Roll Over Chuck Berry," *Rolling Stone*, June 14, 1969, 15–16.
130.   Lennon and Berry apparently did not meet until they both appeared on The Mike Douglas Show, filmed in New York City, in 1972. Berry's Toronto performance can be viewed on YouTube.
131.   McCracken, "Rock joy." The ninety-minute set was filmed by D.A. Pennebaker.
132.   In 1991, D.A. Pennebaker and Chris Hegedus released a forty-five-minute film of most of Berry's set in Toronto: *Chuck Berry Rock and Roll Music, Toronto Rock and Roll Revival*.
133.   Dennis Duffy, "Rock Festival," *Toronto Daily Star*, Sept. 15, 1969, 20.
134.   "Gene Vincent and the Blue Caps," Rock and Roll Hall of Fame: http://www.rockabillyhall.com/gvbio.html.
135.   "The influence of Gene Vincent on the Beatles," Aaron Krerowicz, Flip Side Beatles: https://www.aaronkrerowicz.com/beatles-blog/2.
136.   Batten, "They revived"; Don Shebib director, *Satan's Choice* (National Film Board, 1965).
137.   McCracken, "Rock joy."
138.   Charles White, *The Life and Times of Little Richard: The Quasar of Rock* (New York: Harmony Books, 1985).
139.   McCracken, "Rock joy."
140.   Batten, "They revived."
141.   *Ibid.*
142.   *Ibid.*
143.   Melinda McCracken, "Rock and Roll Revival Surprise: John & Yoko," *Rolling Stone*, Oct. 18, 1969, 1.
144.   Duffy, "Rock Festival"; "McCracken, "Rock joy."
145.   McCracken, "Rock joy."
146.   Duffy, "Rock Festival."

147. McCracken, "Rock joy."
148. Henderson, *Making the Scene,* 167, 195–97; John Marshall, "The Bikers, Menace," *Globe and Mail,* Aug. 13, 1973, 1.
149. *Ibid.*
150. Yorke, *Christ You Know It Ain't Easy,* 54–55.
151. Joe Goodden, *Riding So High: The Beatles and Drugs* (Pepper & Pearly, 2017), 228.
152. Yorke, *Christ You Know It Ain't Easy,* 55
153. Bob Spitz, *The Beatles: The Biography* (New York: Back Bay Books, 2006), 846.
154. Richter, *The Dream Is Over,* 98.
155. Goodman, *Allen Klein,* 181–82
156. Keith Badman, *The Beatles,* 464–65.
157. Wiener, *Come Together,* 105.
158. McCracken, "Rock and Roll," 1, 6.
159. Dave Laing, "Six boys, six Beatles: the formative years, 1950–1962," in Kenneth Womack, ed. *The Cambridge Companion to the Beatles* (New York: Cambridge University Press, 2011), 25.
160. Yorke, "The Lennons."
161. McCracken, "Rock joy."
162. Yorke, *Christ You Know It Ain't Easy,* 55.
163. Eric Clapton with Christopher Simon Sykes, *Eric Clapton: The Autobiography* (New York: Arrow Books, 2008).
164. "From the Music Capitals of the World," *Billboard,* Aug. 9, 1969, 96.
165. Wiener, *Come Together,* 105.
166. *Ibid.,* 91.
167. Batten, "They revived."
168. Badman, *The Beatles,* 465.
169. Yorke, "The Lennons."
170. Godfrey Jordan, "A picture and a thousand words," *Toronto Daily Star,* Sept. 11, 2005, section D.
171. McCracken, "Rock and Roll," 1, 6.
172. Jack Batten, "Jim Morrison: the rock singer who carries demons inside of him," *Toronto Daily Star,* Sept. 16, 1969, 26.
173. Ritchie Yorke, "The Doors Signed to Rock Show," Aug. 22, 1969, 13; Johnny Brower interview with author, Aug. 1, 2018.
174. CBC, "Jim Morrison of The Doors: Rock and Roll Poet for a Generation," Oct. 31, 2014, https://www.cbc.ca/radio/rewind/jim-morrison-of-the-doors-rock-and-roll-poet-for-a-generation-1.2801186.
175. McCracken, "Rock joy."
176. McCracken, "Rock joy"; Marilyn Bekker, "Doting girls toss notes to Doors' Morrison," *Globe and Mail,* April 22, 1968, 17. The audio of the Doors set can be found at: https://www.youtube.com/watch?v=SlmH1AezCl0&t=2964s.
177. Johnny Brower interview, Aug. 7, 2018.
178. *Ibid.*
179. Peter Ames Carlin, *Paul McCartney: A Life* (New York: Touchstone, 2010), 191.
180. Wiener, *Come Together,* 102, 104–105. For a fan website recalling the Varsity Stadium event, see Richard Maxwell's Toronto Rock and Roll Revival, available online at: http://rockandrollrevival.tripod.com.
181. McCracken, "Rock joy."
182. Jack Batten, "The passionless of pop festivals," *Toronto Daily Star,* Sept. 20, 1969, 67.
183. Dennis Duffy, "Toronto Pop Festival," *Toronto Daily Star,* June 26, 1969, 20.
184. Ritchie Yorke, "Pop festival promoters parting company," *Globe and Mail,* Oct. 17, 1969, 15.
185. Ritchie Yorke, "Lennon on Toronto: Bloody Marvelous," *Rolling Stone,* Oct. 18, 1969, 6.
186. Yorke, "The Lennons."
187. Ken Zelig, "John and Yoko Tell It Like It Is," *Winnipeg Free Press,* Jan. 24, 1970, New Leisure, 2.
188. Richard Ginell, "Live Peace in Toronto," All Music: https://www.allmusic.com/album/

live-peace-in-toronto-1969-mw0000653014. The album was re-released twice in the 1980s and as a compact disc in 1995.

189.	Peter Brown, *The Love You Make: An Insider's Story of the Beatles* (New York: McGraw-Hill, 1983), 331.
190.	Martin Knelman, "Sweet Toronto Stresses Music," *Globe and Mail*, July 14, 1970, 13.
191.	Sweet Toronto, https://www.youtube.com/watch?v=ZxDAUNH9J-k.
192.	Carlin, *Paul McCartney*, 192.
193.	Goodman, *Allen Klein*, 181–82.
194.	*Ibid.*, 204.
195.	Norman, *John Lennon*, 621–22.

Chapter 3
1.	Juan Rodriguez, "Lennon Ballad: 'All we need is peace,'" *Montreal Star*, Dec. 23, 1969, 25.
2.	McGrath director, *John & Yoko's Year of Peace*.
3.	"Trudeau on Yacht Vacation," *Globe and Mail*, Aug. 20, 1969, 1.
4.	Susan Kastner, "PM attracts the girls," *Globe and Mail*, Oct. 24, 1969, 12.
5.	Granatstein and Bothwell, *Pirouette*, 17.
6.	Clyde Sanger, "Sharpe says protest note to Washington was 'the strongest possible' he could send," *Globe and Mail*, Oct. 1, 1969, 4.
7.	Powell, "Vietnam," 252.
8.	Canadian Press, "Ottawa pledges control over pollution in the Arctic," *Globe and Mail*, Oct. 24, 1969, 8.
9.	Marc Roby, "U.S. deserters here tell of other Viet 'massacres,'" *Montreal Star*, Dec. 4, 1969, 1.
10.	Powell, "Vietnam," 250–56, 275–76.
11.	Clyde Sanger, "May support Canairelief," *Globe and Mail*, Oct. 28, 1969, 3.
12.	John Burns, "PM again attacks Ojuwuki," *Globe and Mail*, Nov. 18, 1969, 31.
13.	*Ibid.*, 28–29.
14.	"Trudeau says fogies oppose NATO change," *Globe and Mail*, June 25, 1969, 8.
15.	Canadian Press, "Stanfield sees protests as Canadian as Kentucky Fried Chicken," *Globe and Mail*, May 13, 1970, 31.
16.	"The succeeders in Canadian life," *Globe and Mail*, July 28, 1969, 8.
17.	"Hippies, PM do their own thing," *Globe and Mail*, July 16, 1969, 3.
18.	Donald Newman, "Will still talk to demonstrators but not to mobs, PM comments," *Globe and Mail*, Aug. 24, 1969, 4.
19.	"Bombing blackmail in Quebec," *Globe and Mail*, June 17, 1969, 1.
20.	Auf de Maur, *Quebec: A Chronicle*, 14.
21.	Yorke, *Christ You Know It Ain't Easy*, 60–62.
22.	Johnny Brower interview with author, Aug. 9, 2018. According to Hawkins, Brower was a guest of Lennon and Ono at their home for five days: Ronnie Hawkins and Peter Goddard, *Ronnie Hawkins Last of the Good Ol' Boys* (Toronto: Stoddart Publishing Company, 1990), 166.
23.	Fawcett, *John Lennon*, 62.
24.	Yorke, *Christ You Know It Ain't Easy*, 68.
25.	Ritchie Yorke, "Lennons start Toronto drive for peace," *Globe and Mail*, Dec. 15, 1969, 1.
26.	"John Lennon, wife visiting Toronto on peace trip," *Toronto Daily Star*, Dec. 15, 1969, 24.
27.	Terry Ott, "Ronnie Hawkins remembers John and Yoko," http://www.abbeyrd.net/hawkins.html.
28.	Hawkins and Goddard, *Ronnie Hawkins*, 162.
29.	Jack Batten, "He signs gold U.S. record pact," *Toronto Daily Star*, Sept. 5, 1969, 27.
30.	Ritchie Yorke, "John, Yoko & Year One," *Rolling Stone*, Feb. 7, 1970, 18.
31.	Marci McDonald, "Lennon and wife fly in, hide out in singer's farm," *Toronto Daily Star*, Dec. 17, 1969, 62.
32.	Kenneth Bagnell, "The Legendary Ronnie Hawkins," *Globe and Mail*, March 20, 1971, A4; Ott, "Ronnie Hawkins remembers."
33.	Ott, "Ronnie Hawkins remembers."
34.	Yorke, "John, Yoko & Year One," 18; Ott, "Ronnie Hawkins remembers."

35. Richter, *The Dream is Over*, 106.
36. Hawkins and Goddard, *Ronnie Hawkins*, 162; 168–9.
37. Canadian Press, "Two fined 450 for scuffle," *Globe and Mail*, Jan. 29, 1970, 8.
38. Yorke, *Christ You Know It Ain't Easy*, 69–70.
39. Spitz, *The Beatles*, 850.
40. Marcus Collins, "The Beatles' Politics," *British Journal of Politics and International Relations*, 16 (2) (2014), 300.
41. Louis Kaplan, "John and Yoko's Media War for Peace," in J. Keri Cronin, Kirsty Robertson, eds. *Imagining Resistance: Visual Culture and Activism in Canada* (Waterloo: Wilfrid Laurier University Press, 2011), 61–62.
42. *Ibid.*, 62–63.
43. Wiener, *Come Together*, 129.
44. Yorke, "John, Yoko & Year One"; Ritchie Yorke, "A Private Talk with John Lennon," *Rolling Stone*, Feb. 7, 1970, 22–23; Jon Carroll, "Will Moon Attend Peace Festival?" *Rolling Stone*, March 7, 1970, 10.
45. Canadian Press, "RCMP briefed FBI on John and Yoko's Plans," CTV News, July 24, 2007.
46. Fawcett, *John Lennon*, 62; Badman, *The Beatles*, 484; Dan Stafford, "Lennon plans Mosport peace festival," *Toronto Daily Star*, Dec. 18, 1969, 24; Yorke, "John, Yoko & Year One."
47. Ritchie Yorke, "The Press Conference," *Rolling Stone*, Feb. 7, 1970, 20.
48. Dan Stafford, "Lennon plans Mosport peace festival," *Toronto Daily Star*, Dec. 18, 1969, 24; Yorke, "The Press Conference."
49. Fawcett, *John Lennon*, 62; Stafford, "Lennon plans"; Yorke, "John, Yoko & Year One."
50. Some of the Mekas footage ended up in his 1969 diary film *Walden*.
51. Doris Giller, "Can That Be a Lennon Looking at the price tag?" *Montreal Star*, Dec. 24, 1969, 30.
52. Carlyle C. Douglas, "Diogenes Put Down Your Lamp!" *Ebony*, April, 1970, 76, 82; James Bawden, "Gregory to breakfast," *Globe and Mail*, Aug. 20, 1970, W8.
53. Russell, "Yippie's Entry to Canada."
54. Yorke, *Christ You Know It Ain't Easy*, 80; Richter, *The Dream Is Over*, 108.
55. Steven Heller, "Ralph Ginzburg, 76, Publisher in Obscenity Case, Dies," *New York Times*, July 7, 2006, https://www.nytimes.com/2006/07/07ginzburg.html; "Wedded Bliss: the Erotic Lithographs of John Lennon," *Avant Garde*, no. 11, January 1970, 18.
56. "Bag One," John Lennon Dreamsite: http://www.johnlennon.it/showcase-bag-one-eng.htm.
57. Yorke, *Chris You Know It Ain't Easy*, 88–89.
58. "Canadian News Report," *Billboard*, Oct. 9, 1971, 42; Ted Rhodes, "Kelly Jay cherishes musical treasures," *Calgary Herald*, Aug. 26, 2016, C5.
59. Blaik Kirby, "Who says striptease is dead?" *Globe and Mail*, Jan. 14, 1967, 17; John Clarke, "The Only Place where the dog license man is the theatre censor," *Globe and Mail*, July 16, 1969, 8.
60. Jake Noah Sherman, "'They Are a Scum Community Who Have Organized': The Georgia Strait, Freedom of Expression, and Tom Campbell's War on the Counterculture, 1967–1972" (MA Thesis: University of British Columbia, 2018).
61. Ray Connolly, "My part in the Beatles' break-up," *Daily Mail*, Aug. 26, 2016: https://rayconnolly.co.uk/my-part-in-the-beates-break-up/.
62. Gaëtan Tremblay, "From Marshall McLuhan to Harold Innis, or From the Global Village to the World Empire," *Canadian Journal of Communication*, Vol. 37 (2012): 561.
63. John Leo, "New Technology, New War," *Globe and Mail*, May 27, 1968, 2.
64. Litt, *Trudeaumania*, 54.
65. Leslie Millin, "McLuhan Dazzles *W5* Interviewer," *Globe and Mail*, May 1969, 21.
66. Jann Wenner, "Beatles," *Rolling Stone*, Dec. 21, 1968, 10.
67. Brenn Stilley, "Marshall McLuhan: Culture Becomes Show Biz," *Rolling Stone*, Nov. 12, 1970, 1. See also: Brennan Doherty, "50 years ago, U of T had an LSD convention," *Toronto Daily Star*, Feb. 11, 2017; https://www.thestar.com/news/gta/2017/02/11/50-

years-ago-u-of-t-had-an-lsd-convention.html.

68. Stilley, "Marshall McLuhan," 1, 6.
69. "After a Fashion," *Globe and Mail,* Sept. 13, 1969, 32.
70. Yorke, "John, Yoko & Year One," 18.
71. Yorke, *Christ You Know It Ain't Easy,* 86.
72. John and Yoko with Marshall McLuhan, Ontario, Canada, 12/19/1969, The Beatles Ultimate Experience: http://www.beatlesinterviews.org/db1969.1219.beatles.html
73. Yorke, "John, Yoko & Year One," 18; *Christ You Know It Ain't Easy,* 85–86.
74. Television: John Lennon in conversation with Marshall McLuhan, December 20, 1969, The Beatles Bible; https://www.beatlesbible.com/1969/12/20/television-john-lennon-in-conversation-with-marshall-mcluhan.
75. *Ibid.*
76. Matthew Rankin, "The Ballad of John and Yoko," *Beaver,* Vol. 86, Issue 6 (Dec. 2006/Jan. 2007), 45.
77. John Lennon and Yoko Ono are interviewed for CBC Weekend, December 20, 1969: The Beatles Bible; John Lennon 1969 peace interviews, YouTube, March 31, 2016: https://www.youtube.com/watch?v=iuW9x44SVCk.
78. Yorke, *Christ You Know It Ain't Easy,* 95.
79. Rodriguez, "Lennon Ballad."
80. Yorke, "John, Yoko & Year One," 20.
81. "PM says violence won't be tolerated by his government," *Globe and Mail,* Oct. 25, 1969, 4.
82. Ronald Lebel and Clair Balfour, "15,000 students parade in Montreal," *Globe and Mail,* Oct. 30, 1969, 1.
83. Ronald Lebel, "CYC, Parti Quebecois infiltration charged," *Globe and Mail,* Oct. 23, 1969, 1.
84. "Montreal will use anti-protest bylaw to curb radical left," *Globe and Mail,* Nov. 10, 1969, 1.
85. "1969 Bylaw 3926 (Montreal)," Canada's Human Rights History: https://historyofrights.ca/encyclopaedia/main-events/1969-montreal-bylaw-3926; Ronald Lebel, "Montreal will pass anti-protest law to curb radical left," *Globe and Mail,* Nov. 10, 1969, 1.
86. Ritchie Yorke and Ben Fong-Torres, "Hendrix Busted in Toronto," *Rolling Stone,* May 31, 1969, 1.
87. Ritchie Yorke, "The Hendrix dilemma: more artistry or more fire," *Globe and Mail,* May 5, 1969, 5.
88. "Says gifts rain on group: pop star faces 2 drug charges," *Globe and Mail,* Dec. 9, 1969, 5; "Narcotics acquittal 'a Christmas present' for pop star Hendrix," *Globe and Mail,* Dec. 11, 1969, 1.
89. Yorke, *Christ You Know It Ain't Easy,* 76.
90. Yorke, "John, Yoko & Year One," 20.
91. Fawcett, *John Lennon,* 65.
92. Yorke, *Christ You Know It Ain't Easy,* 95–98. See also: Canadian Press, "Ian Campbell attacks drug law," *Globe and Mail,* Nov. 4, 1969, 33.
93. Yorke, *Christ You Know It Ain't Easy,* 97–98; Johnny Brower interview with author, Aug. 9, 2018.
94. Yorke, "John, Yoko & Year One," 20.
95. Owram, *Born at the Right Time,* 196–203.
96. Jon Rudy, "Some of the best people smoke pot," *Maclean's,* January 1969, 35–36.
97. Cynthia Lennon, *John* (New York: Three Rivers Press, 2006), 212.
98. Hampton, *Guerrilla Minstrels, 212.*
99. Goodden, *Riding So High.*
100. Keith Richards with James Fox, *Life* (Toronto: Basic Books, 2010), 207.
101. Connolly, *Being John Lennon,* 304, 312, 316; Elliot, *The Mourning of John Lennon,* 120, 126.
102. Yorke, "The Press Conference," 21.
103. "John Lennon's Drug Testimony: The Le Dain Commission of Inquiry into the Non-

Medical Use of Drugs — The Private Hearing of John Lennon," Dec. 22, 1969, in Montreal, Ottawa, Beatles' Site: http://beatles.ncf.ca/lennon_inquiry.html.

104.   Yorke, "John, Yoko & Year One," 20.

105.   Ritchie Yorke, "I'd Rather Burn in Canada," *Rolling Stone*, Dec. 13, 1969, 10.

106.   Hugh Segal, *No Surrender: Reflections of a Happy Warrior in the Tory Crusade* (Toronto: HarperCollins Canada, 1996), 50.

107.   Olive Patricia Dickason and William Newbigging, *Indigenous Peoples within Canada*, 4th ed. (Don Mills: Oxford University Press, 2019), 270–72.

108.   Hilary Brigstocke, "Lennons in 'beautiful' talk with Trudeau," *The Times* [London], Dec. 24, 1969, 4.

109.   Doris Giller, "Can That Be a Lennon Looking at the price tag?" *Montreal Star*, Dec. 24, 1969, 30.

110.   Brigstocke, "Lennons in 'beautiful' talk."

111.   Hawa, "Old Politics," 8.

112.   Yorke, "John, Yoko & Year One," 21.

113.   Fawcett, *John Lennon*, 67.

114.   Wiener, *Come Together*, 91.

115.   "Editorial," *Montreal Star*, Dec. 27, 1969, 5.

116.   Gerald Clark, "Trudeau without the Trudeaumania," *New York Times*, Jan. 25, 1970, 198.

117.   *Ibid.*

118.   Litt, *Trudeaumania*, 327.

119.   Lawrence Martin, "The Social Conscience of John Munro," *Maclean's*, May 1, 1972, 37.

120.   "Munro says opponents of plan are linked to vested interests," *Globe and Mail*, Feb. 28, 1969, 1.

121.   "Youth may challenge on drug issue: Munro," *Globe and Mail*, May 23, 1969, 4.

122.   Martin, "The Social Conscience."

123.   Canadian Press, "Lennons love beautiful 'Pierre,'" *Montreal Star*, Dec. 23, 1969, 25.

124.   Fawcett, *John Lennon*, 68–69.

125.   Yorke, "John, Yoko & Year One," 20.

126.   Yorke, *Christ You Know It Ain't Easy*, 101.

127.   Yorke, "John, Yoko and Year One," 18.

128.   Fawcett, *John Lennon*, 68–69.

129.   Yorke, "John, Yoko & Year One" 21.

130.   Yorke, *Christ You Know It Ain't Easy*, 101.

131.   Winn, *That Magic Feeling*, 355–56; Canadian Press, "Smile, clap hands and hope and the world will find peace," Dec. 22, 1969, found at: The Ritchie Yorke Project: https://ritchieyorke.com/1969/12/22/smile-clap-hands-and-hope.

132.   Wiener, *Come Together*, 129.

133.   James Eayrs, "Memo to John and Yoko," *Montreal Star*, Dec. 29, 1969, 8.

134.   Jann Wenner, "Man of the Year," *Rolling Stone*, Feb. 7, 1970, 25.

135.   Pete Doggett, *The Art and Music of John Lennon* (London: Wise Publications, 2005).

136.   Graeme Thomson, *George Harrison: Behind the Locked Door* (Overlook Books, 2017), 236.

137.   See the special issue of the *Canadian Historical Review*, Volume 100 (Issue 29), June 2019.

138.   Donald Newman, "Canada may end ties with monarchy, PM says," *Globe and Mail*, Dec. 23, 1969, 1.

Chapter 4

1.   Carlin, *Paul McCartney*, 201.

2.   Bob Bossin, "The Ups and Downs of a Great Canadian Peace Festival," *Maclean's*, July 1970, 49.

3.   Norman, *John Lennon*, 633–36.

4.   Wenner, "Man of the Year," 25.

5.   Yorke, "A Private Talk."

6.   Jann Wenner, *Lennon Remembers* (San Francisco: Straight Arrow, 1971), 74–5; See also: Michael Luckman, *Alien Rock: The Rock n' Roll-Extraterrestrial Connection* (New York:

Simon and Schuster, 2010), 36.

7.   Johnny Brower interview with author, Aug. 9, 2018; Yorke, *Christ You Know It Ain't Easy*, 106.
8.   *Ibid.*, 110–19.
9.   Hawkins and Goddard, *Ronnie Hawkins*, 182.
10.   Bagnell, "The Legendary Ronnie Hawkins."
11.   Yorke, *Christ You Know It Ain't Easy*, 122–66. For an account by Hawkins, see Hawkins and Goddard, *Ronnie Hawkins*, 181–91.
12.   Wiener, *Come Together*, 128–30.
13.   "Area residents 'turned off' by prospect of Lennon Peace festival at Mosport," *Globe and Mail*, Jan. 16, 1970, 37.
14.   "Peace festival possibilities explored," *Globe and Mail*, March 5, 1970, 11.
15.   Bossin, "The Ups and Downs," 50; Carroll, "Moon to Attend Peace Festival," March 7, 1970, 10.
16.   Cited in Yorke, *Christ You Know It Ain't Easy*, 172–77.
17.   J. Patrick Boyer, "Prospects for Tories in the Seventies," *Globe and Mail*, Jan. 7, 1970, 7.
18.   Anthony Westfell, "NDP's Schreyer more a Trudeau than a Socialist," *Toronto Daily Star*, Sept. 23, 1969, 7.
19.   Martin O'Malley, "Ed Schreyer: a nice guy who finishes first," *Globe and Mail*, Oct. 25, 1969, A4.
20.   Duncan McMonagle, "Free radio idea here gets pledge of backing," *Winnipeg Free Press*, Dec. 17, 1969, 2A.
21.   Ken Hingle, "Vietnam protest rally Attacked by Brotman," *Winnipeg Free Press*, March 26, 1969, 13.
22.   Manitoba Museum of Music, 60s press clippings: https://www.manitobamusicmuseum.com/60spressclippings.htm.
23.   Martin DeFalco and Willie Dunn, directors, *The Other Side of the Ledger: An Indian View of the Hudson's Bay Company* (National Film Board, 1972).
24.   Evelyn Bowen, "Fun, pomp mark Manitoba birthday," *Toronto Daily Star*, July 4, 1970, 74.
25.   Arlene Billinkoff, "Schreyer: Lennon Not My Idea," *Winnipeg Free Press*, Feb. 6, 1970, 1, 6.
26.   *Ibid.*
27.   Owram, *Born at the Right Time*, 290–97; 312–13.
28.   Frances Russell, "Reds at root of unrest on campus, PCs warned," *Globe and Mail*, March 12, 1969, 8.
29.   Jayman Heilman, "Offspring as Enemy: How Canada's National Magazine Confronted Youth and Youth Culture in the 1960s," *Past Imperfect*, Vol. 6 (1997): 73–110.
30.   Melinda McCracken, "Hot Seats and Wounded Knees," *Globe and Mail*, Feb. 5, 1977, A17; Rankin, "The Ballad of John and Yoko," 45.
31.   Rankin, "The Ballad," 46–47.
32.   "Importune guests," *Winnipeg Free Press*, Feb. 1, 1969, 6.
33.   Ellen Simmons, "John, Yoko in Centre of a Storm," *Globe and Mail*, Feb. 28, 1970, 8.
34.   Wiener, *Come Together*, 128–30.
35.   "Lennons pull out of peace festival," *Globe and Mail*, March 12, 1970, 12.
36.   "Lennon's peace festival role uncertain," *Globe and Mail*, March 13, 1970, 11; "Klein: It's John's Peace Festival," *Rolling Stone*, March 19, 1970, 8.
37.   Melinda McCracken, "Hostilities have barely started, astronomical profits," *Globe and Mail*, April 18, 1970, 25.
38.   Connolly, "My part."
39.   Manitoba House of Assembly, *Debates*, April 23, 1970, 1228–30.
40.   Quoted in Linda Mahood, *Thumbing a Ride: Hitchhikers, Hostels, and Counterculture in Canada* (Vancouver: UBC Press, 2018), 72.
41.   Julien Kern, *John Lennon: Wanted by the FBI* (Liverpool: Liverpool Revolution, 2014). See also: Wiener, *Gimme Some Truth*; The John Lennon FBI Files website: http://www.lennonfbifiles.com.
42.   Gerard Warren, "Policeman fights rock festival dangers with movies, traffic problems,"

Globe and Mail, June 2, 1970, 1.

43. Kathy Oilloff, "Toronto Peace Festival? Forget it!" *Tampa Tribune*, April 19, 1970, 119.
44. John Lennon, "Have We All Forgotten What Vibes Are For?" *Rolling Stone*, April 16, 1970, 7.
45. *Ibid.*, 7–8.
46. Wiener, *Come Together*, 136–37; Gooden, *Riding So High*, 230–31.
47. Bruce Ballister, "Who killed the Toronto Peace Festival?" *Rolling Stone*, Dec. 24, 1970, 37–43.
48. Johnny Brower interview with author, Aug. 9, 2018.
49. Clair Balfour, "Trudeau tells Indians that Jewish banquet 'is a hell of a place' to hold their protest," *Globe and Mail*, Feb. 9, 1970, 1.
50. Canadian Press, "Negro, labour opposition cited," *Globe and Mail*, March 19, 1970, 10.
51. "Vietnam war protesters try to gain audience with prime minister," *Weekend*, Jan. 10, 1970, CBC Digital Archives: https://www.cbc.ca/archives/entry/anti-war-protesters-camped-out-for-peace.
52. Murray Goldhatt, "Maoists disrupt rally against war Ottawa," *Globe and Mail*, April 1970, 1.
53. "Maoists, police clash in Ottawa, 16 arrested," *Globe and Mail*, April 20, 1970, 1.
54. Peter Churchill et al., "91 arrested at anti-war rally," *Globe and Mail*, May 11, 1970, 1.
55. Canadian Press, "Police blame terrorists," *Globe and Mail*, July 1, 1970, 8; D'Arcy Jenish, *The Making of the October Crisis: Canada's Long Nightmare of Terrorism at the Hands of the FLQ* (Toronto: Doubleday Canada, 2018).
56. "Police invoke anti demonstration bylaw," *Globe and Mail*, July 2, 1970, 29.
57. Hoffman, *Woodstock Nation*, 13.
58. Ennis, *The Seventh Stream*, 350–51.
59. Mark Mattern, *Acting in Concert: Music, Community and Political Action* (New Brunswick, NJ: Rutgers University Press, 1998), 16.
60. Richard Santelli, *Aquarius Rising: The Rock Festival Age* (New York: Dell Publications, 1980), 8–11, 190–91; Jann Wenner, "Rock and Roll Music," *Rolling Stone*, Feb. 10, 1968, 16; Bill Horan, "New youth culture emerges from sixties," *Montreal Star*, Dec. 1, 1969, 47.
61. Kaspars Dzeguze, "Music only incidental: technical problems plague drab rock festival," *Globe and Mail*, March 26, 1970, 15.
62. Eric Spalding, "Turning Point: The Origins of Canadian Content Requirements for Commercial Radio," *Journal of Canadian Studies*, 50 (3) (September 2017), 677–78.
63. *Ibid.*
64. James Cullingham, "Festival Express," *Globe and Mail*, Sept. 5, 2003, R3; Adams, "The tracks of his tears."
65. Canadian Press, "Police, youth clash in BC, 26 arrested," *Globe and Mail*, July 20, 1970, 9.
66. United Press International–Canadian Press, "Vancouver mayor: Bar U.S. Hippies," *Toronto Daily Star*, July 13, 1970, 1.
67. Sarah Hampson, "Sylvia Tyson: Partying with Janis Joplin," *Globe and Mail*, July 31, 2004, R3.
68. "New Left group calls festival a rip-off," *Globe and Mail*, June 24, 1970, 5.
69. Steve Hewitt, *Spying 101: The RCMP's Secret Activities at Canadian Universities, 1917–1997* (Toronto: University of Toronto Press), 169–70; "Festival Express: bashed heads and bad trips," *Globe and Mail*, June 29, 1970, 10; Mark Wilson, "'Peace, love' at Manseau," *Montreal Star*, June 29, 1970, 4.
70. Manitoba Music Museum, "Festival Express": https://www.manitobamusicmuseum.com/festivalexpress.htm.
71. *Ibid.*
72. Andy Marshal, *Thin Power: How Former Calgary Mayor Rod Sykes Stamped His Brand on the City . . . and Scorched Some Sacred Cows* (Victoria: Friesen Press, 2016), 144–48.
73. Jack Batten, "The big pop festival fizzles," *Globe and Mail*, July 4, 1970, 23.
74. Dick MacDonald, "Music famine bugs festival," *Montreal Star*, Aug. 3, 1970. 14.
75. Wilson, "'Peace, love'"; Beverley Mitchell, "Manseau awaits permit"; Susan Altschuk,

"Manseau festival gets go-ahead," *Montreal Star,* July 23, 1970, 3.

75.   Raymond Guerin, "Bank to close door before pop festival," *Montreal Star,* July 27, 1970, 1.

77.   Beverley Mitchell, "Musicians' guild blacklists pop festival," *Montreal Star,* July 30, 1970, 1.

78.   Beverley Mitchell, "Manseau: A phantasmagoria of happiness," *Montreal Star,* July 31, 1970, 25.

79.   Canadian Press, "Missing stars, union row cloud Manseau festival," *Montreal Star,* July 31, 1970, 20.

80.   Beverley Mitchell, "Manseau opening a washout"; *Montreal Star,* Aug. 1, 1970, 1–2; "Manseau: A soggy farmyard of disappointments," *Montreal Star,* Aug. 3, 1970, 25; Susan Altschul, "Manseau festival"; Walter Poronovich,"Festival charges alleged," *Montreal Star,* Aug. 7, 1970, 3.

81.   Robert McKenzie, "Festival's producer says mafia muscles in," *Toronto Daily Star,* July 10, 1970, 1–2; Ritchie Yorke, "Canadian festivals get bleaker," *Billboard,* Aug. 15, 1970, 56.

82.   Ritchie Yorke, "Toronto Peace Festival on again, 1000-acres site fixed," *Billboard,* May 30, 1970, 71.

83.   Bob Bossin, "The Ups and Downs of a Great Canadian Peace Festival," *Maclean's,* July 1970, 49.

84.   William Gerrard, "Toronto Peace fete rejected by township," *Globe and Mail,* June 2, 1970, 1.

85.   "Peace festival off, Brower indicates," *Globe and Mail,* June 8, 1970, 10.

86.   Evelyn Bowen, "Fun, Pomp Mark Manitoba Bash," *Toronto Daily Star,* July 4, 1970, 74.

87.   Don Newman, "Centenary celebrations: Manitoba welcome for PM, cabinet is marred by protest," *Globe and Mail,* July 1, 1970, 1.

88.   Bossin, "The Ups and Downs," 50–53.

89.   Della Margaret Stanley, *Louis J. Robichaud: A Decade of Power* (Halifax: Nimbus Publishing, 1984).

90.   Johnny Brower interview with author, Aug. 9, 2018.

91.   Steven Conn, "Back to the Garden: Communes, the Environment and Antiurban Pastoralism at the End of the Sixties," *Journal of Urban History,* 36 (6) (2010): 831–48.

92.   Gillian Mitchell, *The North American Folk Music Revival: Nation and Identity in the United States and Canada, 1945–1980* (Burlington, VT: Ashgate, 2007), 155.

93.   Images of posters advertising the festival can be found on The Strawberry Fields Festival Facebook site.

94.   Greg Marquis, "Rocking Free North America: The Strawberry Fields festival and the Youth Culture Borderlands," unpublished paper, 2013; See also: "The Concert Led Zeppelin never Gave: The Lessons of the Strawberry Fields Festival," Acadiensis Blog, Oct. 31, 2018: https://acadiensis.wordpress.com/2018/10/31/the-concert-led-zeppelin-never-gave-the-lessons-of-the-strawberry-fields-festival.

95.   Marquis, "Rocking Free North America."

96.   *Ibid.*

97.   *Ibid.*

98.   Norman Hartley, "Le Dain findings win support of ARF analysis," *Toronto Daily Star,* July 29, 1970, 1.

99.   "Le Dain Commission highly critical of police attitudes on drugs, users," *Globe and Mail,* June 20, 1970, 1.

100.   "Lumping of marijuana, heroin is main objection in Toronto," *Globe and Mail,* June 20, 1970, 11.

101.   *Daily Gleaner* (Fredericton), July 17, 1970; Altschul, "Manseau festival"; Marcel Martel, *Not This Time: Canadians, Public Policy and the Marijuana Question, 1961–1975* (Toronto: University of Toronto Press, 2006).

102.   John Burns, "PM says marijuana use is an individual choice," *Globe and Mail,* Aug. 5, 1970, 1.

103.   In a Facebook posting (Jan. 12, 2012), Brower claimed that the manager of Led Zeppelin had been advanced $75,000, which the band subsequently kept.

104.   Marquis, "Rocking Free North America."

105. Mahood, *Thumbing a Ride*, 69–72.

106. Trent Frayne, "Toronto is not prepared for the youthful invasion forecast this summer," *Toronto Daily Star*, July 11, 1970, 9.

107. Santelli, *Aquarius Rising*, 188.

108. Canadian Press, "Nova Scotia residents fear permit for festival," *Globe and Mail*, Aug. 7, 1970, 13; "Tolerance has its limits," *Globe and Mail*, Aug. 17, 1970, 6; Marquis, "Rocking Free North America"; Greg Marquis, "Uptight Little Island: The Junction 71 Affair," *Island Magazine*, 52 (Fall-Winter 2002), 10-14.

109. John Adams, "I've threatened to cut the heart out of any . . . promoter who comes into this field hospital," *Globe and Mail*, Aug. 15, 1970, 1.

110. "OPP seeks injunction to stop weekend festival at Mosport," *Globe and Mail*, Aug. 6, 1970, 1; Adams, "I've threatened"; Marquis, "Rocking Free North America."

111. "Drug Peril Eases at Powder Ride: Thousands Leaving Site of Banned Rock Festival," *New York Times*, Aug. 2, 1970, 58.

112. "OPP seeks injunction"; Adams, "I've threatened."

113. Marquis, "Rocking Free North America"; "Rock festival set to start at Mosport," *Globe and Mail*, Aug. 7, 1970, 1; "Legal move fails to stop festival," Globe and Mail, Aug. 7, 1970, 25; Robert Douglas, "'Pills, hash and grass . . . I got it all,' hawkers shout as drugs freely sold," *Toronto Daily Star*, Aug. 8, 1970, 2.

114. "Rock festival set to start"; "Legal move fails to stop."

115. *Ibid.*

116. Marquis, "Rocking Free North America"; "Missing stars, union row cloud Manseau festival," *Toronto Daily Star*, July 31, 1970, 20.

117. "Good-Time Rockers," *Newsweek*, Feb. 23, 1970, 90.

118. *Montreal Star*, July 28, 1970; *Toronto Daily Star*, July 28, 1970.

119. Leroy was a pop singer who released several singles and one album in the 1970s: The Canadian Pop Encyclopedia: http://jam.canoe.ca/Music/Pop_Encyclopedia/L/Leroy_James.html.

120. James Bawden, "Pop Scene: Mosport: was the music incidental to the smoking and drinking?" *Globe and Mail*, Aug. 14, 1970, 11.

121. James Bawden, "Moods at Mosport: Pop, Pot and Patience," *Globe and Mail*, Aug. 8, 1970, 21; Bawden, Pop Scene: Mosport."

122. John Adams, "Thousands of candles flicker at Mosport; the restless drink, seek drugs and action," *Globe and Mail*, Aug. 8, 1970, 1–2; "Nudes in the Mill Pond," *Globe and Mail*, Aug. 8, 1970, 1; "Mosport expects up to 50,000, 150 police on duty," *Toronto Daily Star*, Aug. 8, 1970, 1–2; Rae Corelli, "Police say fear of riot prevented Mosport drug crackdown," *Toronto Daily Star*, Aug. 11, 1970, 1, 18; Strawberry Fields Festival (YouTube): http://youtube.com/watch?v-y8tpngdUmYk.

123. Ritchie Yorke, "Brower promotes Strawberry Fields Fest into Winner," *Billboard*, Aug. 22, 1970, 80; "Mosport expects."

124. Johnny Brower interview with author, Aug. 9, 2019; "LSD, marijuana sold out in open at Mosport," *Toronto Daily Star*, Aug. 7, 1970, 1, 3; "Medical dispute develops," *Globe and Mail*, Aug. 11, 1970, 5.

125. John Adams, "The Mosport legacy may be to ban future mass rock festivals," *Globe and Mail*, Aug. 15, 1970, 1.

126. Ken Kelley, "Why did New Brunswick Pull the Plug on an Epic Rock Festival in August, 1970?" The Music Nerd Chronicles, Aug. 7, 2016: https://musicnerd.ca/why-did-new-brunswick-pull-theplu-on=an-epic-rock-concert-in-august-1970.

127. "No races and no trophies, but few care as music, drugs and nudity highlight Mosport," *Globe and Mail*, Aug. 10, 1970, 1–2; "Police stay out as drugs sold openly at Mosport," *Toronto Daily Star*, Aug. 8, 1970, 1–2; Allan Dickie, "Police want to bill Mosport rock promoters for $100,000," *Toronto Daily Star*, Aug. 10, 1970, 1, 4.

128. Kelley, "Why did New Brunswick?"

129. Strawberry Fields Music Festival, Facebook site, posts Jan. 12, 2020, June 24, 2013.

130. Jeff Lieberman interview with the author, Jan. 11, 2020.

131. Yorke, "Brower promotes Strawberry Fields"; Corelli, "Police say fear."

132. Adams, "The Mosport legacy."

133.   "After Mosport, Take Drug Dealers Out of Festivals," *Globe and Mail*, Aug. 11, 1970, 6.
134.   "No races and no trophies."
135.   David Churchill, "American Expatriates and the Building of Alternative Social Space, 1965–1977," *Urban History Review*, 39 (1) (2010): 37.
136.   Ross Munro, "Rochdale council urges selling experimental college," *Globe and Mail*, Nov. 13, 1969, 1; Stuart Henderson, "Toronto's Hippie Disease; End of Days in the Yorkville Scene, 1968," *Journal of the Canadian Historical Association*, New Series, Vol. 17 (1) (2006): 205–34.

Conclusion
1.   "City without cops," *Time Canada*, Oct. 17, 1969. See also: Pierre Elliot Trudeau, "Notes for a national broadcast, Oct. 16, 1970," First Among Equals: The Prime Minister in Canadian Life and Politics: https://www.collectionscanada.gc.primeministers/h4-4065-e. html.
2.   Palmer, *Canada's 1960s*, 364.
3.   *Ibid.*, 361–63.
4.   Hawa, "Old Politics," 10.
5.   Dominique Clément, October Crisis, Canada's Human Rights History: https:// historyofrights.ca/history/october-crisis/5.
6.   Clair Balfour, "10 face seditious conspiracy charge," *Globe and Mail*, Nov. 5, 1970, 1.
7.   Larue-Langlois gets ovation in Toronto," *Globe and Mail*, Jan. 18, 1971, 5; "3 in Quebec face new conspiracy charges," *Globe and Mail*, March 11, 1971, 4; "Haven't killed any ministers, not as yet," *Globe and Mail*, March 12, 1971, 1; James Lorimer, "The Trial of Gagnon and Larue-Langlois," *Globe and Mail*, June 8, 1971, 7.
8.   Jack Batten, "Janis Joplin: Sex, drinking, added to image of blues-rock singer," *Globe and Mail*, Oct. 6, 1970, 15.
9.   Wiener, *Come Together*, 140.
10.   Connolly, *Being John Lennon*, 341; Andrew Grant Jackson, *Still the Greatest: The Essential Songs of the Beatles' Solo Careers* (Lanham, MD: Scarecrow Press, 2012), 30.
11.   Canada, *Report of the Royal Commission on the Status of Women in Canada* (Ottawa: Information Canada, 1970).
12.   Churchill, "American Expatriates."
13.   Hampton, *Guerrilla Minstrels*, 19.
14.   Dinerstein and Goodyear, *American Cool*, 33.
15.   Goodman, *Allen Klein*, 225.
16.   Norman, *Days in the Life*, 20.
17.   Jonas Mekas, *A Dance with Fred Astaire* (New York: Anthology Editions, 2017), 379.
18.   Wiener, *Come Together*, 256. The details of the anti-Lennon campaign can be found in: John Wiener, *Gimme Some Truth: The John Lennon FBI Files* (Los Angeles: University of California Press, 1999).
19.   May Pang and John Edwards, *Loving John: The Untold Story* (New York: Time Warner Books, 1983).
20.   Stories from the Montreal Bed-In, Panel Discussion, Fondation PHI, May 6, 2019: YouTube: https://www.youtube.com/watch?v=BpZ7dqe43tQ.
21.   Anthony Elliot, *The Mourning of John Lennon* (Berkeley: University of California Press, 1999), 152–53.
22.   Hampton, *Guerrilla Minstrels*, 34.
23.   CP, Associated Press, Reuters, "Lennon mourned around the world," *Globe and Mail*, Dec. 15, 1980, 1.
24.   Michael Frontani, *The Beatles: Image and the Media* (Jackson: University Press of Mississippi, 2007), preface.
25.   Kim Richard Nossal, Stephane Roussel, Stéphane Paquin, *The Politics of Canada's Foreign Policy* (Montreal: McGill-Queen's University Press, 2015), 114.
26.   Connolly, *Being John Lennon*, 402.
27.   Norman, *Days in the Life*, dust jacket notes; Pang and Edwards, *Loving John*, 333–34; Elizabeth Grice, "'Dad was a hypocrite. He could talk about peace and love to the world

but he could never show it to his wife and son,'"(1998) *The Telegraph*, April 1, 2015; https://www.telegraph.co.uk/culture/4713954/Dad-was-a-hypocrite.-He-could-talk-about-peace-and-love-to-the-world-but-he-could-never-show-it-to-his-wife-and-son. html; Powell, *John*.

28. MacDonald and Ono, "Yoko Ono."
29. Alex Horton, "Why Paul McCartney marched: 'One of my best friends was killed in gun violence,'" *Washington Post*, March 24, 2018: https://www.washingtonpost.com/news/arts-and-entertainment/wp/2018/03/24/why-paul-mccartney-marched-one-of-my-best-friends-was-killed-in-gun-violence.
30. Paul Irish, "Yoko Ono to show art in Kitchener," *Toronto Daily Star*, March 22, 2012: https:/www.thestar.com/entertainment/2012/03/22/yoko_ono_to_show_art_in_ kitchener.html.
31. Murray White, "Yoko Ono's view from the Riverbed," *Toronto Daily Star*, Feb. 19, 2018: https://www.thestar.com/entertainment/visualarts/2018/02/19/yoko-onos-view-from-the-riverbed.html.
32. Imaginepeace.com; Canadian Press, "Yoko Ono posts bed-in video on-line," CBC News, Aug. 17, 2011: https://www.cbc.ca/news/entertainment/yoko-ono-posts-bed-in-video-online-1.1037854.
33. Stories from the Montreal Bed-In, Panel Discussion.
34. Shirin Radjavi, On Instructions, Invitations, and Saying Yes to Imagination: https://fondation-phi.org/fr/article/yoko-ono-instructions-invitations-imagination.
35. Athey, McGrath, Deiter, eds. *Give Peace a Chance*.
36. Levitan, *I Met the Walrus*, 155.
37. In 1983, in response to increased Cold War tension, Trudeau embarked on a global peace initiative where he attempted to use Canada's honest broker reputation to encourage the superpowers to resort to diplomacy and not the arms race.
38. Heather Kitching, "Folk Alliance: 50 Years after Lennon's bed-in for peace another bed-in for peace," Roots Music Canada, Feb. 20, 2019: https://www.roots.music. ca/2019/02/20/folk-alliance-50-years-after-lennons-bed-in-for-peace.
39. Bernard Schissel, *Blaming Children: Youth Crime, Moral Panics and the Politics of Hate* (Halifax: Fernwood, 1997), 16.
40. Marcus Collins, "The Beatles' Politics," *British Journal of Politics and International Relations*, Vol. 16 (2014): 304.

Index

Pictures are indicated with italic references.

244